Performance, Identity, and Immigration Law

Performance, Identity, and Immigration Law
A Theatre of Undocumentedness

Gad Guterman

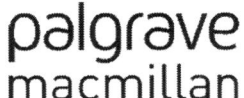

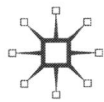

PERFORMANCE, IDENTITY, AND IMMIGRATION LAW

Copyright © Gad Guterman, 2014.

Softcover reprint of the hardcover 1st edition 2014 978-1-137-41248-5

First published in 2014 by
PALGRAVE MACMILLAN®
in the United States—a division of St. Martin's Press LLC,
175 Fifth Avenue, New York, NY 10010.

Where this book is distributed in the UK, Europe and the rest of the world,
this is by Palgrave Macmillan, a division of Macmillan Publishers Limited,
registered in England, company number 785998, of Houndmills,
Basingstoke, Hampshire RG21 6XS.

Palgrave Macmillan is the global academic imprint of the above companies
and has companies and representatives throughout the world.

Palgrave® and Macmillan® are registered trademarks in the United States,
the United Kingdom, Europe and other countries.

ISBN 978-1-349-48959-6   ISBN 978-1-137-41100-6 (eBook)
DOI 10.1057/9781137411006

Library of Congress Cataloging-in-Publication Data

Guterman, Gad.
    Performance, identity, and immigration law : a theatre of
undocumentedness / by Gad Guterman.
        pages cm
    Includes bibliographical references and index.

    1. Hispanic American theater. 2. Hispanic Americans in the
performing arts. 3. American drama—Hispanic American authors—
History and criticism. 4. American drama—20th century—History and
criticism. 5. Illegal aliens in literature. 6. Emigration and immigration in
literature. 7. Citizenship in literature. 8. Identity (Psychology) in
literature. 9. Theater and society—United States. I. Title.

PN2270.H57G68 2014
792.089'68073—dc23   2014000779

A catalogue record of the book is available from the British Library.

Design by Newgen Knowledge Works (P) Ltd., Chennai, India.

First edition: July 2014

10 9 8 7 6 5 4 3 2 1

Contents

Acknowledgments

Many have made this project possible. I am deeply grateful for the mentorship and instruction I have received from incredible teachers, including Marvin Carlson, J. Ellen Gainor, Daniel Gerould, Sally Engle Merry, Judith Milhous, David Savran, and Alison Van Dyke. Jean Graham-Jones, my dissertation director, continues to be a formidable guide even after my time at the Graduate Center, CUNY. Robyn Curtis and Erica Buchman at Palgrave Macmillan have been an ideal editorial team, and Chelsea Morgan and Deepa John have transformed the manuscript into the fine volume you are now reading: thank you. Thanks also to Chris Cecot for compiling the index and to Amanda Swearingen for assisting in the proofreading process. Research for this project was made possible in part by a City University of New York MAGNET Presidential Fellowship and by a Martin S. Tackel American Theatre Research Fund Award. My gratitude extends to the Association for Theatre in Higher Education Latino/Latina Focus Group and to my various working groups at the American Society for Theatre Research, especially the (Re)Positioning the Latina/o Americas under the leadership of Jimmy Noriega and Analola Santana. I am indebted to many at Webster University for giving me the support and resources needed to complete a book project, particularly Peter Sargent, Dottie Marshall Englis, and the rest of the Conservatory of Theatre Arts faculty, staff, and students; Emily Scharf and our library staff; and Gee Gee Johnson and Lorraine LiCavoli. Several artists were most generous with their unpublished work, time, and ideas: Carlo Albán, Elías Cabrera, Daniel Carlton, Kat Chua, Yussef El Guindi, Michael John Garcés, Juan José Mangandi, Lorena Moran, and Caridad Svich. I must thank also my friends and colleagues, in various settings, whose encouragement and feedback have been invaluable: Ritchie Abraham, Linell Ajello, Kevin Byrne, Mark Cosdon, Jody Enders, Rachel Falk, Jennifer Garvey-Blackwell, Lynette Gibson, Patricia Herrera, Jessica Hillman-McCord, Jorge Huerta, Amy Hughes, Elisa Legon, Teresa Marrero, Lara Nielsen, Jon Rossini, Felicia Ruff, Ilka Saal, Carly Smith, Sarah Stern, Christopher Swift, and Tamara Underiner. My family has suffered and celebrated with me at every step of this process. Gracias, abrazos, y besos to my parents, Bernardo and Tania Guterman; my sister, Ruti Smithline; and a family tree that keeps growing stronger with Smithlines, Roitmans, Finkelsteins, Wassermans, Sragoviczs, Gutermans, Florendos, and Gibbs. Finally, this book is as much Alan Florendo's as it is mine (♥).

It has been a joy to engage with theatre artists whose work has challenged and invigorated me. To be sure, it has been less joyful to think through and investigate the harsh realities of undocumentedness. I hope that my work pays service to and honors the millions of individuals living in the United States without papers.

Permission has been granted by the Martin E. Segal Theatre Center to reprint text from my article, "'The, Uh, Immigration Situation': *Living Out* and the Legal/Illegal Divide," which appeared in the *Journal of American Drama and Theatre* 23 (Spring 2011): 51–73.

I

Act § 237(a)(I)(B)—Present in Violation of Law

An Impossible Subject

Near the end of his autobiographical one-man show, *Intríngulis*, Carlo
Albán erases markings that he has written in chalk on the set. What at
first sight appears to be a simple black background has become, throughout the show, a blackboard, a projection screen, and shelves. The set is
deceptively complex. Various oddly shaped geometrical panels transform
the seemingly flat backdrop into a sort of monochromatic jigsaw puzzle.
Once Albán erases words and figures that he has scribbled throughout
the performance, the set gains additional intricacy. Traces of the story
that he has shared both remain and no longer remain. A few chalk letters, or pieces of letters, linger legibly against the dark wall. Others are
completely gone. In this way, Raul Abrego's set for the 2011 production of
Intríngulis at INTAR Theatre in New York City aptly captures the meaning of the title word. "Intríngulis" translates from Spanish to "complex
web" or "tricky situation."

We are often reminded by our politicians that immigration issues
are difficult. They are personal and inspire much passion. But current
immigration debates regularly reduce individuals and their positions
to dangerous binaries. Labels such as "criminal" and "racist" fuel the
flames of intense ongoing discussions. They also ignore messy realities
that make divisions between citizen and noncitizen, between "alien" and
"American," between legal and illegal imprecise and often indetermi-
nate. Historian Mae Ngai deems those living in the United States without
proper authorization "impossible subjects." They are distinguishable in
concrete ways from citizens and legal immigrants but also indistinguish-
able. They are rendered powerless but are not altogether unprotected by
the law. They are needed here and in ostensible need of removal. Ngai

ultimately demonstrates how the "illegal alien," an invention of US immigration law, surfaces as "a person who cannot be and a problem that cannot be solved."[1] Theatre pieces such as Albán's—a play about growing up as an undocumented immigrant in the United States—illuminate these kinds of complexities, which are often ignored in the broader debates.

The acts of writing, rewriting, and erasing performed by Albán evocatively capture realities of what I call "undocumentedness." The term helps to approach the tricky nature of immigration law and highlights connections between identity and law. Much has been made of the dehumanizing and contentious use of "illegal alien" to describe migrants who reside in a country without legal authorization. Other adjectives—undocumented, unauthorized, irregular—deemphasize the criminalization of these immigrants. Nonetheless, as adjectives, such terms retain the power of "illegal" to turn issues of immigration law into individual qualities. I prefer a noun—undocumentedness—to stress how the labels that immigration law creates engender particular conditions. Undocumentedness moves us away from an adjective that dangerously describes people to a noun that describes circumstances under which people must live. These circumstances often create specific stresses and contradictions that inevitably shape an individual's sense of self and of community. Undocumentedness leads to a long list of adjectives that easily attach themselves to individuals forced to live within its constraints: vulnerable, afraid, exploited, persevering, cautious, determined, displaced, and disenfranchised, to name a few. Although inevitably tied to questions of ethnic and national identification, undocumentedness also demands distinct attention. Albán's play fits not only within a long tradition of Latina/o performance but also within a growing repertory of stories that focus specifically on living in the United States without proper immigration papers. Such a repertory has not yet received much dedicated attention. I hope that this study can open up new paths for discussing law, identity, and performance.

Still, it is important to remember that terms such as "illegal" and "alien" link issues of identity to issues of law. "Illegal alien" is firmly established legal language that speaks to a real legal entity. US statutes have used "alien" since the passage of the Alien and Sedition Acts of 1798, some of the federal government's first attempts to delineate processes of citizenship and naturalization. Defined as "any person not a citizen or national of the United States" by the Immigration and Nationality Act (INA), "alien" retains its currency in statutes, executive orders, and court cases.[2] Although the compounds "illegal alien" and "undocumented alien" are far rarer in the immigration statutory and regulatory framework, they do commonly appear in judicial opinions. Even as the Associated Press and the *Los Angeles Times* are leading the way in dropping the use of "illegal" as a descriptor for individuals, both "undocumented immigrant" and "illegal immigrant" remain widely used in political and journalistic arenas. For some prominent politicians, retaining the term "illegal" becomes a matter of principle.[3] With "undocumentedness," I endeavor to move us away from charged and contentious terminology. At the same time, I rely strategically on "illegal" and "alien" to remind us that law constructs categories that contribute to the building of identities, as Albán's work emphasizes.

In development since 2005, *Intríngulis* officially premiered in 2010 as a coproduction between LAByrinth Theatre Company in New York City and Elephant Theatre Company in Los Angeles (subsequent productions have included the one at INTAR as well as at Southern Rep in New Orleans, at the Atlantic Fringe Festival in Halifax, and in Spanish at Two River Theater Company in New Jersey).[4] The one-man show places Albán in direct interaction with his audience. He shares his passage through and out of undocumentedness with candor, focusing on key moments and ideas interspersed with *nueva canción* protest anthems popular in Latin America, which he accompanies on guitar. He depicts his family's journey from Ecuador to the suburbs of New Jersey, their years of residing in the United States with lapsed tourist visas, and their nearly 20-year struggle with the US immigration bureaucracy. He chronicles the shift from living in perpetual fear to finding peace. The tension in Albán's intimate theatre piece does not come from dramatizing opposing viewpoints of the immigration debate. Rather, *Intríngulis* stages Albán's struggles of having to exist day-to-day within those oppositions. It is the boundary between illegal and legal that truly animates the play, as Albán contends with the severe material consequences that illegality can prompt.

In her compelling studies of Salvadoran immigrants, legal anthropologist Susan Coutin describes living in the United States today without proper immigration papers as occupying a "space of legal nonexistence." She proposes that such a space requires its occupants to negotiate between being present and erasing presence, between existing physically and not existing legally. Disallowed or unrecognized by the law, so-called illegal immigrants participate fully in a community and simultaneously exist "underground," in an "otherworld" where their presence must be falsified or altogether denied. Individuals without papers can thus exist as family members, neighbors, consumers, and workers but also strive tirelessly to erase themselves to avoid notice. The incongruities inherent to this process are many, and our current immigration system therefore leads to "incompatible realities [being] true simultaneously."[5] As I describe below, *Intríngulis* ably illuminates some of these contradictions and demonstrates why nonexistence is unsustainable, as Coutin adamantly warns.

I introduce Coutin's work here because legal nonexistence offers students of performance a productive approach to analyze undocumentedness. Performance—construed in this study broadly as an embodied, deliberate practice—surfaces as a way to manage contradictions caused by nonexistence. Moreover, because performance demands presence, it offers a tool with which to combat nonexistence. I am interested in considering how enactment and representation create spaces of existence, even if only fleeting ones. What power does performance hold to interrupt and perhaps modify gradations of existence created by law? What role can performance play in shaping not only an individual but also a collective identity vis-à-vis the law? How might performances make present for audiences a condition predicated on non-presence? More to the point, how does theatre participate in making undocumentedness visible? Coutin briefly discusses how the 2003 Immigrant Workers Freedom Ride, which convened immigrants and their advocates to Washington, DC, after a cross-country journey, helped to combat images of the undocumented as "shadows."[6] But she does not meaningfully engage with cultural products that depict undocumentedness (she does frame *Nations of Emigrants* with a poem and the lyrics to a song). I find in her work an invitation to examine how cultural products generally, and theatre pieces specifically, can bring those forced into spaces of nonexistence out of the shadows and, in so doing, mitigate the violence characteristic to those spaces.

Intríngulis makes clear that spaces of nonexistence are dangerous as well as transformative. Albán submits plainly that without legal status, "there are people who sell themselves into slavery [...,] people dying of thirst in the desert [...,] thousands of men, women and children, held for months, even years at a time in detention centers, caught up in a system that benefits financially from keeping them there" (*I* 18). As a personal narrative, *Intríngulis* becomes less about these distinct circumstances and more about the pressures of undocumentedness. Albán tells us: "We started learning English upon arrival in the U.S. [...] In time, we learned [words like] Visa, Immigration, Green Card, Bureaucracy, Deportation, Naturalization, though I don't remember learning them. [...] You simply absorb and absorb until one day you find that you understand, speak and even dream a different language. It's part of you" (*I* 8–9). How the law and legal categorizations seep into everyday lives, into dreams, is at the core of *Intríngulis*. Albán describes the perpetual "state of unease" in which his family lived, how "fear became the status quo" (*I* 2–3). He equates the fear of immigration authorities with having a bomb set off in his heart, a bomb that can "destroy a person in one big boom" (*I* 8).

Fear fuels the need to erase oneself. Some acts of erasure operate through imitation. Coutin explains that the US immigration system generally encourages migrants to "imitate citizens." They live daily lives "act[ing] on the rights" that citizenship ultimately promises.[7] The angst produced by undocumentedness intensifies the need to imitate. Undocumentedness strengthens the power of a disciplinary apparatus, to tap into Foucauldian language, that compels immigrants to erase marks of foreignness. But in undocumentedness, imitating citizens can never fully cease to be an imitation. So other acts of erasure come into play, and these highlight immigrants' agency. Coutin writes of the "art of not existing."[8] This combination of practices—inventing biographies, manipulating documents, misleading authorities, avoiding exposure—proves necessary in order to withstand the perils of nonexistence. Growing up, Albán sees himself as "play[ing] the role of [an] American teenager to a T" (*I* 10). The theatrical language is noteworthy. It stresses both how legal nonexistence can cause existence to feel put-on and how performance becomes a tool to manage the pressures of undocumentedness.

The frequency with which theatrical language and ideas appear in descriptions of undocumentedness is striking. Josefina López introduces her play *Real Women Have Curves* with an anecdote about encountering immigration officers as a child: "On the way to the store we saw 'la migra' (INS/immigration/Border Patrol). I quickly turned to my friend and tried to 'act white.' I spoke in English and talked about Jordache jeans and Barbie dolls hoping no one would suspect us." The character of Pepe, in John Leguizamo's *Mambo Mouth*, attempts also to deflect *la migra*'s attention by "acting" Swedish, then black Irish, then Israeli, and then, like López, American.[9] Although theatre-makers like Albán, López, and Leguizamo might be drawn to performance metaphors, the use of such comparisons extends beyond those of theatre folk. Chronicling his journey from life without papers to life as a surgeon in New York City, Harold Fernandez peppers his narrative with allusions to the theatre. His initial entry into the United States required planning "similar to rehearsing for a well-choreographed play." Fernandez writes often of *pretending*, of *disguising* himself, of *performing* a role for others. "He should have been an actor in the theatre," offers now-reporter Ramón "Tianguis" Pérez of a fellow border crosser trying to outsmart border patrol agents when the two have been caught. Well beyond the moment and the place of crossing a border, the performance must continue. In her journalistic narrative of four Mexican American teenagers living in Colorado, Helen Thorpe describes the "seamless job of acting," the "escalating theatricality," that often accompanies undocumentedness.[10] As I will explore in subsequent chapters, both immigrants and immigration authorities must become keenly aware of how they present themselves to each other. To paraphrase geographer Joseph Nevins, the kind of boundary policing inherent to immigration law is necessarily about performance as much as it is about particular legal procedures.[11]

Intríngulis further links issues of law and performance when Albán discusses his work as a young actor. A successful stint in a community theatre production of *Oliver!* eventually lands a 13-year-old Albán a regular role on PBS's beloved *Sesame Street.* "What better place to hide than in the spotlight," he tells us (*I* 13). That limelight readily illuminates some of the incompatible realities to which Coutin calls attention. As a denizen of the famous street, Albán becomes a paragon of Americanness. His heritage as a Latin American immigrant actually solidifies his place in the television neighborhood, as he embodies myths of the Melting Pot and the American Dream. But matters of law prevent Albán from belonging fully. He simultaneously represents an idealized, all-American kid and lives with the feeling that he is somehow trespassing. He shares with us another dream, this one a recurring nightmare:

> It would start out with me sitting in my apartment at 123 Sesame Street practicing counting—"One, Two, Three"—when there's a knock at the door. I walk to the door with a cheery disposition and answer with a smile. On the other side of my smile I see Oscar, looking especially green and smelling especially dirty, flanked by Big Bird and Snuffy, both looking especially gigantic and overbearing. Oscar asks me if there's anything I'd like to share with them. I answer that as much as I am a big fan of sharing...and helping...and compromising, I don't have anything for them at the moment, but they're welcome to hang out and count with me if they feel so inclined. Then Oscar gives a signal and the giant yellow bird and the hairy elephant tackle me to the ground and drag me out of the building. And outside an angry mob of children and Muppets and "viewers like you" are throwing Styrofoam letters and numbers and chanting "Why is Carlo crying?!" Then out of Hooper's store they bring a bucket of hot tar, dump it on my head and douse me with a raft of yellow feathers. And just before I'm dumped into Oscar's trash can which leads straight to the Immigration Department's Detention Center, the announcer says "This program has been brought to you by the number one and by the letters U.S.A." (*I* 14)

On television screens across the nation, Albán gains spectacular presence. He is a palpable member of the national imaginary. But as per INA, Albán's presence violates the law. Undocumentedness drives a relentless internal tug-of-war and prevents Albán from truly being himself, on or off-camera. Like the blackboard at the end of the performance, he surfaces as a product of partial writings and erasures. In Albán's words, "I don't belong here. [...] I want to be here" (*I* 17).

Intríngulis offers an obvious—though increasingly difficult to attain—solution for overcoming these struggles: legalization. Albán makes plain that gaining legal status and eventually citizenship afforded him a new way of being in the United States. He also stresses the astonishing complications, cost, and capriciousness of legalization. But with legal status, "There's nothing left to define, nothing left to prove. I am a part of you" (*I* 24). In interviews, he explains that legalization made *Intríngulis* possible. For him, sharing his story was simply out of the question before having the security of a green card.[12] But as an autobiographical exercise, *Intríngulis* also demonstrates how a perfect erasing of the slate is impossible. Years of performing nonexistence are neither immediately nor fully overcome. The "sense of security and stability" (*I* 19) that Albán tells us came with legalization coexisted with echoes of fear. In his words, Albán continued to "put up a wall" (*I* 22). Legalization, and naturalization in turn, can only ever be what Albán describes as a "subtle transformation" (*I* 23). Legal status clearly changes Albán's life. But legal status cannot fully change the individual whose dreams and nightmares were molded in undocumentedness. In other words, legalization solves problems created by undocumentedness but cannot fully dissolve an identity constituted within it.

The trajectory of the play itself points to another means of combating legal nonexistence. The play might narrate a process marked by erasures, but it very much celebrates presence. By delving directly and deeply into undocumentedness, *Intríngulis* becomes a surrogate narrative for the many that are forced to remain invisible. To quote one of many representative reviews, Albán has surfaced as a "reasoned, compassionate face on the immigration issue." He "puts a very human face" and "put[s] soul" on the issue, to quote two others.[13] Interviews and write-ups about *Intríngulis* have appeared in a wide range of outlets, from the ACLU website to Fox News Latino, from *Variety* to the BBC. The play thus becomes more than another polemical voice on the immigration debate and rather a much-needed guide into the realities of undocumentedness. One critic writes that Albán's work "takes us somewhere new, into what is still considered by many to be a taboo underground world." Another concludes that Albán "gives the audience members a peek at a world and culture quite foreign to them."[14] Although Albán is now a US citizen, he has risen as a voice not just *for* but *of* those still living in undocumentedness. His work, for instance, has been featured online by the DREAM Act Union, a collective of artists and educators dedicated to raising awareness about immigrant youth and immigration law.[15] *Intríngulis*'s bold depiction of a life without legitimate immigration papers and Albán's own public revelation of past undocumentedness become the type of assertions to existence that undermine invisibility and nonexistence. Indeed, because undocumentedness requires a kind of self-conscious and state-imposed invisibility, performances about unauthorized immigration illuminate the condition in important ways.

In a contribution to *Time*, journalist Jose Antonio Vargas—who disclosed his undocumented status in a 2010 *New York Times* article—offers "coming out" as a "game changer" for the immigration debate. Vargas writes: "While closely associated with the modern gay-rights movement, in recent years the term *coming out* and the act itself have been embraced by the country's young undocumented population.... [Each individual who comes out as undocumented] becomes another walking conversation. We love this country. We contribute to it. This is our home. What happens when even more of us step forward? How will the U.S. government and American citizens react then?"[16]

Vargas's article appeared just as US policies experienced major shifts. In 2012, Barack Obama's administration announced a new stance toward eligible young undocumented immigrants brought into the United States as children. Through an executive order, Obama halted deportations of and began to issue work permits to self-described DREAMers. The executive action therefore realizes some of what the proposed but yet-to-be-enacted DREAM Act (an acronym for Development, Relief, and Education for Alien Minors) has sought to accomplish legislatively since first introduced to the Senate in 2001.[17] The policy comes from the same administration that also has, as Albán narrates in the play, "mercilessly gone after immigrants, with record numbers of deportations" (*I* 18). Ten days after the president's announcement, the United States Supreme Court ruled on Arizona's SB 1070 law, a controversial statute that has garnered much public attention. On the one hand, SB 1070 raises difficult questions about policing immigration violations and targeting ethnic minorities in the process. On the other hand, the law marks an invigorated desire by some local governments to control what has historically been viewed strictly as a federal effort. Although *Arizona v. U.S.* maintains that state governments cannot contradict federal immigration policy, the Court has allowed local police officers to question the immigration status of those they detain. Other states—Utah, Georgia, Indiana, Alabama, South Carolina—have passed or have tried to pass their own versions of Arizona's restrictive law. In the meantime, cities like Baltimore, San Francisco, and Chicago as well as states like California, Massachusetts, and Rhode Island have enacted policies that are increasingly friendly to those living in undocumentedness. The 2012 presidential election and the marked attention on Latina/o voters placed a very bright spotlight on immigration issues. As I write, Congress continues debating immigration reform. Even if a much-deliberated path to citizenship is approved to ensure that some estimated 11 million immigrants currently living in undocumentedness can someday "come out of the shadows," to use the White House's own words,[18] it is clear that a system that continues to label immigrants "legal" and "illegal" will remain in place. Moreover, the policing efforts and mechanisms of punishment that so crucially shape undocumentedness will not only persist but also possibly intensify. The debate is far from settled; contradictions will inevitably endure.

Vargas's questions therefore become all the more pressing. How will coming out change things? If theatre's participation in the broader LGBTQ rights movement is an indication, should we begin to look more adamantly at a theatre of undocumentedness and what such a theatre could do? We could approach the undocumentedness that Albán presents as "*abject* in relation to Americanness," to borrow Karen Shimakawa's ideas about Asian American theatre. Following Shimakawa, I see undocumentedness appearing as a shifting frontier. It becomes a "movement between visibility and invisibility," a necessary element that "must be both made present and jettisoned" in order for "U.S. Americanness to maintain its symbolic coherence."[19] By making undocumentedness visible, tangible, present, the play begins to unhinge—however slightly—the imbalance between visibility and invisibility that pushes those living in undocumentedness into abjection. Policies and political rhetoric might aim to reduce those living without papers to nonentities, but total erasures are impossible. On the stage, Albán's presence demands our attention, the attention that undocumentedness sought to erode. And on the stage, Albán bears witness to ways in which US laws jettisoned him out of existence all the while he was becoming an American. "I am part of you." I quote Albán again. He not only claims membership through legalization, he charges us to see the paradoxical reality of undocumentedness: he's been a part of *US* all along.

What follows is a study of intersections among performance, immigration law, and identity. I raise interrelated questions about law's participation in identity formation, contemporary US theatre's engagement with immigration issues, and performance's role in immigration debates. Although the plays I discuss do not themselves offer the word "undocumentedness," I find it an apt term on which to center my analysis. The theatre pieces at the core of this study bring undocumentedness to life for their audiences. As a collection, they have urged me to rethink how issues of identity are discussed in the field of theatre and performance studies. Moreover, the plays at hand illuminate the power of law to shape identity and practices of belonging. Undocumentedness forges ways of being, seeing, and existing. By considering such plays together, I seek to highlight some of the disjunctures intrinsic to US immigration law and the *intríngulis* inherent to undocumentedness. Furthermore, by considering a variety of theatre pieces that engage directly with immigration debates, I hope to make the difficult subject of immigration law, at least as we are forced to encounter it today through the screaming rhetoric of political debate, a little less impossible to evaluate.

My analysis and organization of the texts seek in some way to follow the framework of US immigration law. Accordingly, I have titled each of my chapters with headings from various areas of the Immigration and Nationality Act. Rather than opting for an arrangement based on chronology (of laws, of plays, of dramatized subjects), geography (of productions, of play settings), or ethnicity (of playwrights, of characters), I have created a structure that parallels the manner in which US immigration law operates to define and constrain both individual and collective identity. Thus, questions of movement, of labor, and of family take precedence over questions of national origin or ethnicity.

Moving across borders is the focus of chapter 2. I consider connections between performance and border crossings, noting especially how legal boundaries function. Through what I call "border scenarios," I examine the performative nature of immigration law. My reading of Genny Lim's *Paper Angels*, Culture Clash's *Bordertown*, and López's *Real Women Have Curves* focuses on ways in which performance serves to manage and to disrupt legally defined borders. Additionally, I consider the borders created within the field of US cultural production that propel the productions as specifically Latina/o or Asian American, questioning how such categories affect conversations about immigration law.

I move in chapter 3 to discuss workers in undocumentedness and issues of labor and class. Specifically, I concentrate on the theatrical representation of a well-worn character, the undocumented maid, and her necessary antagonist, the privileged homemaker. By studying Milcha Sánchez-Scott's *Latina*, Lisa Loomer's *Living Out*, and Octavio Solis's *Lydia*, I explore a set of interdependent questions: How do the plays reproduce as well as challenge a conception of class relations in which, as Linda Bosniak speculates, "first-world women's citizenship [could come] at the expense of the citizenship of their household workers"?[20] How does undocumentedness structure the experience of work? What is the role of undocumented labor in US theatre production? Through what I deem "undocumentedface," I propose that we must be attentive to ways in which professional theatre production in the United States precludes the active participation of immigrants lacking papers, even as it presents their stories.

La víctima by the collective Teatro de la Esperanza, *Deporting the Divas* by Guillermo Reyes, and *Away Alone* by Janet Noble anchor the discussion in chapter 4, which reflects on particularities of family life and personal relationships in undocumentedness. I turn to the plays to discuss how immigration law keeps some families together and breaks others apart. To that end, I approach US immigration law as a disciplinary apparatus that compels certain ways of performing "family." I pay particular attention to a growing trend in the United States: the mixed-status family that is composed of members of different citizenship and immigration categories. The three theatrical examples allow me to contemplate both how stage narratives can sustain categorical distinctions that immigration law seeks to protect and how performances potentially problematize such familial categories, many of which sustain traditional notions of gender and sexuality.

In view of policies and debates that increasingly focus on illegality, I dedicate chapter 5 to stagings of those criminalized for their undocumentedness. Ntare Mwine's *Biro*, Yussef El Guindi's *Back of the Throat*, and Michael Garcés's *Los Illegals* serve my consideration of ways in which all sorts of daily activities are legislated, disciplined, and often criminalized through immigration and citizenship policies. Against this background, I ponder how the plays illuminate processes of activating rights. I am interested here in looking at how performances might successfully interrupt nonexistence, even if only for a moment.

For the most part, the plays that I highlight in this study easily exemplify ideas explored in various chapters. *Real Women Have Curves*, for instance, is as much about labor as it is about legal borders, *Living Out* depicts realities of families split apart by challenging laws, and *La víctima* attests to the criminalization associated with unauthorized immigration. In an effort to keep my arguments focused, I do not underscore these overlaps. Bringing a range of examples into the discussion allows me to engage more fully with broadly circulating images of undocumentedness on US stages and thus make bolder claims about a shared legal consciousness rooted in distinctions between legal and illegal statuses.

The plays at the core of my arguments should also be readily available to most readers. I have selected them in part for that reason. Still, the accompanying bibliography identifies a growing catalog of other theatre pieces that directly engage issues of immigration law in diverse ways. The scope of my project has not allowed me to explore in depth other kinds of performances especially those emerging in nonprofessional, community, and educational contexts or those created outside the United States. Perhaps this book can offer tools with which to study these cultural texts as well. In an effort to open up the discussion, I conclude the book by moving outside the walls of theatres and into the streets. Specifically, I turn to Times Square in New York City, where men and women daily perform the contradictions and disjunctures of immigration law. Dressed as globally recognized characters like Mickey and Minnie Mouse to pose for photographs with tourists, they make themselves invisible under masks and full-body costumes to participate in an underground economy in plain sight. By examining these generally overlooked street performers, I seek to explore how legal boundaries come undone, yet are simultaneously reinforced as immigrant bodies, many of them donned illegal, become spectacularly present at an iconic location. Their performances offer a productive opportunity to observe the material effects of immigration law as well as its limits.

In the remainder of this chapter, I introduce concepts developed by legal anthropologists in order to outline crucial connections among law, identity, and performance. I then offer a brief sketch of immigration law as well as of theatre history to provide a solid basis from which to understand the performances that I take on in later chapters. My attention turns to two mid-twentieth-century theatre texts that featured undocumentedness prominently: *A View from the Bridge* by Arthur Miller and *Flower Drum Song* by Richard Rodgers and Oscar Hammerstein II.

Law, Identity, Performance

Intríngulis attests to a budding trend of staging stories about undocumentedness. Since the May Day street marches of 2006 that saw immigrants and their advocates rallying nationwide through the 2012 presidential election that reenergized immigration reform, theatre artists in the United States have and continue to engage increasingly with immigration law onstage. A list of representative works is appropriate here to call attention to the growing mass of theatre pieces dedicated to exploring issues of immigration law directly: *Stuck Elevator* by Byron Au Yong and Aaron Jafferis; *The Dreamers* by Cara Mía Theatre Co.; *American Jornalero* and *La Ruta* by Ed Cardona Jr.; *14* by José Casas; *Undocumented* by Kat Chua; *Dream Acts* by Mia Chung, Jessica Litwak, Chiori Miyagawa, Saviana Stanescu, and Andrea Thome; *Los Illegals* by Garcés; *Boxcar* by Silvia González; *No Roosters in the Desert* and *Trash* by Kara Hartzler; *Tres Niñas* by Michael LaChiusa and Ellen Fitzhugh; *Nowhere on the Border* by Carlos Lacámara; *In the Labyrinth* by Dan LeFranc; *Detained in the Desert* by Josefina López; *Lush Valley* by Kristin Marting, Mahayana Landowne, and Tal Yarden; *American Night: The Ballad of Juan José* by Richard Montoya, developed by Culture Clash and Jo Bonney; *Visitor's Guide to Arivaca (Map Not to Scale)* by Evangeline Ordaz; *Kita y Fernanda* and *Our Lady of the Underpass* by Tanya Saracho; *Lydia* by Solis; *De Novo* by Jeffrey Solomon; *Tortilla Curtain* by Matthew Spangler (based on T. C. Boyle's novel); *Aliens with Extraordinary Skills* by

Stanescu; and *Aliens, Immigrants & Other Evildoers* by José Torres-Tama. This list reflects a variety of styles and approaches, from docudramas to fantasies, from realist dramas to musicals. It does not include theatre pieces developed outside of the United States, which have nonetheless been presented in the country and participate in discussions about immigration law (e.g., Peky Andino's *Medea llama por cobrar*, Saulo García's *El Insomnio Americano*, Victor Hugo Rascón Banda's *La mujer que cayó del cielo*, Roland Schimmelpfennig's *The Golden Dragon*, and Teatro Línea de Sombra's *Amarillo*).

Like *Intríngulis*, the majority of these performances have taken place in relatively small venues across the United States. The Lillian Theatre where *Intríngulis* had its Los Angeles premiere, for example, seats 99 patrons. Albán's show played in New York City at INTAR, a fourth-floor flexible performance space of even smaller capacity. (One rides up in an elevator with a first-person sign in which the machine confesses, "I am NOT dilapidated, just a bit old and a little cranky. Please be patient with me and I will take you to INTAR"). My research in New York has taken me to the Julia Miles Theatre (~200 seats), Theatre 80 (~160 seats), Repertorio Español (~140 seats), New Dramatists (~90 seats), and Spyer Hall (~70 seats). Larger regional theatres have dedicated some of their season slots to theatre pieces that tackle immigration law directly. Solis's *Lydia*, discussed in chapter 3, premiered at the Mark Taper Forum in Los Angeles and then moved to the Yale Repertory Theatre. Thus, this particular production played to larger audiences. Nonetheless, even these auditoriums, with approximately 740 and 490 seats respectively, are both unusual for the plays I examine in this study and still smaller than commercial venues across the country.

Despite the small playhouses, theatre of undocumentedness is a flourishing phenomenon. The proliferation of stage pieces about unauthorized immigration remains predominantly rooted in small not-for-profit theatres whose missions are often focused on promoting ethnically defined and/or marginalized voices, from Borderlands Theater in Tucson to Teatro Luna in Chicago, from Diversionary Theatre in San Diego to the Women's Project in New York City. Historical trends that have kept the issue mostly invisible in larger, more commercial venues therefore continue. As a result, the mechanism through which such performance pieces are produced bolsters and plays into the belief that undocumented immigration is not an important issue for all Americans but rather only for so-called hyphenated Americans. I endeavor in this study to showcase theatre pieces that have achieved some measure of circulation and visibility. The plays on which I focus my arguments have either enjoyed multiple productions or taken on lives beyond the stage through publication and/or adaptation. By gravitating toward material with varied trajectories and considerable reach, I hope to make a stronger case for connections between cultural production and processes of identity formation. In juxtaposing the various examples and in bringing different histories and contexts of migration together, I seek also to combat trends that displace immigration law from taking center stage in our analyses of identity.

Law and identity are intricately linked. I propose we consider *legal identity* with as much attention as we do gender, ethnic, or national identities. These are all inevitably correlated, but I find that the direct impact of law is oftentimes overlooked in today's identity-based studies. At the risk of creating yet another taxonomic cubbyhole, I see much potential in exploring a type of identity that can cut across divisions that, by now, have been naturalized. We need not look much further than current book titles, conference groupings, or academic structures to understand that identity-based studies favor certain lines of distinction. Although students of Asian American and Latina/o theatre, for instance, share many questions and concerns, opportunities for active dialogue are limited. Looking specifically at legal categorization has allowed me to make connections across long-standing disciplinary lines such as those that demarcate ethnicity. At the same time, considering legal difference points to critical differences that Pan-Asian or Pan-Latina/o approaches must necessarily overlook.

To be sure, as Bosniak reminds us in her studies of citizenship and alienage, categorical legal differences do not necessarily create cohesive or self-conscious groups. Immigration status works only through other forms of identification and social distinction. Nonetheless, in Bosniak's words, "it seems clear that there are certain characteristics of alienage that structurally shape the lives of most noncitizens, usually in disadvantaging forms." The most powerful of these characteristics is the always-present threat of deportation. Such fear is intrinsic to undocumentedness. With deportation—and, more recently, with long-term detention—looming over their heads, those living in undocumentedness frequently fear taking any legal action or claiming any rightful due. Bosniak summarizes: "The collateral effects of these deportation provisions on undocumented immigrants arguably structure their experience in this country more than any other single factor." Studying connections between immigration law and labor rights, Shannon Gleeson recommends we approach undocumented status as a "master status" that, like gender, class, or race, shapes an individual's sense of self.[21] Since legal status can cut deeply across certain familial, cultural, and community ties, a category like "illegal alien" might therefore prove more powerful today in determining who a person is and how he or she acts than a label like "Mexican," "Chinese American," or "Irish."

It is therefore critical to consider how identities forged around legal labels might in fact create cohesive groups, both to raise visibility and to bolster political agency. In this sense, I seek to follow Joshua Takano Chambers-Letson's investigation into "the unique relationship between law and performance" and its power to make and unmake subjectivities. While Chambers-Letson focuses specifically on Asian America, I deliberately look across ethnic lines to examine performances that illuminate undocumentedness. Such a strategy offers another method for understanding how legal labels function in processes of identity formation and heeds Bosniak's call to make visible law's crucial participation in the subordination of noncitizens. Because alienage is so often relegated to what Bosniak describes as "mere proxy for other forms of oppression," the legal identity that immigration spawns can go unobserved.[22] Legal identities indeed remain under-examined, especially in theatre and performance studies.

In order to alter patterns of organizing and analyzing theatre through the lens of ethnic categorization, I turn to the field of legal anthropology to reconsider the overdetermined question of identity. Legal anthropologists have advanced the concept of "legal consciousness" as a way to approach how lay persons think about the law, understand legal concepts and institutions, and live daily lives within and against the constructs of the law.[23] Legal consciousness becomes a constructive force, one that shapes the way people make sense of their world and determine their place as active agents. Sally Merry, perhaps one of the scholars most commonly associated with the concept of legal consciousness, defines it broadly as the "ways people understand and use law."[24] Merry connects these ways of interacting with legal agents, institutions, and procedures to active processes of building self-awareness. As Patricia Ewick and Susan Silbey explain, "Our social roles and statuses, our relationships, our obligations, prerogatives, and responsibilities, our identities, and our behaviors bear the imprint of law." Ewick and Silbey's major contention—the law is present in our everyday lives—echoes a number of studies supporting the notion that legal processes and ways of thinking can mark individual bodies and subjectivities.[25]

Importantly, Ewick and Silbey encourage an expansive definition of "law." The law is not a solid structure, but rather a historically varying combination of practices and agents often resulting in contradictory and unrelated trends and actions. An act by Congress, a judge's opinion, a sheriff's arrest, an airport security check, a visa, a vote: all fall easily under a discussion of law. Ewick and Silbey further urge us to see how phenomena that occur outside courtrooms, the legislature, and lawyers' offices also fall into the realm of the "legal," especially as they pertain to legal consciousness. As I propose below, cultural representations of these practices and agents also share in a community's conception of law.

Using legal consciousness as a springboard, I conceive of a legal identity as the confluence of legal definitions imposed upon an individual (e.g., "criminal," "minor," "wife," "domestic partner," "Hispanic," "illegal alien") and the manner in which the individual lives with, through, against, and around those impositions. A legal identity must take into account how the subject fits into, is created by, and behaves according to a legal apparatus, as well as the individual agency that allows for the manipulation, use, and resistance of the law.

Given that a legal consciousness is necessarily variable and always in a process of development, a legal identity, too, is a powerful but ever-changing phenomenon. A legal identity need not be the strict result of ideological indoctrination, and it serves as a useful theoretical construct to navigate the contradictions and connections between an individual and a group or social identity. In their study of people with disabilities, David Engel and Frank Munger, convincingly posit identity as "protean," a "concept of self" that necessarily changes through interpersonal and group interaction and that inevitably functions in reaction to cultural influences. Identities, they tell us, "are the products of already familiar images and stereotypes, and they also emerge spontaneously from surprising acts of creativity and struggle."[26] These identities, Engel and Munger remind us, must be understood above all within the context of an individual's perception of boundaries. In particular, one's consciousness of rights—a pivotal structural component of individual identity—depends not only on explicit knowledge of the law or access to legal institutions, but also, and perhaps more importantly, on general recognition of inclusion and exclusion.

Cultural products such as *Intríngulis* can play an important part in (re)shaping an individual's legal consciousness and his or her engagement with the legal field. As I have argued elsewhere, the cultural and legal fields are deeply enmeshed, and symbols frequently migrate between them, undermining their separateness and distinctness.[27] Ewick and Silbey's *The Common Place of Law* supports the conclusion that cultural influences can affect the development of a legal consciousness. Seeking to move beyond a study of formal or official legal agents, Ewick and Silbey note that the law operates through a "prominent cultural presence."[28] Trials, lawyers, crimes, courts, and law are ubiquitous in US cultural production, intimately tying our experiences of law to our experiences with cultural products. Law's power and significance in people's lives thus operate in constant collaboration with other forms of discourse. Albán's play not only offers insight into the author's personal sense of legality, but also exemplifies the available cultural models through which other individuals might forge their own legal identities. An immigration statute might well wield a different kind of power than a play about immigration, but it is crucial that we note the porous nature of both the cultural and legal spheres.

In her 2011 study of legal consciousness in gay and lesbian lives, Rosie Harding stresses the importance of fictional narratives and published texts to explore connections between law and identity. Harding acknowledges that in considering works of fiction and works that have been produced for publication, she departs from the traditional approach to examining legal consciousness, which focuses almost exclusively on in-depth interviews. But she finds in her "novel" reliance on fictional and public texts a new path for "accessing discourse about the place of law in everyday life."[29] As legal anthropologists venture into investigations of cultural products, I offer their theories here in my own attempt to engage in an equally novel exploration of identity in theatre and performance studies.

Moreover, I submit that theatre texts are particularly productive in a study of legal consciousness. First, as I discuss throughout this book, issues of law and identity are inseparable from issues of performance. Onstage narratives illuminate such connections. Second, much of the theatre about undocumentedness that is produced in the United States speaks to relatively small audiences. The conversations theatre prompts can therefore proceed with certain finesse. Of course, some theatre speaks in the overgeneralizations that are common in other media. But the theatre pieces on which I focus invite their audiences to listen deeply to issues often relegated to simplistic sound bites in other contexts. Finally, theatre gives breath and substance to an issue marked by invisibility. Performances of undocumentedness can offer an embodied substitution for the subjects whom the legal system endeavors to banish or erase. As Joseph Roach makes clear, such a process of surrogation is inherently imperfect and incomplete, and the performances of absences can call forth what is now nonexistent only through (re)invention, so that what is made manifest inevitably alters that which it replaces.[30] The possibilities that arise from this gap are significant; performance surfaces as an opportunity for change. In particular, the potential for theatricality that performances of surrogation allow can offer the types of poses, presumptions, projections, and futurity—to borrow Martin Puchner's conception of theatricality[31]—that may lead to a radical reconceiving of immigration law and the legal identities it produces. Standing on a stage in front of us, Carlo Albán defies legal categories. According to the law, he should not be there, at least not through the trajectory he describes. His real presence, however, is undeniable. We are watching him live. His performance of himself therefore challenges the limits of law without becoming a simple rant against immigration law.

By inspecting together the work of artists who make undocumentedness visible, I seek a window into the law's power to mold our sense of identity. I see Ewick and Silbey's proposal that stories are "expressions and forms of legal consciousness" as an invitation to consider performances in a similar manner. I see their subsequent proposition that "a story by its telling extends temporally and socially what might otherwise be a discrete or ephemeral victory" as an imperative to examine how theatre of undocumentedness participates in debates over immigration law.[32] As a group, the performances that I analyze—spanning a range of production styles, conditions, and trajectories, and engaging with different aspects of US immigration policies—illuminate both an individual and a collective understanding of what it means to be "illegal" under the law. The performances point to ways in which identity, law, and performance are inextricably connected.

Impossibly Possible Subjects

Today's conception and legal treatment of migrants without proper papers rests predominantly on the foundations laid by the 1965 Immigration and Nationality Act (INA). Therefore, my focus throughout this book is on theatre pieces from a period that starts in the early 1970s, when the material effects of Congress's Act began to arise, and that brings us to the present day. Still, the appearance of characters marked as undocumented on US stages goes further back than 1965. As long as there have been immigration laws, there have been artists engaging with those laws onstage. In sketching a brief history of a theatre of undocumentedness, I urge us to remember that today's debates about immigration law are part of a long-standing, ongoing negotiation. Despite the explosion of theatre concerned with immigration law that I describe above, I also stress here that some of the most prevalent theatre pieces that tackle the subject of undocumentedness come from a pre-1965 era.

The federal government's first broad attempt to restrict entrance into the United States was the Chinese Exclusion Act of 1882. Legitimizing the racism and nativism that plagued a fast-growing nation, the Exclusion Act made it a crime to be Chinese (of a certain social class) in the United States. No Chinese laborers were to enter the United States until at least 1892 and no Chinese individual already in the country was to become a citizen. Ironically, as Dave Williams has pointed out, while the Exclusion Act severely curbed the influx of Chinese men and women into the country, Chinese characters began to surface more and more frequently in the work of Euroamerican playwrights in the late nineteenth century.[33] Most of these were gross stereotypes that, in fact, helped to fuel anti-Chinese sentiments and justify legal exclusion (a powerful example of cultural production bolstering activity in the legal field).

Still, the first "illegals" represented on the US stage served also to question the practicality of immigration law. Onstage, crafty trespassers defied the law's desire to keep individuals out of the United States. Frank Powers's *The First Born*, for instance, boasts among other figures "the excellent" Duck Low, a savvy traveler who proudly enters the United States by first landing in Canada and then "cross[ing] over into this country disguised as an Indian, a savage race much favored by the white devils." Once in San Francisco's Chinatown, Duck Low is able to shed his costume, but it is clear he is entering into a life of constant struggle against the laws of these white devils. His first onstage action, after relating his tale, is learning of new and innovative ways to trick US officials: "Let me hear of anything that has deceived these barbarous people."[34] A small role in the play, Duck Low does manage to win some sympathy. At the very least, Powers allows him to succeed in his unlawful crossing. Even though the figure then reinforces an image of the Chinese as lawbreaker, the creative and resilient Duck Low combats the mostly powerless, impotent Chinese characters that were prevalent in the period. More to the point, Duck Low's presence onstage—even if played by a white actor in yellowface as was common at the time—rebels against the non-presence the Exclusion Act sought to enact. After all, the character of Duck Low reminds audiences that total exclusion is an impossibility. As a surrogate for Chinese immigrants actually living in the United States, Duck Low therefore ceases to be fully emasculated or ineffective, as Sean Metzger posits many Chinese characters were in his study of nineteenth-century yellowface performance.[35]

The Chinese Exclusion Act fundamentally altered the ways in which the United States approached its national borders. Julian Samora argues that concerns for securing the US-Mexico border, for example, developed from the desire to keep Chinese immigrants out of the country. "In the eyes of immigration authorities, the Chinese were the first 'wetbacks,'" Samora writes, alerting us to the fact that the derogatory appellation would then gain prominence in the 1920s.[36] Following the model set by the Exclusion Act, US law also continued to focus on restricting immigration based on national origin. The "new immigrants" of the early twentieth century, who came increasingly from southern and eastern Europe, exacerbated nativist xenophobia. Congress responded with a series of acts designed to curb particular waves of immigrants. The Quota Laws, beginning in 1921 and remaining in effect until 1965, aimed to maintain open borders but also shape more stringently the ethnic composition of incoming immigrants.

Yet, with the passing of the Johnson-Reed Immigration Act of 1924, US immigration policy undertook a major change, one that remains constitutive of immigration policy today. Whereas previous restrictions to entering the country had all been of a qualitative nature (e.g., no criminals, no paupers, no Chinese), the quotas imposed for the first time a ceiling to the number of avowedly desired immigrants. Hence, many potential entrants, who otherwise fit the qualitative criteria for coming into the United States, now became undesirable. As Ngai convincingly explains, this quota-based immigration policy in essence created the "illegal alien" by severely restricting the number of people allowed to settle in the country, by inventing hierarchies of racial and ethnic difference, by insisting on passport and visa controls, and by drawing increasing attention to the idea of the US border as a space in need of protection and patrolling (the Border Patrol was established in 1924).

Alterations to the immigration policies of the United States throughout the first half of the twentieth century attested to the difficulties of managing the impossible subjects that Ngai describes. The economic pressures of the Great Depression and the subsequent boom from the United States' participation in World War II required a patchwork of policies that could satisfy the needs of a changing labor market. At the same time, participation in World War II placed the US government in a moral quandary, exacerbating the clash between the two ideological poles most prevalent in shaping immigration policy: Is a society obligated to aliens to whose presence it did not consent, or is it fundamentally obligated to them because of their humanity?[37] The sweeping 1952 Immigration and Naturalization Act (also known as the McCarran-Walter Act) attempted to reconcile some of these contradictions. It abolished the racially based conception of naturalization, creating a supposedly color-blind system for citizenship and establishing a preference for skilled workers and relatives of residents and citizens to enter the United States. It provided for fairer deportation hearings. However, the 1952 INA maintained, over President Truman's veto, the obviously racist national quotas, and it called for stricter expulsion regulation that could possibly protect the United States from Communists.

Ngai notes that, for decades, "illegal aliens" were not a matter of broad national concern; they were perceived as problematic only in limited areas of the United States, particularly in the Southwest. Calls for curbing the presence of undocumented workers in the US labor force were weak at best, and what was known as "drying out wetbacks," or legalizing those in undocumentedness, became a prevalent practice. Indeed, yielding often to the demands of politically powerful farmers in need of laborers, authorities sometimes adjusted the status of immigrants through the symbolic performance of having them put one foot on the southern side of the border so that they could then "return" tc the United States. Up to the late 1940s, Ngai tells us, the Immigration and Naturalization Service (INS) worked predominantly to apprehend unauthorized border crossers and smugglers only at the moment and site of entry.

In this context, theatres in the United States that raised questions about immigration law in the early part of the twentieth century tended to address narrowly defined audiences, often in non-English-language stages and also often in the Southwest. Nicolás Kanellos describes a rich tradition of Spanish-language theatre that regularly tackled the subject of immigration and, more specifically, the legal challenges faced by immigrants. Plays like Gabriel Navarro's *Los emigrados* (The Émigrés), Antonio Helú's *Los mexicanos se van* (The Mexicans Are Leaving), and Eduardo Carrillo's *El proceso de Aurelio Pompa* (Aurelio Pompa's Trial) epitomize the concerns and experiences of 1920s Mexicans and Mexican Americans facing an increasingly strict and unfriendly US justice system in the nation's Southwest.[38] These titles testify to the concern for legal themes in portrayals of immigrant narratives. Indeed, since the Chinese Exclusion Act, courtrooms have regularly fielded the battles over immigration status, a contradictory phenomenon in which a challenge to the US legal system requires participation in, and thus deference to, that very system. As plaintiffs and defendants, as court winners or losers, immigrants on and offstage take part in that most cherished American tradition—litigation—and so assert their "Americanness" perhaps more than in other arenas when they join the most litigious society in the world.

By the 1920s well before characters with ties to Latin America had become a palpable presence on non-Spanish-language stages, Asian American figures began to lose the type of visibility described above. Contrary to the phenomenon noted by Dave Williams, the Johnson-Reed Immigration Act managed to push Asian American characters off US stages. Esther Kim Lee's study of Asian American theatre suggests that while many "oriental" shows in the United States regularly presented "alien residents" before the 1924 legislation, the Act inaugurated new treatment. Asian figures in US theatre ceased to represent US residents and were increasingly confined to Asian settings. In Lee's words, "It was as if the Immigration Act of 1924 erased Asian Americans from the national domestic imagination."[39] Early-twentieth-century practices thus point to connections that exist between immigration law and cultural production.

On the one hand, the plays offer models of the immigrant within the legal system. On the other, as Lee proposes, immigration law serves not only to control the population of the nation; it also alters the demographics of its theatrical characters.

Mid-century measures and policies caused fluctuations in the broad meanings of both "immigrant" and "illegal alien." As Ngai explains, preferential treatment for certain groups coupled with a stringent consulate bureaucracy in Mexico ensured that Mexicans, above all, "emerged as iconic illegal aliens" with the "construction of the 'wetback' as a dangerous and criminal social pathogen [feeding a] general racial stereotype 'Mexican.'"[40] Ngai demonstrates how immigration law not only reflects and reacts to social and cultural trends but also participates actively in the constitution of society. Law naturalizes relations and routines; it normalizes social practices. The various quota laws, in particular, constructed the "illegal alien" as well as the "alien citizen"—born in the United States and granted formal citizenship but perceived by most as alien due to his or her ethnicity.

While Ngai considers the law at three distinct levels—legislative and political discourse, court cases, and the practical or everyday articulation of the law—she pays only passing, if any, attention to cultural products, limiting her examination of "everyday articulations" predominantly to political discourse and press coverage of such. Still, legal issues and the immigrant experience did take center stage in various cultural performances, participating in the development of individual and collective legal consciousness so integral to formulating one's position in society and, by extension, one's identity. Theatrical treatments of illegal immigration during the period that Ngai examines attest to and help produce or maintain a legal imagination in which the undocumented are simultaneously problematic and completely normalized—in short, impossibly possible.

Relatively invisible to most US citizens, "illegal immigrants" nonetheless surfaced as central characters in two renowned mid-century theatrical pieces: Arthur Miller's *A View from the Bridge* and Richard Rodgers and Oscar Hammerstein's *Flower Drum Song*.[41] Perhaps because they each treat a distinct ethnic population (and because one is a musical comedy while the other a tragic play), the two have not invited serious joint consideration. I discuss them here as a unit; their pairing well attests to the impossible subjectivity and effective nonexistence that resulted from immigration policies of the first half of the twentieth century. Together, *A View from the Bridge* and *Flower Drum Song* attest also to a legal consciousness that made impossible subjects in fact quite possible.

The works probably do not need much introduction. *A View from the Bridge* premiered in the United States as a one-act verse drama in 1955. A year later, Miller rewrote the play into a full-length prose play that opened in London under Peter Brook's direction. It is this production's script that has endured and been regularly revived. Set in Red Hook, the play focuses on Eddie Carbone, an Italian American longshoreman, whose marriage to Beatrice is threatened by his increasingly intense feelings for his niece, Catherine. The arrival of two cousins from Italy, Rodolpho and Marco, exacerbates Eddie's tumult, as Catherine begins a relationship with one of these "submarines" (waterfront slang for those who entered the United States illegally in order to work). *Flower Drum Song*, based on a novel by C. Y. Lee and directed by Gene Kelly when it premiered on Broadway in 1958, was Rodgers and Hammerstein's third collaboration to treat an exoticized Asia, following *South Pacific* (1949) and *The King and I* (1951). Although not as commercially successful as some of their other musicals, *Flower Drum Song* nevertheless led to a London production, a national tour, and a film version within just three years of its premiere. The musical follows Mei Li's illegal arrival as a picture bride from China to California. Complications arise when her promised husband opts not to marry her. Eventually, Mei Li wins the heart of Wang Ta, a young Chinese American man whose father operates a theatre in San Francisco's thriving Chinatown.

To date, Rodolpho and Mei Li remain some of the most broadly performed and circulated characters defined by undocumentedness on US stages. On the surface, both *A View from the Bridge* and *Flower Drum Song* propose that immigration laws are inherently unfair. Rodolpho is in the United States to "work, that's all" (*VB* 627) and Mei Li has "no papers" only because "com[ing] in under the quota would take another five years" and make her "too old to get married" (*FDS* 25). Beatrice's defense of her undocumented cousins, "Who're they hurtin', for God's sake, what do you want from them?" (*VB* 627), aptly captures the attitudes toward Rodolpho and his brother Marco as well as toward Mei Li and her father, if I may apply one play's line of dialogue to the other. Indeed, Rodolpho and Mei Li quite easily fit into their new respective communities despite their illegal status. Little separates them from those already living in the depicted Italian American Red Hook or in San Francisco's Chinatown.[42] Such portrayals support and reflect common mid-century practices of unmaking illegal status via administrative policies, such as the "drying out" described above. The portrayals thus point to the limits of exclusionary immigration legislation.

Still, undocumentedness propels much of the action in both theatrical pieces, with illegality engendering a kind of fear that fundamentally alters a sense of self. Quickly, Rodolpho learns that if he "were not afraid to be arrested [he] would start to be something wonderful here!" (*VB* 614). The law seemingly curbs his possibilities, his dreams, even as we witness his success. Despite consistent employment and despite a blossoming relationship with Catherine, his time in the United States can end at any moment. His romantic intentions, especially, become suspect. Is Rodolpho after Catherine's heart or her citizenship? "Purposely," Miller has confessed, "we are left to wonder about [Rodolpho's feelings]."[43] Although there is less to doubt about the earnest Mei Li, and although her time in the United States seems less explicitly threatened, her illegality crucially serves to construct her identity as an active agent.

It is the cultural production of such an illegal identity that sparks a moment of recognition for Mei Li. She emulates the heroines of television movies to woo her preferred partner and fulfill the American Dream. One such figure, a "Mexican girl," provides Mei Li with a definitive solution to the mismatches of partners around which the musical's plot revolves. "Señor Sheriff, I must give myself up!" pleads the girl in the film Mei Li watches. The voice from the television confesses that she "came to the United States illegally across the Rio Grande," that she is a "wetback," and that she "cannot marry with Rodriquez [sic]" because "he is in love with another woman, and he is a wetback too!" (FDS 137). The overly melodramatic delivery makes little legal sense; the girl's problem is unrequited love and not her or her beloved's immigration status. But recognizing herself in the performance, Mei Li finds in her illegality an exit strategy from her impending nuptials to Sammy Fong, a man she does not love and who clearly loves another. Just one scene later, Mei Li confronts Sammy, his mother, and the rest of the community with the purportedly awful truth: "I came into this country illegally—across the Pacific Ocean. It is for that I cannot marry with your son. My back is wet!" What has not mattered before now becomes critical, and Madame Fong insists that her son "cannot marry a wetback!" This is a term used multiple times within the production's final minutes and one that easily sticks to Mei Li. Madame Fong suddenly remembers—and reminds the audience—that such a wet back is dangerous, problematic, and lowly. The perfect leading man, Ta offers at this last moment that he will "gladly marry a wetback!" (FDS 139–40). A plot convenience, Mei Li's illegal status serves predominantly to untie all the knots. Almost.

Ta's eagerness to wed an illegal alien does not fully satisfy the musical comedy's necessary ending. The true happily-ever-after here is possible only because, through marriage, Mei Li's illegal status will be undone, just as Rodolpho's is when he marries Catherine. In the world of each piece, undocumentedness cannot possibly be sustained. Indeed, there are no impossible subjects left on either stage at play's end. Following the familyties logic of the 1952 INA, Ta's proposal means not only that Mei Li will gain citizenship through marriage but also that Dr. Li—the only other illegal immigrant in *Flower Drum Song*—becomes a candidate for legal residence and eventual naturalization. The riddance of illegal immigrants in *A View from the Bridge* proves even more sweeping. Rodolpho will gain legal status through marriage. His brother, we gather from Marco's conversation with the lawyer Alfieri, has no prospects of staying in the country (*VB* 630–31). Furthermore, Eddie's informing the immigration authorities about Marco's and Rodolpho's illegal status results, from the audience's perspective, in the arrest of *all* the known submarines. The two nonspeaking "strange immigrants," whom both audiences and characters perceive to be undocumented, must also endure the roundup and are removed from the stage by the Second Immigration Officer (*VB* 627, 629). With Marco's insistence that Eddie's betrayal has robbed and killed his children back in Italy, we could surmise as well that a new generation of potential immigrants dies within the world of the play.

But the "naturalization" of Rodolpho and of Mei Li fails to be transgressive in either case, as the only seeming solution to their condition is to accept a system in place and become citizens. This they do through marriage, at a time when "there's no law, [when] the law is not interested" (*VB* 603) in the substance of a marital relationship in relation to immigration status. Heteronormative unions manifestly solve the problem of illegality, using one legal label—"wife," "husband"—to naturalize the unnatural "wetback" or "submarine."[44] The seeming correction of Rodolpho's and Mei Li's status then results, in both cases, because the fulfillment of individual desires requires legalization, not, to be sure, because the system is inherently flawed. The two portrayals just prior to a period of drastic immigration reform suggest a broad legal consciousness that very much can accept the illegal status as natural. They each depict a community—albeit a relatively isolated (and, especially in the case of *Flower Drum Song*, exoticized) community—in which undocumentedness can easily exist. They both suggest that the exit strategy out of undocumentedness—created in the first place by a logic of quantitative restriction—rests strictly on individual qualitative conditions and individual agency. Mei Li and Rodolpho, at bottom, should not be illegal aliens, because they simply do not fit the bill. He can become "something wonderful here" and she will "like it here" (*FDS* 47), because neither appears threatening to the "here" at hand. Of course, such an argument comes with a tacit dark side, an implication that someone else, or other personal qualities, be those physical prowess or Mexicanness, can and should be deemed illegal and alien.

On multiple levels, Rodolpho and Mei Li defy common mid-century notions of "the wetback" as criminal, male, and Mexican. Their exit from undocumentedness can therefore maintain stereotypes even as it critiques an unfair legal system. As he seemingly pushes the boundaries of traditional masculinity (at least in Eddie's and his fellow longshoremen's view), Rodolpho also queers the role of submarine. Much attention has been paid to the question of Rodolpho's sexuality, but less has been made of the fact that it is precisely this more feminized and more Nordic-looking figure that gains legal acceptance into the United States. Richard Davalos, cast as Rodolpho in the 1955 premiere of *A View from the Bridge*, helped to underscore the difference of the particular undocumented immigrant at hand and laid a baseline of sorts for all Rodolphos to come. Compared to his über-masculine castmates Jack Warden (Marco) and Van Heflin (Eddie), the preppy, platinum blond Davalos, known to the 1955 audiences predominantly as "the sweetheart of Brother Aron" in the film *East of Eden*,[45] presented a candidate for legalization who lacked his brother's roughness and explicit manliness. Even the biographies in the program prepared the audiences for this distinction: spectators read that Warden was a "former professional boxer and baseball player"; that Heflin, a "mixture of college-bred gentleman and two-fisted sailor," "had desires of only traveling the seas [...and journeyed] on a coastwise cargo boat for New York via the Panama Canal"; and that Davalos, instead, "acted with the Chapel Theatre Group, which presented plays for children at various schools in New Jersey [and] learned dancing from Martha Graham and Erick Hawkins."[46] Accordingly, Miller creates a submarine with "bright lights in his head," lights that potentially blind him to the realities and responsibilities by which a "regular slave" like Marco lives (*VB* 597, 594). Such lights figuratively illuminate a way of existing without papers that displaces the norms of what undocumentedness might mean, both within the world of the play and for the audience that watches. Rodolpho knows, for example, that he must not sing, a more than symbolic reminder that he must not call attention to himself. But Rodolpho quickly becomes a center of attention both on the docks and in the Carbone home with his song and sense of humor. He proves to be an active lover and an active entertainer of sorts; he succeeds in areas not conventionally associated with the invisible undocumented laboring population to which his brother more fittingly belongs.

Mei Li also surfaces as a queered illegal alien. She is not supposedly in the United States to work. Despite her cartoonish accent, Mei Li speaks English quite fluidly. Even if this is merely a theatrical convention (why would she speak English to her father?), the use of accented language follows the same model as *A View from the Bridge*, offering "fresh off the boat" characters who communicate effortlessly in their new environment and whose speech blends quite easily with that of others around them. The casting of Miyoshi Umeki as the original Mei Li, much like the casting of Davalos, further highlighted the frailty and meekness of the undocumented figure. As the production's press release promised, the "Japanese singing doll" was a "petite and lovely 22-year-old singing actress [...] whose first name means 'beautiful life,' [and who] single-handedly stole the hearts of the United States military forces in Japan with her lilting voice and demure smile."[47] Mei Li and Rodolpho, crucially, are not of Mexican origin. In this, they certainly defy prevalent stereotypes, then and now, about illegal aliens and corroborate the position of European and later of Asian immigrants as "model minorities." The two cultural products thus serve to reinforce and naturalize, even as they criticize, the idea that immigration can be deemed systematically illegal.

The 1965 amendments to 1952 INA attempted in some manner to address the ambivalences in US immigration policy captured by *Flower Drum Song* and *A View from the Bridge*. Born in part from the momentum of the Civil Rights movement, the new immigration policies abolished the system of national quotas that had increasingly been criticized as racist. The 1965 INA thus abolished a hierarchy of immigration based on national origin and replaced it with a system of preference based predominantly on family reunification and labor skills. While a more liberal policy on the surface, the new law did curb immigration in serious ways and, more than before, called national attention to the "problem" of illegal immigrants, especially by conceding that migrants from the Western Hemisphere needed for the first time to be counted among a newly established world quota. Illegal immigration—and the Mexican border more specifically—was indeed becoming a subject of broader interest, although it would still take some years before it received serious academic attention, attesting perhaps to a more general legal consciousness unconcerned with the undocumented.

Issues of labor and family have remained structuring principles for post-1965 immigration policy. But subsequent legislation, including the 1980 Refugee Act, the 1986 Immigration Reform and Control Act (IRCA), the 1990 Immigration Act, and the 1996 Illegal Immigration Reform and Immigrant Responsibility Act (IIRIRA), has both responded to and fueled a heightened public anxiety over the undocumented. Post-1965 laws have turned illegal immigration into a pivotal—*the* pivotal?—way of conceiving immigration generally. Since the September 11 attacks of 2001 and the passage of the Patriot Act, the Homeland Security Act, and the Enhanced Border Security and Visa Entry Reform Act (EBSVERA), concerns over terrorism and national security have also become driving forces behind the kinds of legislation and court tests that continue to amend the 1965 base upon which our immigration policy rests today. Crucially, post-1965 immigration law has had to manage the increased presence of undocumented immigrants more than in periods past—reminders that the system of law and border patrol does not always accomplish its set goals.

Theatre production in the United States also changed significantly in the wake of the 1960s. With the Civil Rights movement and the subsequent explosion of identity politics, the emergence and proliferation of self-identified minority theatre companies and artists radically affected and continue to affect the performance of undocumented characters. The institutionalization and promotion of "Chicana/o," "Latina/o," "Asian American," "Chinese American" artists and cultural products, for example, have ensured that undocumentedness remains an actively staged phenomenon on ostensibly specialized stages. For the most part, it has been artists of the hyphen who have treated and challenged the undocumented condition onstage, concentrating on stories about "their" brothers and sisters.

Immigration statistics help to underscore the fact that undocumentedness as a theatrical subject tends to attract particular attention, first and foremost, from artists with ties to Mexico and other Latin American countries, and then from those with ties to Asia.[48] Throughout the 1970s and 1980s, Latina/o and Asian American playwrights and theatre collectives set a precedent for so-called artists of color to create theatre pieces calling attention to the undocumentedness, whether head-on or more subtly. Prominent examples of this trend include Frank Chin's *The Year of the Dragon*, Rodrigo Duarte-Clark's *Brujerías*, David Henry Hwang's *FOB*, Genny Lim's *Paper Angels*, Estela Portillo Trambley's *Sun Images* and *Puente Negro*, Dolores Prida's *Beautiful Señoritas*, Milcha Sánchez-Scott's *Latina*, Luis Valdez's *Quinta Temporada* and *Los Vendidos*, and Teatro de la Esperanza's *Guadalupe* and *La víctima*. Into the 1990s, theatre artists like Guillermo Gómez-Peña, Miguel González-Pando, Velina Hasu Houston, John Leguizamo, Josefina López, Cherríe Moraga, Kabu Okai-Davies, Edit Villarreal, and Teatro Raíces challenged audiences more directly to consider the phenomenon of illegal immigration in the United States.

In the face of legal media circuses like Zoë Baird's 1993 "nannygate," in which President Clinton's derailed nominee for attorney general brought unprecedented national attention to undocumented domestic workers but nonetheless depicted Baird's chauffeur and child-care provider mostly as invisible, nameless abstractions, theatre artists sought more aggressively to surrogate the humanity erased in such debates. John Leguizamo, as the undocumented Pepe in *Mambo Mouth*, charges: "What are you so afraid of?"[49] The question well encapsulates how many of the performances of the period challenged audiences and their legal consciousness, even if the works sustained conceptions of illegal immigration as a specifically ethnic rather than a national or global phenomenon.

The focus on (il)legal status has allowed at times for productive movement across ethnic lines. Some artists have endeavored explicitly to collapse different immigration histories and experiences into a single stage event (JoAnne Akalaitis's *Green Card*, Mary Gallagher's *¿De dónde?*, Elizabeth Wong's *Letters to a Student Revolutionary*, Chay Yew's *A Beautiful Country*, and Oliver Mayer's *Conjunto* are notable illustrations). While such efforts can reinscribe particular stereotypes even as they critique cruel immigration policies, the bringing together of different groups productively interrupts the kind of cultural and political isolation that results when unauthorized immigration is treated predominantly through ethnic categorization.

Other interesting and effective interruptions can also occur through adaptation and casting. A 1978 production of *A View from the Bridge* by the Four Seas Players in New York City, for instance, transferred the tragedy from Red Hook to Chinatown, changing little of the submarines' story. The Source Theatre Company in Washington, DC, offered a Dominican community at the center of its 1995 production of the play.[50] Such alterations, I think, pinpoint the crucial role that US immigration law plays in constructing a hostile environment and a fragile identity for all those without papers. Miller himself seemed to appreciate a cross-ethnic approach to staging his work. Of a production at City College in New York City in the late 1970s, he commented, "The Eddie Carbone character was played by a Korean; his wife was Jewish; the young people were all Chinese. The cast was terrific—and not one resembled the other! I thought it was inspiring."[51] Similarly, for David Henry Hwang, who rewrote the book for the musical in 2001, what is at the core of *Flower Drum Song* is the clash of cultures coming together in a century marked by increased movement of people across national borders. Theatre and film historian Laurence Maslon supports Hwang and offers the view that the "smuggled" Mei Li and her father represent one pole in a broad experience: these characters are "archetypes for anybody in any city in America. Whether they're Chinese or Jewish immigrants or Irish immigrants or whatever. They represent all the different aspects of trying to come to grips with what it means to live in this country."[52]

Even if it could speak to a universal immigrant experience—a difficult claim to make—*Flower Drum Song*'s trajectory into the twenty-first century demonstrates how the meaning of legal status has shifted and how the occupants of the pole Maslon describes adjust with it. As a film in 1961 (directed by Henry Koster), the piece heightened the audience's awareness of Mei Li's illegality by adding an opening sequence that detailed her and her father's surreptitious entry into the San Francisco port. But when the show was reconceived by Hwang, Mei Li's back was no longer wet. A self-proclaimed "refugee," the character is explicitly escaping a violent Communist regime and is presumably legally permitted into the new country.[53] While Hwang writes a darker piece in which the immigrant experience is far more painful than in the original musical comedy, his narrative no longer has room for an undocumented protagonist. Hwang's character list and stage directions consistently refer to refugees as well as to "new immigrants"; there are no indications that the characters have crossed US borders illegally. NBC/Universal, which released the DVD of the 1961 film in 2006, likewise chooses to describe Mei Li in its synopsis as a "young Chinese girl who travels to the United States as part of an arranged marriage."[54] *Flower Drum Song* is thus officially advertised today without reference to immigration status, despite both the 1958 Broadway musical's and the movie's insistence on such plot point. The revised *Flower Drum Song* suggests that an unauthorized immigrant might no longer prove as viable a protagonist for a major commercial endeavor as might have been the case in the late 1950s. Indeed, at the extreme edge of the commercial pole of theatre production, the undocumented remain today virtually invisible.

New York Times reviews of major productions of *A View from the Bridge*, from the premiere in 1955 to a 2010 Broadway revival, indicate similar trends in approaching undocumentedness. A preoccupation with illegality begins to surge in the 1960s; by the twenty-first century, illegal status becomes an increasingly suspect trait for a sympathetic stage character. Brooks Atkinson writes in 1955 that the play involves "two Italians smuggled in aboard a cargo ship," a phrase he repeats twice, not once using the word "illegal" (or "undocumented" or "submarine"). Rodolpho and Marco, seemingly, are not the subjects of their actions, but rather victims of a system. Richard Coe chose to introduce the brothers in a review of a 1956 transfer from London without any mention of their immigration status. Nearly a decade later, as immigration reform was very much in the air, an off-Broadway revival earned John Voight as Rodolpho the label of "illegal Sicilian immigrant" in Howard Taubman's critique. By the early 1980s, reviews of a new Broadway production more consistently referred to Rodolpho and Marco as "illegal immigrants," dropping all qualifiers and letting the two single words tell a presumably well-known story to their readers. With Ben Brantley's 1997 review we find a new approach, as Marco and Rodolpho become men who "have entered the United States illegally to seek work." Here, they are active agents who have made a decisive choice. Brantley addresses the issue of illegality much more hesitantly in his review of the 2010 revival. He introduces "two Italian cousins of Beatrice's—young men in need of work (and illegally in the country)— ... " Brantley relegates Marco and Rodolpho's unauthorized entry to parentheses within dashes, privileging now their necessity for employment over the condition of their immigration. Although I present different critics here, each reviewing a distinct production with his own style of writing, this short sample of articles does indicate a changing attention to the roles of the submarines and thus, perhaps, to a changing national legal consciousness.[55]

As we move toward the more restricted pole of twenty-first-century cultural production, we find a flourishing variety of performances interested in scrutinizing illegal immigration. Sarah Jones, Rick Najera, and Ntare Mwine, like Leguizamo, have in recent years challenged stereotypes of the illegal alien directly in their much traveled and broadly acclaimed solo and monologue-based performances. Off-Broadway and on the regional theatre circuit, playwrights such as Lisa Loomer and Octavio Solis and companies such as Culture Clash and The Civilians have managed to garner attention for the topic of undocumented immigration from relatively wide-ranging audiences. And in community-based theatres across the United States, artists have countered the intensified anti-illegal immigration vitriol of the 1990s and 2000s—Proposition 187, English Only, Border Fence Project, Light Up the Border, Minuteman Project, Lou Dobbs, Bill O'Reilly, Tom Tancredo, Pat Buchanan, Ann Coulter, and Arizona SB 1070 law and its copycats—with renewed interest in stories about undocumentedness. We thus approach the moment that I describe earlier in the chapter, a post-2006 era to which *Intríngulis* belongs.

These are but some of many examples, but they serve here to pinpoint certain trends. First, at a basic level, there is a demonstrably growing interest in performances that implicate undocumentedness. Second, most of these performances approach the topic from a predominantly pro-immigrant point of view. It is not difficult to see that, as they participate actively in furthering a dialogue about the border more generally, most artists seek to call attention to the unfair, problematic, and often catastrophic consequences of living in undocumentedness. Third, as each of the subsequent chapters will explore, the performances broaden the visibility of legal nonexistence. And in creating a space of existence, these performances often succeed not just in calling attention to but also subverting legal identities. At times, however, such performances can reiterate and naturalize certain legal categories and perpetuate economic and political structures that create illegal immigration in the first place. Finally, these most recent performances, together with earlier examples, attest to a common understanding of immigration law that is increasingly filtered through the issue of illegal immigration, highlighting the power of legal consciousness to shape our individual and our collective sense of self. Within this context, I turn to specific case studies in the ensuing chapters so that I can more deeply examine performances of legal nonexistence on the contemporary US stage.

2

Act § 275(a)—Improper Entry by Alien

In Culture Clash's interview-inspired *Bordertown*, the character Julia tells us, "To cross the border is a big decision, it's like being reborn."[1] Legal borders indeed suggest lines of consequence: cross them and something will, or at least should, happen. That something involves performances of various sorts, as I explore in this chapter. After all, the national border cannot establish its power without requiring some material interaction between those entering a country and those charged with guarding the literal and metaphoric gates. Borders thus become sites that demand concrete performances from its crossers and custodians. When we imagine the national border as a phenomenon that operates through performance, we begin to understand the power, as well as the fragility, of such a legally constructed boundary. And perhaps in the legal act of crossing a border, and through the performances it requires, one is reborn.

Analyzing modern European borders and the movement of refugees, Sophie Nield has explored the border's "theatricality." She suggests that crossing national boundaries requires specific types of appearance: border crossers must present themselves physically and also represent their legitimacy. These appearances resemble the performances of actors, who are simultaneously a physical body and a representative figure onstage. Nield posits border encounters as moments "at which 'you' are produced" for an audience of "observers, inspectors, judges" through the conjunction of actual and represented presence.[2] US immigration law likewise demands that those seeking entry into the country present and represent themselves as legitimate candidates.

In fact, US law today insists on a live performance from border crossers. Until the early twentieth century, immigration procedures stressed the inspection of bodies at the border. In the 1920s, new procedures began to focus on the inspection of documents (some of which attested to healthy bodies inspected abroad rather than at the point of entry). US immigration officials have moved increasingly, and especially after the attacks of 9/11, toward inspecting border crossers' biometric traits as well as their documents. None of these innovations has altered the fact that immigration processes continue to rely on face-to-face interactions. The 1965 Immigration and Nationality Act (INA) still requires that "all aliens (including alien crewmen) who are applicants for admission or otherwise seeking admission or readmission to or transit through the United States shall be inspected by immigration officers."[3] Penetrating the national border thus involves an actual or a potential interface with a border official. Papers, fingerprints, and retinal scans may be the focus of these exchanges, but the legally required encounter necessitates embodied, live contact. Such an interview does not always occur at a geographic border and does not always coincide with the time of entry. The encounter can take place at an airport in St. Louis or at a road stop deep in a Texas highway. It can take place at the moment of arrival into the United States or months later. The border that immigration law creates is therefore much more fluid than the Rio Grande and less precise than the forty-ninth parallel.

Borrowing from Diana Taylor's conception of scenarios, I propose we approach interactions at this fluid border as repeatable, transferable, meaning-making templates.[4] I offer the "border scenario" as a tool to understand how immigration law operates through performance. Since they combine a textual/narrative component with an embodied experience, border scenarios extend opportunities for reiterations and restagings that potentially disturb the power dynamics at play. Border scenarios center on the performances of two central figures: border crosser and border monitor, each in various permutations and always mutually constructed. These key players engage through intricately related strategies in a contained drama, whose repetitions and variations prove critical in continuing imaginings of national borders. A great number of theatre pieces tackling the issue of immigration into the United States offer versions of the INA interrogation integral to the border scenario. Be it an immigrant–immigration officer encounter (e.g., *A Beautiful Country, Aliens with Extraordinary Skills*), an immigrant–security enforcer run-in (e.g., *Detained in the Desert, Walking to America*), an immigrant-vigilante confrontation (e.g., *Nowhere on the Border, American Jornalero*), or an immigrant-judge interrogation (e.g., *FOB, !Bocón!*), onstage repetitions of border scenarios provide a glimpse into ways in which the national border is imagined and surfaces as a materially consequential site.

Taylor carefully distinguishes scenarios from case studies. She reminds us that scenarios operate hypothetically and offer "not what *is* but what *if.*"

As works of art, theatre pieces that stage border scenarios ably play in the hypothetical and allow for a reconsideration of the border. Nield advocates that theatre opens "an alternative form of border space" in order to frame and problematize questions of nation and identity. However, border scenarios, especially when staged in an interview-based piece such as *Bordertown*, remind us that the line between hypothesis and observation is not clear-cut. *What if*, the stage piece insists, can alert us to *what was* or *what is*. As Taylor herself has suggested, "simulation produces the new real."[5] We must therefore pay attention to how representations of border interactions can both propel cultural imaginaries and direct real-life exchanges between border crossers and managers.

Studies of real-life immigration screenings demonstrate that US officials at international airports and road crossings tend to operate mechanically, submitting to routine. These studies help contextualize one of the key players in a typical border scenario, one that has changed little since the early twentieth century.[6] Despite the shift toward document-based transactions, border officials remain involved in human-to-human processes that ask them to assess the believability of entrants' claims without recourse to exact guidelines. Discrete characteristics of an individual's appearance, behavior, and speech can sway an officer's decision to grant or deny entry or recommend further inspection. Prior experiences in the job (both personal and organizational) and a work culture that demands speed and caution often prove influential in shaping the decision-making process.

As for border crossers, the border interview essentially creates a legally conscious figure with a distinct goal: entry. I call attention to the entrant's basic desire, since legal consciousness and performance converge here. Whatever personal feelings or knowledge about immigration law the entrant may have, crossing a border reflects a conscious legal choice and requires the type of credible performance that potential entrants believe will grant them passage. Entrants must consider how best to manage or avoid altogether the face-to-face interaction that border scenarios demand. Their approach thus relies on imagining the possible actions of a border monitor.

Elsewhere, I have discussed how a legal process can push participants beyond the everyday and into a performance, if we follow Eugenio Barba's description of such as an extra-daily phenomenon.[7] While border interactions might prove routine for monitors (and thus their mechanical approach), the border scenario places crossers in a type of extra-daily situation. Indeed, the role of applicant for admission offers a clear, powerful purpose for the player, one that must be pursued in a focused and determined manner. Extending Barba's understanding of the actor, we might say that the applicant is a "decided body" resolute in his or her desire to enter the country. Driven by a Stanislavskian supertask, the applicant in a border scenario is, theoretically at least, fully prepared to dismiss the extraneous and irrelevant, anything that might prevent him or her from remaining true to the throughaction.[8] For those crossing a national border without proper authorization, the border scenario proves especially pressing, so that they become especially decided. Their embodied participation in the performance that immigration law requires must take one of two forms to increase the likelihood that the border official will permit entry. We could call these "performances of invisibility" and "performances of credibility."

The Pew Research Center has estimated that roughly 55 percent of unauthorized immigrants in the early 2000s entered the United States without passing through inspection.[9] In order to avoid this requirement, entrants must actively disappear themselves, be it by hiding, by traversing unmonitored borders, or, in many cases, by doing both. Performances of invisibility thus erase crossings and presence in order to avoid the playing out of a border scenario. Such tactics also postpone or transfer the potential interaction to a different, perhaps unknown, place and time. So, the probability of a border scenario lingers, and the fear of an encounter with immigration officials ultimately still structures experiences within undocumentedness.

Many entrants do present themselves at the border, in which case a performance of credibility becomes necessary. For those with forged papers or the knowledge that they will violate the terms of their visas, these performances of credibility inevitably become more acute. The stakes are raised, as the type of appearance made necessary involves a conscious effort to bridge the gap between the physical person and its paper representation, to revisit Nield's proposition. The decided border crosser, like an actor, must convince his or her audience, even for just one moment, of a particular truth. The performance will depend on personal experience and the experiences and stories of other border crossers. The tactics utilized anticipate what an immigration official might be like and so reveal and transmit "cultural fantasies, fears, and values," as Taylor avers all scenarios do.[10] The need for performances of credibility requires theatrical attention to a range of details, from what to wear and say to how to move and breathe. Of his own crossing into undocumentedness, Harold Fernandez depicts a preparation process similar to rehearsing an intricate piece of theatre. Rubén Martínez describes how *coyotes* (smugglers) serve as acting coaches, directing their *pollitos'* (literally, chicks') speech, wardrobe, and storyline to achieve a credible performance for immigration officials. There is a "Look," a specific combination of garments and ways of wearing them that can attract or prevent the Border Patrol's attention, explains Debbie Nathan. And in his auto-ethnographic study of borders in an era of transnationalism and globalization, Shahram Khosravi insists that border crossings are matters of performance: "If you are self-assured, you can cross any border even with the worst passport in your hand. But your body can betray you, and border guards can recognize the tell-tale signs at once." In short, as Susan Coutin succinctly describes, unauthorized migrants must "act by appearing *not* to act."[11]

Critically, performances of invisibility and performances of credibility can both alter their actors' legal consciousness and shape a sense of self. In her analysis of migrants crossing into undocumentedness, Cecilia Olivares concludes that "crossing the border for the illegal migrants is a uniquely politicized experience." It leads to the "formulation of identities that exist within particular spaces of the border" precisely because the means of achieving entrance into the United States requires extraordinary feats vis-à-vis increasingly fatal obstacles. Moreover, neither performances of invisibility or of credibility offer a reprieve from the border scenario, whose threat continues to exist even after the moment of crossing. The border, as Linda Bosniak explains, follows noncitizens inside.[12] We can thus begin to understand performances at the border as rituals of transition, or baptisms, as *Bordertown*'s Julia does.

I will continue in this chapter to consider the role that performance plays in crossing legally defined borders and the ways in which border scenario performances can drastically mold an entrant's identity. Through Culture Clash's *Bordertown* and Genny Lim's *Paper Angels*, I focus on the material consequences of initial interactions between border crossers and monitors. The plays stage different historical moments, but both explore immigration law's dependence on performance and performance's potential to disrupt the law. I then read Josefina López's *Real Women Have Curves* as evidence for the lasting effects on identity that crossing a legal border can prompt as well as for tactics used to counter the performances demanded by immigration processes. In the chapter's final section, I consider the trajectories of the three plays, noting how the field of cultural production in the United States naturalizes and solidifies other borders. Ironically, as the plays criticize the power of seemingly arbitrary boundaries, they also exemplify the ease with which ostensibly imagined lines continue to divide. Together, the plays point to ways in which theatre can activate border scenarios, play with the dynamics of the exchange, and ultimately reimagine the concept of a national border.

Performances at the Legal Border

Genny Lim's *Paper Angels*, premiered in 1980 by the Asian American Theater Company in San Francisco, centers on several Chinese men and women awaiting entry into the United States. The play is set in 1915 at the Angel Island Immigration Detention Center, where nearly one million immigrants were inspected and processed by government agents between 1910 and 1940 while the Chinese Exclusion Act was still in effect. In the late 1970s, Lim collaborated with historians Him Mark Lai and Judy Young—all descendants of immigrants processed at Angel Island—to collect poems recently discovered on the walls of the detention center and to interview surviving detainees. The oral histories and poetry led to a publication, but Lim feared that "more people wouldn't find out about this period of history and [so] decided that drama was the best way to reach more people."[13] Indeed, *Paper Angels* has been produced regularly in the United States, as well as in Canada and China, especially after a 1985 televised presentation for PBS's *American Playhouse*. As a documentary drama drawing directly from experiences of individuals who passed through Angel Island, the play complicates a neat division between scenario and case study. *Paper Angels* rehearses hypothetical interactions and simultaneously presents phenomena that are observable, recordable, and actually lived.

Also an interview-inspired work that blurs lines between the hypothetical and evidentiary, the 1998 *Bordertown* presents the performance troupe Culture Clash's inquiry into the San Diego–Tijuana region. The San Diego Repertory Theatre commissioned Richard Montoya, Ric Salinas, and Herbert Siguenza—the writer-performers who make up Culture Clash—to create the piece after the trio's foray into a similar exploration of Miami in *Radio Mambo*. Cultural Clash presented *Bordertown* in several regional stages beyond San Diego, including the Mark Taper Forum in Los Angeles and the Actors Theatre in Phoenix. Additionally, Culture Clash included portions of *Bordertown* in its *Culture Clash in Americca*, which toured in the early 2000s, and audiotaped *Bordertown* for L.A. Theatre Works. *Bordertown* offers a satirical, but compelling, portrait of the intricately linked San Diego–Tijuana border area and their inhabitants at the end of the twentieth century.

Quite different in tone, subject matter, and trajectory, *Paper Angels* and *Bordertown* both reveal how immigration law participates actively in shaping personal identity and notions of national boundaries. The two plays begin similarly with border scenarios materializing out of darkness and operate on suggestive rather than concrete stage designs. *Bordertown* was presented on a sparse set, with colorful costumes and an intricate soundscape locating the piece's action; the original production of *Paper Angels* conveyed barracks through the use of exposed pipes. In both cases, performances of recognizable immigration interrogations instantly conjure border spaces.

In *Paper Angels*, a recorded interrogation begins to play over "*a darkly lit*" tableau: "*Chinese immigrants...are suspended in silent postures of expectation, longing and fear. An interpreter translates and a typewriter is heard in the background*" (*PA* 19). The disembodied dialogue emphasizes the everyman nature of the exchange; a nonspecific inspector probes the credibility of an individual who could be any of the bodies on display. Even if some productions decide to stage fully the 40-line prologue rather than rely on a voice-over, Lim's dialogue offers few indications about the sole Applicant. Not included in the list of characters, the Applicant surfaces only as male (from a stage direction about "his" hands) and as possibly 20 years old (from his answer to a question about his birthdate). The information requested of the Applicant suggests a rather bizarre nightmare; the government agent presses to discover details about the Applicant's mother's feet and the number of stairs to his doorstep. The vagueness for which Lim calls, the detached presence hovering over still and fearful bodies, and the mechanical typing foretelling the creation of a menacing record evoke for her late-twentieth-century audience a Kafkaesque bureaucracy. Lim's character descriptions further insist on the sinister atmosphere by guiding actors and directors to create government officials who are slaves to a machine. For the Interpreter, Lim suggests someone who performs his or her duties "with distinction and objectivity" (*PA* 18), a figure whose loyalty, above all, is to the job. The playwright specifies that the Interpreter can be played by a man or a woman or both, if two actors are desired. It matters little for the structure of the piece who the individual playing the Interpreter is. Likewise, the Inspector, as one of few unnamed characters (the Warden is the other one), functions as a cog. He is "a civil servant, who's come up through the ranks"; a man defined by his title (*PA* 18). The cold, generic figures do not reveal individual personalities and portray instead a heartless system. They are part of a structure wholly devoid of humanity.

Lim's reliance on unnamed, utilitarian characters fits a broader pattern for staging border scenarios. Characters in the role of border monitor often go by generic names, even as the border crossers are individualized (e.g., *¿De dónde?*, *El Otro*). Through machinelike government servants, Lim recalls the type of behavior observed in studies of immigration officers and critiques oppressive policies. Her border scenario not only reveals the power dynamics between immigrant and officer but also the system dynamics that rob officers of their souls. Lim purposefully metes out flesh and blood unevenly, and the dramaturgical strategy of dehumanizing the officers serves to direct the audience's focus and allegiance toward the more humanized border crossers. The bodies waiting onstage at the outset of the piece—all possible Applicants—will transform after the prologue into individualized, named, and complex characters with which the audience can more easily identify.

The opening darkness that *Bordertown* demands is much more violently interrupted. Indeed, by 1998, when Culture Clash developed its piece, the border—especially along the southwestern United States—had seen a surge in violence and vigilantism against immigrants. The 1990s had ushered in an era of heightened attention to unauthorized immigration as a national security concern and to those living in undocumentedness as criminals rather than job-seekers (see chapter 5). Military-style campaigns—such as Operation Blockade (later renamed Operation Hold-the-Line) and Operation Rio Grande in Texas, Operation Gatekeeper in California, and Operation Safeguard in Arizona—attested to the federal government's ramped-up efforts to police the national border, efforts bolstered also by private-led endeavors such as the Minuteman Project and Light Up the Border.[14] *Bordertown* thus evokes the border as a site of peril and chaos. The sounds of a chase—panicked voices speaking Spanish, the word "Halt!" repeated in English, running feet, a vehicle screeching—and truck headlights sweeping the stage pull the audience immediately into the action. When the stage lights come up, "*Two Mexican illegals are caught, frozen like deer in the harsh lights. The Militia Man in head-to-toe army fatigues has captured them*" (*B* 9).

Culture Clash's opening scenario shifts quickly from an aggressive encounter to a comedy of mistaken identities. "We're not Mexicans," repeat the ironically named Mexican 1 and Mexican 2. With an armed, foul-mouthed vigilante in the position of gatekeeper, the initial contact is explosive and the "two wets," as Militia Man refers to them, clearly face physical danger. They are made to lie on the ground, a shotgun cocked and pointed at them. Carefully placed jokes snap the audience out from the nerve-racking situation. "I'm volunteer 1-8-7," the Militia Man announces into his walkie-talkie. A reference to the infamous Proposition 187 (the ultimately unconstitutional "Save Our State" initiative that Californian voters approved in 1994 to ban unauthorized immigrants from a range of social services), the moniker draws laughs.[15] The vigilante's stereotypically gringo Spanish—"cállate la boca" becomes "cayateh la book-ah"—also proves amusing to the audience. But it is Mexican 1's plea to Volunteer 187 to stop speaking in the language that garners the show's first riotous laugh: "He doesn't speak Spanish, sir. He's a Chicano!" (*B* 10). In just over a minute, Culture Clash transforms the border scenario into a situation comedy by stretching the participants into extremes: an overly hawkish, self-appointed, and thus self-important sentinel and two US citizens who are self-referentially members of a theatre troupe conducting interviews for a performance piece about the border region. The conversation quickly metamorphoses from a recognizable immigration interrogation into a discussion about the San Diego Repertory Theatre and its production of *A Christmas Carol*. While the Militia Man's gun and his doubts about the actors' claims to citizenship keep the tension high in this scenario, it is clear that Culture Clash wants the audience to laugh at the inanity immigration law creates. Rather than defining an inside and an outside, the law here seemingly leads to chaos. The legal border is bared as both potentially dangerous and completely preposterous.

Lim's and Culture Clash's scenarios expose the role that performance plays in maneuvering border interactions. Lim draws from a specific immigration practice in which successful performances of credibility facilitated entry into the United States despite severe restrictions. Before its repeal in 1943, the Chinese Exclusion Act offered little hope for Chinese laborers to immigrate to the United States. Yet, as perhaps all legislation does, the Exclusion Act also prompted the invention of ways to circumvent the law. These tactics involved well-crafted performances of credibility to substantiate fictitious claims to legal status. After all, the Exclusion Act left two viable loopholes, with immigrants from China gaining permission to enter the United States by attesting that they were either (1) a merchant with local business involvements or (2) a US citizen, natural-born or derivative (non-US-born children of citizens). Pre-exclusion practices facilitated proving the latter: Cultural traditions, coupled with previous restrictions on female immigrants from China, had normalized the practice of having male US citizens of Chinese descent travel to China to marry and father children. The reporting of sons upon return to the United States was not uncommon (reporting daughters was much less prevalent, although *Paper Angels*'s female characters remind us that the practice was not fully focused on male offspring). These reported children, or "paper sons," in essence opened up legitimate slots for specific individuals to enter the United States if they so desired.[16] Chinese immigrants developed a set of interrelated strategies to overcome immigration restrictions. Available slots were often sold to laborers otherwise ineligible to enter the United States, and additional slots were created by the reporting of fictitious births. In either case, applicants at the border needed to convince immigration authorities of their paper identity to gain entrance.

Such performances of credibility became increasingly complex when immigration authorities were literally shaken to scrutinize applicants more rigorously. One of the many casualties of the 1906 San Francisco earthquake was the municipal records. Suddenly, noncitizen members of the city's Chinese community saw an opportunity to claim natural-born citizenship. Without the available documents to prove otherwise, the San Francisco authorities legitimized fictive accounts of birth alongside genuine claims by (re)granting citizenship to its suddenly undocumented inhabitants. Immigration officials soon understood what was happening and designed a painstaking, face-to-face examination procedure to assess the supposed validity of each claim.

Importantly, as the typing sounds in Lim's prologue suggest, the official procedures together with court challenges brought on by would-be citizens generated a brand new written record. This paper trail that had not existed before, forged in an effort to enforce exclusion, ironically allowed for an explosion of paper sons to enter the United States. The record created "facts that could be coached, memorized, and recited," to quote Mae Ngai.[17] Harsh and convoluted immigration interrogations like that depicted in *Paper Angels*'s opening became standard procedure for Chinese immigrants asserting citizen parentage, and many Chinese applicants mastered the ordeal through careful and persistent performances of their alleged paper identities. As *Paper Angels* stages, applicants relied on script-like "coaching papers," which were to be memorized and promptly destroyed (usually by swallowing), in order to create viable characters corresponding to recorded family biographies. Chinese laborers whose performances did not counter these biographies managed to bypass exclusion more easily than less convincing performers. The eerie interview that opens *Paper Angels* therefore stages a specific and all-too-real historical moment.

Lim's Inspector compares his efforts to catch laborers' circumventing immigration laws to "outwitting a fox." Frustrated by the fact that, in his opinion, "a good ninety-five percent of the Chinamen coming through here are bogus," the Inspector nevertheless expresses a sense of thrill. He sees himself vying against a "little bastard," a "smart little devil," a "little fella" that ultimately deserves admiration. In a back-and-forth with the interviewee, the Inspector is "determined to trip him up," recognizing that his opponent is "just as determined to toss every curve back" (*PA* 37). Although Lim is concerned with the gravity and consequences of Chinese exclusion, she does portray the immigration process as a competitive match, albeit a highly unfair one. She juxtaposes seemingly able competitors alongside other characters who are, by their natures, unable to survive the procedures. Ku Ling's, Lee's, and Mei Lai's passage into Gold Mountain (their nickname for California) is predicated on their individual abilities to withstand a cruel game. They are not "temperamental and cocksure" (*PA* 18), as is the young Lum, whose aggressive disposition drives him to escape rather than submit to the proceedings.

The game's rules are preposterous, as the character of Chin Gung discovers when he cannot reenter a land he has nurtured and loved for decades. Despite his adamant claims—"I answered all the questions,"

"I'm a U.S. citizen," and "I'm a longtime Californ'!" (*PA* 41)—the old man finds himself stuck in detention because of a technicality. He is suffering from an infection, and as the Warden dismissively makes clear, "Liverfluke cases are all deported without appeal." When Chin Gung begins to protest, the Warden immediately retorts with "I don't make the rules" (*PA* 41). The sentiment might betray the official's uncaring nature, but it also reflects the reality of a legal system seemingly beyond any individual's control. The game's logic is problematic because the power dynamics are so uneven. "It's their country," Fong explains about Chin Gung's predicament, "It's their right" (*PA* 42).

Paper Angels thus restages an unfair game that, at least in the early 1980s, continued to be seen as such. Julian Samora's seminal study carefully connects the history of "the Mexican illegal alien" to practices stemming from Chinese exclusion and paints the phenomenon of undocumented immigration as a contest of wills and wits between border crossers and officials. By today's standards, Samora's language seems flip: "Much of what happens to illegal aliens in the United States upon being apprehended resembles a game rather than a serious violation of the law with international consequences." Before the passing of the Immigration Reform and Control Act (IRCA) in 1986, immigration law indeed sought to halt illegal immigration predominantly at points of entry rather than attempt any serious control anywhere other than the physical border.[18] Within the framework of such practices, the nation surfaces as an entity with discernible and defensible edges. It is only at its legal borders—conceived as and marked by processing centers—that undocumentedness becomes tangible. *Paper Angels* calls attention to the ways in which clever performances can lubricate passage and make use of the processes demanded by law to break through the exclusionary border. The system can be beaten, if at extraordinary costs.

While *Paper Angels* participates in promoting images of the national border as a processing center, Lim strives to underscore the long-term effects of the immigration process. What happens at the border, in other words, does not and cannot stay at the border. The playwright admits that her piece is an effort to make sense of the present, to better understand her parents and, in turn, herself. Lim posits that her parents' silence—their "isolation and distrust, which discolors everything"—stems directly from their experience at Angel Island. The rifts she senses between her generation and the previous one originate in that one square mile of land on the San Francisco Bay. "After Angel Island," she summarizes, "we [Chinese in the United States] hid from you." Her project of historical reconstruction and revision urges us to consider how US immigration laws critically altered the nation, creating a population itself profoundly changed by the performances these laws engendered. "Anytime you have immigration laws aimed at a particular race, you will pay for decades," avers Lim.[19] While such a statement relies on the idea that racial categorization somehow precedes legal actions, it reminds us that the law perpetuates and intensifies divisive conceptions of society.

Although *Bordertown* also stresses the importance of performance to manage the border scenario, Culture Clash's work highlights a shift in the kind of credible performance immigration structures seemingly require. In his studies of immigration and citizenship law, Hiroshi Motomura contends that policies in the late twentieth century pulled away from considering (legal) immigrants as future citizens, opting instead to view "new immigrants as outsiders until shown otherwise."[20] What this might mean, for a broad national consciousness, is that the process of immigration is imagined less as transitional and more as contractual or affiliating. Immigrants need to earn their membership in the nation; membership is not guaranteed with entry. The repercussions of this shift are complex, but *Bordertown*'s opening scenario alerts us to two crucial consequences. First, as Militia Man represents, the task of patrolling the border and thus the imagined affiliation of nationhood falls to everyone, not just an official immigration authority. Indeed, the late twentieth and early twenty-first centuries have not only ushered in a rise in citizen activism, from legal neighborhood watch programs to illegal and violent vigilante activities. Legal mandates such as IRCA have at the same time placed the responsibility of determining legal status in the hands of private employers and nonfederal authorities (see chapter 5). Second, as demonstrated by the play's opening scene, a performance of credibility becomes increasingly a sort of cultural litmus test. It is not enough to perform one's paper identity; one must now also enact cultural belonging.

Militia Man's willingness to protect—and define—his nation makes legal realities insufficient: passports and driver's licenses "don't mean shit" to him (*B* 10). Only San Diego's Horton Plaza Mall Monthly Parking Pass, which one of the Mexicans carries in his backpack, serves as a defining paper document. With its discovery, Militia Man begins to change his tune about Mexicans 1 and 2's citizenship. He is only convinced of their Americanness when they are able to recite the various fruits and vegetables by which the parking lot levels are labeled. The power of the parking pass draws attention to a slippery distinction between citizenship and consumerism. Immigration status and legal existence become consumer goods, a point substantiated by the economic costs associated with gaining authorized entry to the United States. Entrants are certainly excluded based on financial evidence; immigration authorities disqualify applicants who might become public charges. Moreover, there are bureaucratic, legal assistance, and travel costs associated with immigrating into the United States. In *Bordertown*, the parking pass ultimately attests to a certain form of conspicuous consumption, through which the goods we purchase and the businesses we patronize serve as markers of distinction and belonging. The Mexicans' possible consumerism becomes, for Militia Man, a most convincing indication of their patriotism.[21] With their express connection to an upscale mall, Mexicans 1 and 2 can indicate to Militia Man that they are an active part of US consuming culture.

In this way, Culture Clash's work aptly captures a broad understanding of the legal boundary as a threshold that coincides with an imagined cultural boundary. This not only turns unauthorized crossers into cultural outsiders but also implies that economic capital, practices of consumption, and cultural affiliation can somehow trump the legal border. The appearance that Nield depicts becomes a test of cultural belonging rather than one of paper legitimacy. Culture Clash's Mexicans do not rely on official documents but rather on a local savvy to prove their right to be on one side of the border.

Furthermore, *Paper Angels* and *Bordertown* capture how border crossings—particularly those involving entry into undocumentedness—meaningfully mark and alter the identities of migrants. Onstage, the phenomenon of disappearance necessitated by performances of credibility and invisibility surfaces through portrayals of the national border as a haunted site. Lim and Culture Clash are not alone in utilizing ghostly or otherworldly metaphors and aesthetics to evoke a national border (e.g., *Boxcar*, *In the Labyrinth*). The prevalent invocations of supernatural elements to stage the US borders attest to an understanding of the legal boundary as a powerful and truly life-altering threshold, one whose crossing prevents full reemergence. Ghost imagery serves to account for some of the paradoxes that nonexistence engenders. Coutin explains that, once migrants are placed outside of the law, their legal selves, in a way, remain in their countries of origin. Unauthorized immigrants cannot "complete" their journeys, always remaining, "in certain senses, outside of the United States." The plays thus prompt images of the border as a kind of "no man's land" that occasions "the changing of one's very sense of 'self,'" to quote Olivares.[22]

In Lim's play, the character of Chin Moo mourns the harrowing process at Angel Island by noting that "this room is full of ghosts!" She laments:

> At night the women do not go to the bathroom for fear of seeing ghosts. Ghosts of all the people who have died here. When all's still, you can actually hear the walls breathing. You think, "It's only the wind!" But it's not. It's the sighing of spirits. Everytime the floor creaks, you say, "It's only the wood!" But it's human bones—stretched beneath the floorboards ... (*PA* 45)

Trapped in a torturous immigration procedure, the old woman senses the physical violence and destruction of life caused by anti-Chinese policies. Yet, *Paper Angels* relies on a phantasmal atmosphere to present more than the trauma of death on the island. The entire play, from its disembodied prologue onward, calls for bodies to come in and out of focus, floating through space and time. The historical underpinning of Lim's play encourages in the first place a sense that the characters at hand are ghostlike. The haunted nature of Angel Island is further emphasized by production choices that underscore the reality of immigration processes. John Lone, who directed the 1982 New York City premiere of *Paper Angels* at the Henry Street Settlement's New Federal Theater and later directed the PBS teleplay, opted in both endeavors to use narrow spotlights through which characters could enter and exit. Spotlit actors in an otherwise mostly dark space conjured up bodies suspended in an unearthly limbo. Lim's close collaborator, Lone well served the playwright's back-and-forth structure (from the men's barracks to the women's, from dialogue to monologue, from the presentational to the representational) with such staging. Even the characters that succeed in gaining admittance into the United States thus appeared as somehow ethereal. Whether a production chooses to keep the actors' bodies visible to the audience at play's end—only two characters physically remain inside the processing center at the conclusion of the drama—Lim's script begs for all the characters' ghosts to live in the space beyond their exit. When Fong remains alone in the men's dormitory at play's end, he *"prepares for the next group of recruits"* and, one by one, refers to the men who have just left: "I'm not a scholar or a poet like Lee. I'm not a dreamer like Chin Gung. I'm not a hero like Lum" (*PA* 51). Once uttered, the names populate the dormitory, and Lee, Chin Gung, and Lum remain spectrally present in the room they have physically left.

I see this reliance on ghosts as a way to manage the loss that the immigration process requires. Lim makes clear that prevailing in the intense interrogation necessitates a full commitment to a false identity. She also demonstrates that this commitment can lead to a shift in self-perception. The clearest example of this process occurs when Lee, after adamantly defending his true identity to his fellow dormitory mates, finally accepts his paper name. Even if it is just a ploy to bypass the exclusion laws, the moment tellingly captures the necessary transformation that the border demands. "I am Lee Sung Fei, not this Moy Fook Sing or whatever his name is! I am from Shekki not Sunning. I am a scholar, not a merchant's son!" he desperately pleads in the play's first scene (*PA* 22). When it is time to leave the island, when he has succeeded in offering a convincing interview to the immigration officers, his simple but momentous "I am" in response to a guard's call for "Moy Fook Sing" attests to the compromise that entering the United States under false pretenses entails (*PA* 51). Lee Sung Fei must somehow be no more, and at least part of that person is lost during the process of legally becoming Moy Fook Sing. The actor playing Lee (as does Ping Wu in Lone's televised production) pauses before replying to the new name. We see in his face a progression from unawareness (who is Moy Fook Sing?) to despair (right, that is my new name) to acquiescence (I *am* this person you are naming). Lee demonstrates in this crucial moment that he is forever changed.

Betty Lee Sung explains in her studies of Chinese Americans that the paper sons "studied their stories and memorized them so well they knew their cover stories better than their true ones." What might have been just a mask to pass through the gates at Angel Island therefore became, for many, much more than an alias. Well into the 1950s and well after the repeal of the exclusion laws, what Sung depicts as the "long shadow of the immigration inspector" forced the Chinese American community to remain bound and tied to the fictions undocumentedness demanded.[23] The fictions ceased to be fictional. Paper sons, as did paper daughters and paper brides, existed materially in the United States—breathing, laboring, consuming, creating bodies—their faces and the masks melding together.

Bordertown tackles the loss necessitated by unauthorized immigration through a similarly ghostly strategy. In a show in which 40 or so multigenerational, multiracial, multinational, and differently gendered characters are played almost exclusively by Culture Clash's three male performers, the only specifically undocumented figure is staged uniquely. Instead of having a single actor embodying the role and speaking the lines of Julia, a faceless body and a prerecorded voiceover (by Zilah Mendoza) create the young domestic worker for the audience. Dorinne Kondo has argued that Culture Clash's "cross-racial, cross-gender performances" transcend mere stereotyping as well as "the liberal humanist desire to escape borders and boundaries" and highlight historically contingent processes that form political subjects.[24] With this in mind, I would add that playing across the legal immigration boundary (cross-documenting, we could say) challenges audiences to consider the specific circumstances that create legal labels in the first place.

The fact that this cross-document performance necessitates a unique technique of stagecraft alerts us to particularities of an undocumented identity. Erasing Julia's face is a not-so-subtle reminder that undocumentedness means only partial existence in San Diego (even if we just read the published script, we are adamantly told three times that we are not to see Julia [*B* 19–2C]). The faceless character also reproduces oft-circulated images of border crossers in the 1990s and 2000s, as increased reliance on night-vision cameras to patrol the southern US border has exploded images of unauthorized border crossers as "ghostly white figures on a softly glowing screen."[25] Julia becomes a mere shadow, a haunted silhouette that once made herself invisible to enter the country and has not been able to reemerge fully. The audience sees her labor—she brings coffee to the wealthy La Jolla woman whom the troupe is interviewing, carries a basket of dirty laundry across the stage, and crosses again with a pile of folded clothes—but Julia herself is never fully visible. Tellingly, costume design sketches for *Bordertown* reveal how Culture Clash planned to keep Julia from being seen: hers is the only character depicted from the back.[26] The audio-only version of the play also highlights Julia's nonexistence. In the monologue that immediately precedes Julia's (still in Mendoza's voice), La Jolla Woman calls out, "Julia, where's the coffee?" and adds a reprimanding "Oh that girl" to punctuate disapproval with her maid's efficiency. Before we even hear from Julia, we are asked to imagine her labor in the wealthy woman's home. Culture Clash then adds a bit of narration to transition from one monologue to the next, telling us that later they "venture back to the laundry room to interview Eleanor's maid, Julia." In this manner, they aurally locate the interaction in an isolated workspace. Finally, the audiotaped version uses collages of radio transmissions to separate sections in the play, and we hear news reports about California's efforts to build a "sturdy steel barrier" and about "evening shadows retreat[ing]" back into Mexico as we leave Julia behind. We are thus reminded of the maid's existence as a shadow.

These choices betray a certain hesitancy. Have Montoya, Salinas, and Siguenza reached an ethical limit? Why can they take on a great diversity of roles but not fully embody the one undocumented character in the play? Recalling the type of queered illegal alien that I investigate in chapter 1, Culture Clash's decision to portray the only explicitly undocumented character as a 15-year-old girl surfaces perhaps as a strategy to engage the audience's sympathies more readily. The socioeconomic and political circumstances of undocumented labor are muddled in a deliberately heightened sentimental appeal. Julia is somehow too delicate a subject for the kind of broad-stroked comic style with which all the other characters are played. The recording offers a voice that is manifestly youthful and female. It is blatantly *not* that of Culture Clash's three male performers. And the words narrate a cruel and transformative journey:

> To cross the border is a big decision, it's like being reborn. I never walk so much in my life. Two days to cross. Not just one mountain, but mountain after mountain. In the day I was so hot and thirsty, it hurt to swallow. At night I was so scared. I couldn't see in front of me and I kept falling down.

My feet were bleeding. I had to keep up with the men. And it was so cold, I couldn't stop shaking. (*B* 20)

Rebirth comes with loss. Julia's presence onstage is deliberately haunting. Culture Clash appropriately creates a border space that, like Lim's, is swarming with spectral presences. Although these are more extraterrestrial in nature, *Bordertown* paints a border region in which "futuristic space music" (*E* 17), "shaft[s] of light from above," and "spaceship sounds" (*B* 37) regularly alert the audience that human materiality and corporeality might be transcended. Indeed, the otherworldliness at hand propels the fictional actors depicted in the play to pursue the investigation of a place that is "driving [them] a little crazy" (*B* 62). Characters continuously appear and disappear in front of the audience. Aliens are everywhere, and the very idea of a concrete border is problematized. We are told by a celestial Bald Man that "there are no borders in the cosmos, only infinitesimal possibilities." Our body "disintegrates" when it transcends space and time, when we "become in tune with the infinite" (*B* 17).

Bordertown's and *Paper Angels*'s ghostly borders emphasize the frailty and ambivalence of immigration law, and in turn, of nation. Legal boundaries might dictate the experiences and shape the sense of self for border crossers such as Lee or Julia; immigration law might turn exclusion into a feasible strategy for men such as Militia Man or Lim's Guard Henderson. Nevertheless, "America" is no more than "a faraway place in the mind—a piece of dream that scatters like gold dust in the wind," to quote Lim's character of Chin Gung (*PA* 25). The United States becomes an illusion not only for those seeking entry into its borders but also for those claiming ownership to the nation. Henderson complains to the audience that "America is for Americans" (*PA* 42), much like a distraught Shamu in *Bordertown* mourns that his fellow whale entertainer, Free Willy, is really the Guatemalan Guillermo (*B* 58). As audiences listen to these trite and still-reiterated complaints, they also watch how the makeup of the nation changes. In the world of the plays, immigrants manage to bypass immigration laws. In the world of the theatre, audiences gather to watch ostensibly minority casts in plays by marginalized authors. After all, given its content, most, if not all, productions of *Paper Angels* rely on actors who are of Asian descent. Likewise, Montoya, Salinas, and Siguenza, although playing characters of various ethnicities, see themselves and are read as ethnically marked bodies.[27] The performances are therefore celebrations of changes achieved despite, not because of, immigration restrictions. They enact rather than merely represent the porosity of even the strictest of immigration policies in US history. A 2009 production of *Paper Angels* ended with all the actors onstage creating a tableau of present-day

San Francisco.[28] The very bodies that in the fiction of the play had been denied entry into the United States now boldly peopled its streets.

Bordertown likewise relies on its actors' bodies to problematize the logic of national borders. This is especially evident in a scene that stages a naturalization ceremony. Ellen MacKay has depicted the naturalization interview—which we may posit as akin to the border scenario—as a "performance of Americanness" designed to accentuate and amplify difference. By requiring citizens-to-be to speak a highly bureaucratic jargon and articulate a "dunderheaded, even primitive, understanding of America," the naturalization ritual essentially confirms the impossibility of perfect inclusion.[29] *Bordertown* includes a performance of naturalization with the characters of Oscar and Paolo. A Ugandan American and a Filipino American, respectively, Oscar and Paolo chat about life in San Diego as they wait to be sworn in as new citizens. The audience erupts in laughter when a "*Pakistani-American with a turban, mustache and suit enters*" to lead Oscar and Paolo, who also wear purportedly foreign clothes, in the ceremony. Waving "*little American flags with pride and hope*" and underscored with "America the Beautiful," Oscar, Paolo, and the Pakistani American recite the pledge of allegiance with markedly exaggerated foreign accents (*B* 51). The audience again laughs at what seems incongruous. Here, dress and language become, as MacKay insists, "the sign of difference that distinguishes the natural from the naturalized citizen, or, more plainly, the citizen who belongs from the citizen who is lucky to be here." The legal proceeding seems to insist on a performance of foreignness at the moment in which that foreignness is supposedly being erased. Like immigration law, naturalization law hence attempts to draw national borders boldly and allow for the imagining of inside and outside. It naturalizes the nation's power to decide that some people belong and others do not. Especially when the legal border collapses into a cultural boundary, markers of foreignness imply that full membership in the nation might be impossible.

But Oscar and Paolo share the stage with Donna and Amy, two evidently American women discussing the detrimental influence of "all these foreigners" in San Diego (*B* 48). Salinas and Siguenza play all four characters in this scene, seamlessly transitioning between the women in their living room and the men at City Hall. Oscar's and Paolo's symbolic and legal entry into full citizenship is thus juxtaposed with Donna's and Amy's complaints that Mexican, Vietnamese, Afghan, and Chinese immigrants denigrate the nation (*B* 49–50). Culture Clash's reliance on instantaneous, fluid double-casting quite literally blurs the boundaries between Amy and Oscar, Donna and Paolo, natural and naturalized citizen. In so doing, the group offers a strategy for rethinking the solidity of national (as well as ethnic and gender) boundaries. The dialogue between the women might heighten the foreignness of the men, but the fact that the naturalized citizens are the natural ones as well—they inhabit a single body—urges us to consider how the national body is necessarily contradictory. Law might seek to define its edges, but where one entity begins and another ends is difficult to determine. At the beginning of act 2, *Bordertown* repeats its opening border scenario, although we are now supposedly in Mexico. Mexican Militia Man's attempts to assess the legitimacy of Americans 1 and 2's claim for being across the border are as inane as those of his US counterpart. Again, the scenario shifts to a conversation about *A Christmas Carol* at the San Diego Repertory Theatre (*B* 40–41). By restaging the interaction—and casting the three actors in the same roles—the play proposes that the legal border does little to define two regions that are, ultimately, the same.

In what is perhaps *Bordertown*'s most iconic moment, a Woman lying atop the Mexican flag shares a bed with a Man, whose blanket is the US flag. The dominant husband "*makes love to his wife, roughly,*" and the wife gradually realizes that she "play[s] the victim" and "wear[s] another face" when she is with her mate (*B* 42–43). Man confesses his need for his wife, but keeps her on her side of the bed, shines lights on the border between them, and whines that her children "are sucking the tit of [his] country dry" (*B* 43). Accusing Man of being "abusive" and "thoughtless," Woman demands respect. Such a gendered portrait of the border easily paints an uneven, stereotypical power dynamic: the wife is pushed to tears by a husband who believes he owns the woman. At the same time, the short scene ends with unexpected tenderness. After she is left weeping, Woman "*crosses the fence to his side of the bed*" and confesses that

> our marriage is political. It is a physically imposing monument, a symbol impressed into our consciousness. Crucé el cerco. "I crossed the fence." This is a spiritual passage and a specific space of struggle and transgression. It is that between fiction and nonfiction. (*B* 43)

Agustín Lara's "Rival" begins to play, a bolero whose words bemoan an impossible love: although my heart has betrayed me, I do not know how I will live without your love.[30] Even if the audience misses the meaning of the Spanish lyrics, the melancholic tone underscores a "*slow and loving dance* [in which Woman and Man] *embrace like tango dancers, locked together, draped by their flag blankets*" (*B* 43). The lights fade on this affectionate image. It is not a romanticized border; this is a sorrowful dance. With it, Culture Clash pushes the audience to see how intimately interconnected Mexico and the United States are. Despite the power struggles and harsh attempts at creating a divisive line, the border is neither wife nor husband alone but rather a single unit, albeit an unhappy one. Amy, Donna, and Shamu—like Henderson in *Paper Angels*—might desperately want to believe that their country is a distinct entity, one painted with solid borders, but we see onstage that such separateness is illusive.

Paper Angels and *Bordertown* attempt to confront the material consequences of a legally defined border by boldly depicting the limits of that border's logic. Unlike the stage pieces I examine in chapter 1, *Paper Angels* and *Bordertown* thus exemplify a much more anxious portrayal of the national border. Both plays highlight immigration policies that construct individual and group identities; crossing a border means a new sense of self for its crossers. Nonetheless, such a border is simultaneously ineffectual. We can transgress it, but at a price. In *Bordertown*'s final moment, when actors-as-themselves Richard and Ric meet the alien Bald Man, the space music that has underscored much of the piece builds and readies the characters for a sendoff from earthly San Diego. The three figures onstage transform gradually into the iconic freeway sign warning drivers in the southern United States that undocumented migrants might be crossing the road. As "Good Vibrations" plays, the lights come down on this recognizable image. If they are to reach the "higher self" that the Bald Man promises (*B* 17), they must, like Julia, find rebirth in sacrifice, in loss, and in danger. The utopian future that the Bald Man paints—"a place where there are no borders"—is ironically a border away. To cross it will require a defiant and possibly unauthorized act. Like the men onstage, we will only leave behind the "hatred, the fear, the unresolved conflicts" (*B* 63) that define the present-day Bordertown if we hazard an illegal crossing.

Leaving the Border Scenario Behind

The performances required at national borders, especially those demanded by illegal crossings, affect lives inside the nation. In other words, the legal notions through which borders are constructed and managed seep deeply into the ways in which immigrants create notions of self and community once across those borders. The border scenario can be life altering. In subsequent chapters I discuss questions of labor, personal relationships, and rights for those living in undocumentedness. I pause here to consider Josefina López's *Real Women Have Curves* in order to examine how leaving undocumentedness can prove as intense as an initial border crossing into legal nonexistence.[31] As the play suggests, performance surfaces as an efficacious tactic to counteract the marks and erasures that undocumentedness engenders.

Real Women Have Curves introduces audiences to five women working in a small sewing factory in Los Angeles. Soon after premiering in
1990, it became one of the most-often produced Chicana/o theatre pieces
in the United States.[32] It has been performed in English and in Spanish,
by professionals and amateurs, at home and abroad. The play is included
in *Latino Boom: An Anthology of U.S. Latino Literature* and was adapted
into film in 2002 (and fundamentally altered, as I describe below). This
broad visibility has ensured *Real Women* a prominent position in discussions about what it means to be Chicana and/or Latina. With its famous
disrobing scene, in which the women shed their clothing to combat the
heat of their suffocating workspace, the play has also surfaced as a prevalent reference in conversations about female body image and conceptions
of beauty. In short, López's work features substantially in examinations of
identity, especially in regard to gender and ethnicity. But the play is very
much about legal boundaries, which are often overlooked in studies of the
play.[33] As I contend below, Ana's self-perception is predicated greatly on
her new legal status.

López's own experience with immigration law is key to entering the
world of her play. She makes clear in an introduction to the script that
the work is semiautobiographical; her "Playwright's Notes" concentrate
almost entirely on legal issues. In just four paragraphs, López writes about
immigration laws, immigration documents, immigration enforcement,
and the hurtful label of "illegal alien." She uses the word "undocumented"
five times. López discusses briefly the summer in which she worked at
her sister's sewing factory, where she came to admire her colleagues. She
explains that *Real Women Have Curves* celebrates her experience bonding
with the women. Still, she adamantly states that the purpose of her play is
to change minds about the categories created by immigration law:

> In the U.S. undocumented people are referred to as "illegal aliens" which
> conjures up in our minds the image of extraterrestrial beings who are not
> human, who do not bleed when they're cut, who do not cry when they feel
> pain, who do not have fears, dreams and hopes…Undocumented people
> have been used as scapegoats for so many of the problems in the U.S. […]
> I hope that someday this country recognizes the very important contribu-
> tions of undocumented people and remembers that they too came to this
> country in search of a better life. (*RW* 6)

Furthermore, López underlines how legalization brought opportunities
otherwise denied to her: "When I finally got my legal residence card,
[I knew] I would never have to hide and be afraid again" (*RW* 5). In discussions of her work, López links the new legal status to her ability to attend
college and her educational experiences to a fulfilling artistic career.[34]

Mirroring López's real-life experience, *Real Women Have Curves* follows the character of Ana's journey to self-discovery and acceptance as she works in her sister Estela's factory. Believing at first that the job is beneath her, the college-bound teenager shifts her ideas about what it means to be a "real woman" after laboring alongside Estela, their mother Carmen, and two other dressmakers, Rosali and Pancha. The collective experience, in which the women challenge and support one another, urges all of them to reposition themselves as individuals as well as members of a broader community. The 1986 IRCA catalyzes these shifts. This law provided, among other things, a limited opportunity for the US attorney general to "adjust" the immigration classification of some undocumented individuals.[35] Like López herself, Ana counts herself among those newly legalized under IRCA. Because the play stages such a particular moment of change, it illuminates how legal categorization can powerfully affect those it seeks to label. At the same time, the play showcases how a transition out of undocumentedness is not necessarily easy. López emphasizes these points in two major ways. First, she keeps one of the characters from obtaining legal residency, offering a foil for the rest of the group. Second, López ensures that the value of the new legal status is clearly depicted as the play progresses.

Estela is unable to benefit from the newly enacted IRCA. López bitingly comments on the harshness of immigration policy, even so-called amnesty, by presenting a character disqualified from lawful status because of her "criminal record." As Estela confesses to the others, she was once arrested for "illegal possession" of an out-of-season lobster (*RW* 15, 16). Coupled with some outstanding debt incurred for purchasing sewing machines, Estela's record has made her ineligible for legalization. The consequences of this are nothing less than dreadful, as Estela must exist in a state of unrelenting fear. When Ana bursts into the factory one day, kicking the door because she is carrying lunches in her arms, Estela reveals the full extent of her anxiety. She is determined to remain invisible: "From now on these doors are to remain closed and locked at all times, okay? If you go outside, you knock on the door like this... *(She knocks in code rhythm.)* ... so we know it's just one of us." Pancha's protests—we will be just like caged chickens—are met only with flat resignation. "We just have to be careful," Estela rationalizes (*RW* 25). Fear leads Estela to alter not only her working environment (no open doors) but also the behavior within the closed space. "No more stories," she charges her mother after Carmen suffers a brief spell of uncontrollable laughter. Estela's desire for invisibility necessitates vigilant control: "If we gossip people are gonna hear everything outside and even if we close the doors they'll know it's a sewing factory because only women talking **chisme** can sound like chickens cackling" (*RW* 27). This type of self-altering behavior points to the ways in which legal nonexistence prompts new ways of existing in the world. Marked as an **"ilegal"** (*RW* 15), Estela must think, behave, and live differently from those labeled otherwise.

Estela's lack of papers provides the major tension in *Real Women*. The tiny factory space in which the entire play takes place becomes additionally claustrophobic by the potential threat of immigration authorities lurking outside. The women spend much time speculating whether vehicles, sounds, and individuals that they can see through the windows or hear through the walls are *la migra*. Stories about raids and deportations exacerbate the distress under which Estela must live, making clear the power of narrativized border scenarios to affect everyday lives. In the middle of the play, a radio voiceover briefly announces that "twenty illegal aliens were captured today at the Goodnight pillow factory" (*RW* 41). Clearly, Estela's distinct legal label makes her vulnerable, transforming her almost into an object of prey. The possibility of a border scenario thus lingers within the confines of the factory; a forever delayed encounter with immigration authorities underpins daily experience.

In her essay about López's play, María Figueroa rightly describes a tangible threat for all five women. She goes as far as to say that "specific communities in the United States, *despite* their sociopolitical status (i.e., documented or undocumented, legal or illegal), are still stigmatized and relegated to second-class citizenship as the abject subjects who exist 'outside' of a capitalist society."[36] Indeed, the immigration authorities could, at any point, demand a performance of credibility from any of them. But the stigmatization at hand results not only from the marks of gender and ethnicity shared by the five characters, nor by the bonds of sisterhood that inevitably turn Estela's problems into problems for all. She is, after all, vital to the other women, as a sister, a daughter, a friend, and an employer. Instead, and crucially, the stigmatization results from their previous shared experience as undocumented immigrants. Despite legalization, López's characters cannot easily leave their fears behind.

The playwright relies on humor to explore how difficult it is to leave a space of nonexistence. At one point, Carmen sees a van through one of the factory windows and screams, "**¡La migra!**" All five women "*scatter and hide.*" It takes a moment for them to understand what they are doing. Pancha urges calm, "Why are we hiding? We're all legal now." "**¡Ayy, de veras!** I forget!," responds Carmen (*RW* 14–15). She then concedes that she cannot easily adjust to her newfound legality. We observe here, as well as in subsequent moments throughout the play, the type of back-and-forth negotiation that the characters maneuver as they adapt to a new legal category. By creating quickly diffused tension and showcasing her characters' miscalculation about the van (we eventually learn that Carmen does not even know what a real *migra* van looks like [*RW* 63]), López aims for laughs. Still, the fear underlying her comedy requires actors to approach the material with intensity. The various exclamation points as well as the double "y" of "ayy" serve as guides for the performer in this regard. This intensity, I believe, points to the mix of excitement and anxiety that accompany the turn out from nonexistence.

López certainly allows the newly documented characters a different subjectivity than that of Estela. The initial instinct to hide from immigration authorities does not necessarily reflect the kind of generalized stigmatization that Figueroa finds. That instinct might rather speak to the adjustment pains of learning to live with a new legal label. With the exception of Estela, López's characters periodically remind each other that, in Pancha's words, "We're all legal now." Indeed, Pancha reveals an almost defiant attitude attesting to the newfound confidence that comes with her Temporary Residence Card: "Let those men in their van come! Who cares?" (*RW* 14–15). Even the much quieter Rosali admits that legal status is changing her. Without fearing immigration authorities, Rosali begins to reinvent herself. "I used to work in factories and whenever they did a raid, I'd always sneak out through the bathroom window, **y ya**," she proudly announces. The definiteness of her *y ya* ("that's all" or "that's it") marks emphatically not only the desire for but also the commitment to existing anew in the world. Her sneaking days are over, she promises. "Yesterday I got my first credit card," Rosali then discloses (*RW* 15). Although she had to fib on the application, presumably about her financials, Rosali's changed perception of what is possible prompts her to take actions she would or could not have taken in undocumentedness. Her decision attests to an altered sense of self following a change in her relational social position. It also attests to links between practices of belonging and conspicuous consumption, as explored above. Rosali's newfound legitimacy propels a desire for material goods. Misguided or not, such a desire reflects urges fomented by undocumentedness "to emulate Americans," as described by Ramón "Tianguis" Pérez in his *Diary of an Undocumented Immigrant*. Pérez portrays the sense of "contentment" that purchasing a car brings: "I haven't met [an American] who doesn't have a car."[37]

As Estela's legal foil, Ana serves well to showcase how legalization prompts an identity tug-of-war. The play's first monologue, in which Ana shares with the audience a journal entry she is writing, invites us immediately to view the character in a state of transition. Ana has just received the Temporary Residence Card made possible under IRCA. The timing coincides with her high-school graduation. This new immigration status

seemingly comes with unpredictable consequences. "I'm happy to finally
be legal, but I thought things would be different," Ana confesses (RW 10).
Just months after shedding her undocumentedness, she believes she is
stuck. Ana finds herself performing menial labor in a sweltering factory,
assisting in the manufacture of dresses whose style and price make them
inaccessible to her (RW 50). She finds herself stuck in a position generally
associated with undocumented workers. They are to labor but not consume. They are to make things that only others can afford to enjoy. "It's
as if I'm going backwards," Ana ponders. She shows disdain for having to
do "the work that mostly illegal aliens do" (RW 10). Ana's awareness that
she is working in a system that fails to recognize her as a full participant
could offer evidence that the new legal status means little.

Yet, I would argue that Ana's discontent with her new status does not
result from the inconsequence of legal categorization but rather from the
resilience and formidable power of legal labels. Ana's initial dissatisfac-
tion must be understood alongside the growth and maturing that López
stages. Thus, Ana's desire for an immediate life change upon receiving
her residency betrays an adolescent impatience. Her mother, Carmen,
offers the audience a more adult conception of what legalization means:
"All those years of being an **ilegal**, I still can't get used to it" (RW 15). The
label, in other words, is not something that can be easily shed. After all,
living in legal nonexistence necessarily involves intensified vulnerability
with dire material consequences. The dehumanization brought on by the
label "illegal" that López describes in her introductory note is not merely
symbolic or semantic. Unauthorized immigrants face physical limita-
tions and psychological stresses created by curtailed legal protections.
The harrowing nature of spaces of nonexistence inevitably participates
in identity formation.

Moreover, López stresses Ana's awareness of her new legal label: "Thank
God, I'm legal," she avers (RW 15). The same young woman who just minutes earlier has complained to the audience about the lack of changes following legalization does understand that changes will come. Precisely
because legal nonexistence has made mobility and transformation difficult, improvements to one's position do not all arrive instantaneously. For
example, as López did in real life, Ana must postpone attending college
for a year. While her new status allows her to continue her education, she
must spend some time securing financing (RW 34). But it is quite clear
to all—characters and audience members—that Estela and Ana occupy
markedly different spaces as long as they are on opposite sides of a legal
boundary. As sisters, Ana and Estela might share much in common. But
once Ana leaves legal nonexistence, their tactics for living life become
quite contrary (see chapter 4 for a discussion of mixed-status families).

Estela seeks invisibility; Ana seeks a bolder presence in the world. She preaches, "We can't allow ourselves to be abused anymore. We have to assert ourselves. We have to realize that we have rights!" (*RW* 33–34).

Real Women stresses the importance of such assertions in order to combat nonexistence. This requires shifts in self-consciousness made difficult by living in undocumentedness in the first place. As the characters strive to adjust to a new legal label, they are caught in a back-and-forth struggle between deep-rooted fears and newfound confidence. This tension plays out, in part, as anxiety over body image. *Real Women's* iconic scene involves all five women stripping down to their underwear following Ana's lead. It is hot, but as the women shed their clothing it is much more than cool comfort that they find. In addition to a collective self-assurance and self-acceptance, the women joyously rediscover in that moment the freedom that legalization brings. They choose to celebrate not only their "fat and beautiful" bodies but also the fact that, in Pancha's words, "All of us, most of us, finally [are] legal." Carmen goes one step further and, feeling triumphant, exclaims, "once you get the [green] card you can do anything you want" (*RW* 61). She begins to convince Estela that a new life is possible. The elation continues and Ana urges her mother to open the factory's door. Carmen actually ventures outside as the others stare in disbelief (*RW* 62). The moment comes to a sudden end when Carmen reenters the factory; she erroneously believes that the immigration van is parked outside. Still, the shedding of clothes has altered the characters. They have asserted themselves in a new way, and their immediate fears are dispelled. Later that evening, Estela will return to the factory alone and, "*measuring herself with pride and pleasure*" (*RW* 64), design a dress for someone like her, someone her size.

Although the climactic turn during this undressing scene is undeniable, it is the ensuing fashion show that marks the characters' full exit from legal nonexistence. The play's final runway show proves a bold endpoint to the difficult journey. When they "*parade down the theater aisles voguing*," wearing original Estela Garcia designs (*RW* 69), the women defiantly pronounce their new relationship to the world. The audience ceases to witness a private environment and partakes instead in an event in which the women know they are being watched and admired. They become performers, whose actions directly counter the pressures of legal nonexistence. With purpose, they contend that they are not undocumented, ugly, or invisible, but rather legal, beautiful, and present. Their self-assured performance as fashion-show models draws directly from their self-acceptance as legal residents. At the same time, the new fighting spirit marked by power and "resistance," to quote Ana's final monologue (*RW* 69), emerges directly from experiencing nonexistence. Although the women have crossed over the legal boundary, their connection to an undocumented status continues to influence who they are. Certainly, López's opening note as well as her ongoing work attests to a lasting commitment to combatting legal nonexistence. Thus, even as the play stages the transition that occurs as individuals move from one legal category to another, it reminds us that the marks left by a space of nonexistence can be long-lasting. Still, with their performance in the fashion show, López's characters are reborn.

A comedy, *Real Women Have Curves* operates generically through inclusion and resolution. In a final address to the audience, an older Ana reflects on her experience at the factory and shares the comic denouement: she gets to attend New York University to pursue a writing career while Estela gets to fulfill a dream of opening up her own boutique (*RW* 69). Both of these achievements, we surmise, stem from legalization, which Estela eventually achieves through the help and sacrifice of the other women—they give up their paychecks to help cover Estela's legal fees (*RW* 67). Indeed, the play builds to an image of the women smiling together for Ana's camera, holding up their Temporary Residence Cards and smiling as they say "Green!!!" (*RW* 68). The green card and the legal status that it brings thus surface as the only means for achieving a happy ending. But unlike the kind of resolution offered by *Flower Drum Song* or *A View from the Bridge* (see chapter 1), the characters in *Real Women* do not overcome undocumentedness to exist in a world that already accepted them. Instead, the characters here carve a new space for existing, one that was not there before. While López then celebrates legal status as essential to any type of success, and in so doing sustains a notion of nation as a legitimate construct, the play also insists on an imagined community that changes. Linda Saborío persuasively argues that López's characters do not blindly adopt the American Dream, but rather "defy it with their performance of difference and re-enact instead their own Latina Dream."[38] I would suggest we distinguish between a Latina Dream and an Undocumented Dream. In both cases, through the women's performance, the United States as a nation is also reborn.

Borders in the Field of Cultural Production

In crucial ways, *Paper Angels*, *Bordertown*, and *Real Women Have Curves* epitomize the minority discourse that Homi Bhabha explores in his essay "DissemiNation." Considering both the physical and metaphoric border, Bhabha suggests a project of dissemination to problematize the construction of wholeness that underpins images of nation. He offers minority discourses as disruptions to "nation" as a "narrative strategy." Each of the three plays I analyze here functions, in Bhabha's words, to "continually evoke and erase [the nation's] totalizing boundaries—both actual and conceptual—[and to] disturb those ideological manoeuvres through which 'imagined communities' are given essentialist identities."[39] The stagings of border scenarios, at both ends of an immigration process, draw attention to the power that legal boundaries have in shaping individual identity as well as to the ultimate elusiveness of national borders. Following Bhabha, we could say the three pieces supplement narratives of the United States, and thus change radically the modes of articulating nation by not only adding to but also disturbing its calculation.

Still, I want to question how the plays' containment within categories perpetuated in the field of cultural production limits their ability to *disseminate* such disturbances. It is not my aim to engage in a discussion about the many ways in which ethnic identity is mobilized to battle prejudice and build political coalitions. The three works I examine in this chapter were created during a period of heightened identity politics in which questions of representation and visibility took center stage and in which marginalized groups made significant strides to rearticulate what "Americanness" might mean. Rather, I want to home in on the particular mechanism by which products like *Paper Angels*, *Bordertown*, and *Real Women Have Curves* seek to undo rigid systems of categorization and borderization, yet simultaneously move through the field of cultural production by claiming clear-cut labels.

Especially given their emergence in the 1980s and 1990s, it is difficult to find descriptions or critiques of the works and artists I treat here without the use of labels such as "Latina/o," "Chicana/o," "Mexican American," "Asian American," or "Chinese American." The artists themselves, who at times yearn to do without such labels, ultimately rely on their use to propel their works forward. Much like the field of cultural production described by Pierre Bourdieu demands that artists legitimate their work by disavowing necessary economic capital, cultural producers in the United States often disavow the rigidity of identity categories, even as these categories prove necessary for securing positions within the field.[40]

The members of Culture Clash, for example, seem keen to problematize a term such as "Chicano." They assert their ties to the Chicano movement of the 1960s and 1970s. But Montoya, Salinas, and Siguenza also insist that the work of Culture Clash—even the collective's name—plays with and evolves from the contradictions inherent in simplistic categorization. They have "moved on" from strict explorations of the "Chicano experience."[41] Notwithstanding, Culture Clash and its producers regularly tag the company a "Chicano performance group" or "Chicano/Latino performance troupe" for quick identification.[42] Similarly, López distances herself from a "Chicano theatre movement" in a 2003 interview, suggesting that her work seeks to "define ourselves" through different strategies, but then acknowledges that *Real Women* "got around" precisely because it fit a defined category for funding: the play was "Latino" theatre. López's preoccupation with labels to mark her ethnicity is often anxious. In the introduction to her play, *Unconquered Spirits*, López explains her adoption of "the title of 'Chicana,'" as opposed to "Hispanic" or "Spanish," as a political and personal choice. Yet, the same play's inside cover—as do other publications by López with Dramatic Publishing—describes the playwright as "Latina," a term she does not discuss in her explanation of the importance of terminology. (The Dramatic Publishing website does introduce López as "one of today's preeminent Chicana writers.")[43] Finally, Lim asserts that "I don't think in terms of types [and that] labeling is a preoccupation of mass media, marketers, and politicians who need to classify their products or politics for consumers and constituents." She expresses interest in dealing with Latin American and native American subjects as her "own attempt at cultural border-crossing."[44] But it is precisely under the label "Asian American" that her cultural production finds a platform. Lim's plays have been anthologized in *Unbroken Thread: An Anthology of Plays by Asian American Women* and *The Politics of Life: Four Plays by Asian American Women*. Her work has been staged by companies such as the Asian American Theater Company, the Asian Theater Group, Asian Improv aRts, as well as the San Francisco Chinese Culture Center.

The field's demand for tidy labels not only erases differences in varied histories of immigration and community-building in the United States, but can also stunt the creation of possibly productive connections. The construction of tactical coalitions around ethnic identities has certainly led to significant steps in ensuring broader and fairer representation as well as in combating official and more informal discriminatory policies. Pan-Latina/o and Pan-Asian organizations and structures of cultural production have, especially since the mid-1960s and 1970s, lifted the visibility of Latinas/os and Asian Americans in the United States. However, we must also recognize how such coalitions foster new borders and potentially create blind spots. For instance, a push to understand Chicana/o, Cuban American, and Puerto Rican American theatre as a coherent unit leads to conclusions we might read differently with express attention to immigration law. Jorge Huerta and Alicia Arrizón, for instance, explain that Chicana/o cultural products do not yearn for "home" and do not display a "circular" nature when compared to Puerto Rican and Cuban American works.[45] A stricter focus on legal realities that affect contact with and travel to a homeland, however, might offer us alternate groupings through which to see those cultural products anew.

Juxtaposing ostensibly Chicana/o theatre with Chinese American theatre might allow for a different manner of understanding circularity or
nostalgia. Given certain ties in patterns and structures of legal exclusion
and legal nonexistence, the lens for studying identitarian duality developed by scholars of Asian American literature can shed useful light in
examining the situation of *Bordertown*'s Julia or *Real Women*'s Ana as
migrants living in undocumentedness in the United States. Following
Stephen Sumida's review of Asian American literature of immigration,
we can productively unpack the young women's shared sense of "awe-
some loss" as one produced by the rifts that harsh laws create between
immigrants living in the United States and their countries of origin.
"Home," Sumida explains, "shifts from being the place where one is *from*
to the place where one is *at*, or nowhere."[46] Such an understanding of
Bordertown and *Real Women* seems more fitting than their characters'
comparison to a Puerto Rican migrant experience, which immigration
law structures differently and therefore sustains a more tangible notion of
"home," one that, legally at least, is not so far out of reach.[47]

Likewise, the trauma of entering the United States staged in *Paper
Angels*, a play that Miseong Woo has examined not as "Asian American"
dramatic literature but rather as "diaspora literature," might transcend
the former label more readily, as Woo advocates, if we examine it alongside Chicana/o products and their analyses. However, Woo does not consider this possibility and limits her discussion to current approaches in
the study of Chinese, Korean, Japanese, and Filipino American dramatic
literature. In short, she seeks to problematize an "Asian American" category without leaving the academic and cultural space of such a label.
Woo insists that the term "Asian American" prevents us from viewing a
"diaspora discourse [that] focuses more on fluidity of identity, the process of constructing subjectivity, and the historical moment of crossing the borders."[48] Viewing *Paper Angels* together with a piece such as
Bordertown helps us precisely to discuss the processes of loss and identity restructuring associated with the immigration process to which Woo
alludes. By focusing first and foremost on the legal structures that forge
such a process, we might avoid repeating and essentializing categories
and ways of knowing that overlook crucial differences in mechanisms of
immigration.

Yet, the field of cultural production regularly precludes such connections, pushing producers, critics, and scholars to mind closely the borders
created along ethnic and racial lines. Attempts to make *Paper Angels*,
Bordertown, and *Real Women Have Curves* accessible to broader audiences
have required modifications to their engagements with undocumentedness. In these modifications, we can find evidence for ways in which the

logics of cultural production and analysis have limited reconsiderations of immigration law, identity, and nation.

Fueled in part by Lim's descriptions of her play as an effort to educate audiences about an unknown history,[49] early productions of *Paper Angels* were received predominantly as history lessons that reconciled a specific and alienated identity within the US cultural landscape. Critics seemed to agree that *Paper Angels* "awakened all kinds of ghosts" and that it opened audiences' eyes about California's "equivalent of Ellis Island."[50] Lim's work surfaced as a play about the past, not so much about the present. Although it asked audiences to grapple with an ugly history, one that even illuminates the contemporary estrangement of an older generation of Chinese Americans, the play's production and reception as an "Asian American" piece in essence concealed its broader Americanness. This is a well-worn argument. But it is striking how a play about immigration becomes segregated from other immigrant populations.

With voices like the Inspector's, the play easily transcended its 1915 setting and evoked a present-day immigration system. Mid-play, the government officer addresses the audience:

> But the law is the law. I have my job to do. You've got to have a system! Because if you don't, they'll take advantage and next thing you know, not only will you have droves of illegal aliens swarming into the country, but they'll be bringing over their wives, children, sundry aunts, uncles, and relatives, not to mention the little yellow ones they'll be propagating all over the U.S. I mean you've got to be systematic about it. If they're coming in fraudulently, we've got to do our best to keep them out! (*PA* 37)

Replace "yellow" with the derogatory color-du-jour, and this invective well captures, and effectively foreshadows, late-twentieth- and early-twenty-first-century immigration debates in the United States. Strikingly then, the speech was altered for *Paper Angels*'s PBS appearance. The charged phrase, "droves of illegal aliens swarming into the country," was struck from the telescript (one of many cuts made to fit the television program's shorter time slot). Consciously or not, Lim aided with this choice to distance the play from current immigration debates.

Subsequent productions of *Paper Angels* have entrenched the play as an Asian American piece, one that presumably does not or cannot speak to other populations. Even the Performance Project @ University Settlement and Direct Art's 2009 staging of the play, promoted as part of a mission to produce "work that is not just multi-cultural, but inter-cultural [and in so doing] challenge the ghettoization of minorities in mainstream media,"[51] ultimately advertised through websites such as the Asian American Theatre Revue, Asians in America, and AsianConnections. Although channels dedicated specifically to Off-Off-Broadway theatre also picked up the production's press release, websites such as NY1 Noticias, NY Remezcla, or NY Al Día, all of which cater to the city's Latina/o populations, made no mention of the event.

Culture Clash faces similarly limiting choices, even as the company has managed to expand its audience base.[52] In streamlining *Bordertown* for a more concise performance piece (as recorded for L.A. Theatre Works), one of the few characters that gets cut altogether from the full script is the Chinese Man. Beautifully integrated with Julia's monologue in the uncut script, this figure appears at the end of her address to the audience: the lights fade on her as they come up on *"an elderly Chinese Man in classic leisure wear as he prepares to tee off on one of the region's countless private golf courses"* (B 20). After listening to the faceless maid discuss rebirth and baptism, the Chinese Man, who we will learn has been elected to San Diego's City Council, describes his father's journey to the city in 1914. It, too, is a story of circumventing immigration law and of donning a new name. It is a story of loss and perseverance, of overcoming intense prejudice. At the heels of Julia's address, Tom's perspective not only offers some hope for migrants such as Julia but also comments on the sluggish nature of change: anti-immigrant hatred is deep-rooted, and witnessing acceptance requires multiple generations. The Chinese Man's words frame Julia's experience as a historical process. The specific choices she had to make are of the moment, but her existence is not a historical aberration. US immigration policies have persistently sought to keep immigrants out in order to justify unequal treatment. Without the Chinese Man, the leaner *Bordertown* transitions from the undocumented figure's monologue directly into the sounds of a helicopter and a radio announcement alerting us to the construction of Operation Gatekeeper's sturdier, better-lit border fence. The sheriff of San Diego County then appears onstage to tell us about his work to curb "4.5 million" monthly illegal crossings at "the busiest international border in the entire world"—4.5 million "Mexicans," he quickly adds.[53] The comment reflects the sheriff's prejudices, but, ironically, by eliminating the Chinese Man, the recorded version of *Bordertown* similarly flattens and dehistoricizes the story of illegal immigration in the San Diego area.

Real Women Have Curves's trajectory attests to a different but related phenomenon. Adapted into film in the early 2000s, the cultural product has enjoyed marked visibility—the kind of recognition Ana so ardently wants for the women in Estela's factory. This has come at a cost: the film completely erases undocumentedness. Perhaps like in the 2001 adaptation of *Flower Drum Song* that I discuss in the previous chapter, the film version of *Real Women Have Curves* cannot offer an undocumented

immigrant as a viable protagonist. López explains the decision predominantly as a structural necessity: "The main plot in the play was the whole
immigration paranoia, which would not work in the movie because we
would have to go out of the factory and as soon as we would do that we
would realize it was not the immigration but the DEA." Linked to this
decision is perhaps the choice to move from an ensemble comedy to a
dramedy centered on the character of Ana, whose journey López believes
is the most universal.[54] If, as Jorge Huerta has claimed, the popularity of
Real Women in mainstream theatres rests partly on the play's indirect
engagement with "the power structure" (the INS threat is never concretely
embodied),[55] then López and co-screenwriter George LaVoo's choice to
disengage entirely with immigration law fits neatly into the desire to succeed with a so-called non-Latina/o audience. However, given the vital
importance of immigration status in the play (and in López's own life),
the shift in characters and action might also reflect, I suggest, a push to
make the product fit the broader and more marketable "Latina/o" label
under which various groups are often squeezed. By disengaging from the
particularities of immigration law, the film version of *Real Women Have
Curves* might more directly speak to Puerto Rican and Cuban American
audiences, who do not share with Mexican Americans a long history of
undocumented immigration, as well as to the large portion of legal residents and citizens. Without attention to the specificities of immigration
law, Ana's story becomes, in fact, more generically "ethnic."[56] While this
strategy perhaps does allow for broader appeal, it comes at the expense of
including the undocumented in the celebratory expression of minority
discourse. The invisibility that the play's Ana so desperately fights against
thus haunts the film.

I am not suggesting that Lim's, Culture Clash's, or López's work somehow falls short. Their individual trajectories are impressive. We can and
should applaud their achievements. They been able to transcend well-
entrenched barriers to minority artists, and, as exemplified by their
attempts above, have also sought to forge new connections. My point here
is to emphasize how difficult such attempts become for professional artists, whose work is pushed to fit expected ethnically based categories. I
call attention to the way in which their products are absorbed into and
discussed by the field of cultural production in the United States and to
the repercussions of such a process. Do we run the danger of perpetuating
problematic policies and of repeating rather than improving our analyti-
cal tools? I am reminded of a Brookings Institution panel on the subject
of the media and the immigration debate. One of the major reasons why
immigration reform has proven difficult, Roberto Suro suggested during the panel, is that immigration is treated predominantly as the story

of immigrants (and to a lesser degree of its policy enforcers). Rarely is immigration discussed as a broad phenomenon in a politico-economic system in which *all* US residents and citizens partake.[57] Media coverage of immigration oversimplifies what is intricately complex.

A machinery that propels cultural products into ethnic cubbyholes similarly oversimplifies networks of connections and multifaceted links. Even as individual performances aver complicated identities, the field of cultural production itself resorts back to simplified labels in order to motorize the system. In this way, the field operates much like a legal border. After all, the legal border demands a certain simplicity and relies on seemingly clear-cut labels to manage the traffic of bodies. Immigrants seeking entry into the United States must fit predetermined categories ranked according to a system of preferences. The system demands such strict delineations that, for instance, a noncitizen woman with a job offer in the United States and a US citizen husband must decide whether to apply for a green card as a wife or as an employee. Such an applicant must only be treated as one or the other. *Paper Angels*, *Bordertown*, and *Real Women Have Curves* offer demonstrations against such problematic reductivism. If the erasures of connections and the flattening of complexity experienced by the three pieces are any indication, we must consider that labels in the field of cultural production can solidify rather than disrupt notions of borders, of edges, and of nation.

3

Act § 274A—Unlawful Employment of Aliens

Zilah Mendoza and Kathryn Meisle shared the final bow in Second Stage Theatre's 2003 premiere of *Living Out*.[1] There is nothing remarkable about such a curtain call. The two actors shared most of the stage time, and they portrayed the protagonists in the play about a nanny and her employer. Director Jo Bonney's choice recognized the two performers' collaborative and comparable labor in bringing Lisa Loomer's script to life. The two bodies bowing together also emphasized *Living Out*'s parallel structure and this particular production's interest in parallel staging. The bow, like the two-hour play before it, encouraged the audience to consider the partnership forged by domestic workers and their employers. The production explored the complications and injustices of a relationship based on skewed power dynamics while stressing the intricate connections and intimacies that exist between a predominantly white, upper-middle class in the United States and an immigrant workforce.

With Mendoza and Meisle's joint bow in mind, I explore in this chapter issues of identity formation in a political economy that categorically divides people on the basis of immigration status. I question how professional theatrical performances can illuminate these issues but also participate in the maintenance of problematic hierarchies. In proposing the dyad of undocumented domestic worker and privileged employer as an inseparable unit—the identity and consciousness of one is tied to the other—I hope to spotlight a segment of the US workforce in dire need of recognition and to interrogate how we use each other to form our sense of self. Is it possible, following Linda Bosniak's rhetorical proposition, that "first-world women's citizenship comes at the expense of the citizenship of their household workers"?[2]

In what follows, I examine how three different theatre pieces—Loomer's *Living Out*, Milcha Sánchez-Scott's *Latina*, and Octavio Solis's

Lydia—advocate for immigrants living in undocumentedness by making visible realities of working without papers.[3] I then complicate the plays' advocacy by considering a broader context of theatre production and consumption. Given that hiring practices and access to performances limit the possibilities for those in undocumentedness to partake in professional theatre in the United States, the plays' efforts to raise the visibility of workers without papers are inevitably problematized. I propose that we approach professional productions of such plays as instances of what I call "undocumentedface." Evoking practices like blackface or yellowface, the admittedly charged term indicates a phenomenon in which members of a dominant social group perform as marginalized Others. I am certain that prominent, professional productions of these plays—which offer smart, well-developed Latina characters—would have come under fire had they not cast Latina actors. But what are the repercussions of representing undocumented characters, however positive the portrayals, if those in undocumentedness are precluded from partaking directly in processes of theatre-making and theatre-going? Given Loomer's, Sánchez-Scott's, and Solis's admirable insight into life and work without papers, their participation in a production system that shuts out unauthorized immigrants offers an intriguing opportunity to consider the legal/illegal divide so prominent in the US socioeconomy.

A focus on stage representations of domestic workers and homemakers allows me to hone my discussion of undocumentedness and labor. Several theatre pieces do showcase undocumented workers in a range of industries. Some notable examples include Cherríe Moraga's *Watsonville*, which centers on California cannery workers; Byron Au Yong and Aaron Jafferis's *Stuck Elevator*, about a Chinese food deliveryman in the Bronx; and Saviana Stanescu's *Aliens with Extraordinary Skills*, which depicts the experience of two undocumented professional clowns and whose title references US immigration law's evaluation of talent in determining who should enter the country with permission to work. But my emphasis on domestic workers illuminates key trends. First, as Pierrette Hondagneu-Sotelo explains in her paramount study of Latina domestic labor, undocumented workers in that arena are particularly marginalized; their labor remains today especially disregarded. The figure of the undocumented domestic worker therefore lends itself well to an examination of legal nonexistence and identity. Second, undocumented immigrant labor is increasingly female. Third, because the work done by domestics occurs in homes and hence blurs some of the distinctions between public and private spaces, it offers a particularly fraught, intimate setting in which undocumented workers and their employers must interact.[4] Loomer explains that "in this relationship between a nanny and the family, there [is] everything…every dynamic of race, class, and especially of power, but within the most personal, human family story."[5]

I have also purposely chosen to focus on theatrical representations of undocumented maids hailing from Latin America. That choice highlights how immigration law prompts a kind of ghettoization prevalent in domestic work as well as the cyclical nature of immigrant labor. Hondagneu-Sotelo reports that, into the twenty-first century, the field of paid domestic work has become increasingly homogenized, with women from Latin America comprising more and more of the domestic labor force, especially after the immigration reform of 1965.[6] *Living Out* comments on these trends ("Good God, everyone is from El Salvador these days!" [*LO* 8]). It also notes that present-day policies might change the nature of domestic employment in the future ("So in a couple of years we can hire a nanny from Iraq" [*LO* 62]).

My parameters help me to highlight ways in which immigration law, work, and identity converge. Questions of undocumented migration and of legal identities are inseparable from issues of labor. That International Workers' Day has, since 2006, become synonymous in the United States with immigrants' rights alerts us to the crucial and tactical self-identification of those living in undocumentedness as workers, first and foremost. As Shannon Gleeson argues, work becomes a central means of forging an identity for laborers in undocumentedness as well as a key building block to their sense of legitimacy and belonging.[7] Protesters at a May Day rally in New York City's Union Square chanted, "Deportations must be stopped, *workers* must be free," "Fight for the rights of *workers*," and "For immigrants, *producing* and *working* mean family unity."[8] Immigrant workers and their advocates thus combat depictions of illegality with notions of labor and production.

Law prompts further and deeper connections between work and identity. On the one hand, immigration law restricts the kind of labor and production that is available to immigrants. A vast number of court cases and much legislation dictate how immigrants can and cannot work while in the United States. One's citizenship status prescribes, for example, whether one can serve as a state trooper, probation officer, or even cemetery sexton; whether one can be certified as a public school teacher or gain admittance into a state's bar association; whether one can continue in a job like airport security.[9] Such restrictions not only shape one's present material conditions but also mold one's broader sense of possibility and, hence, of belonging. On the other hand, regardless of the kind of job involved, legal categorization significantly structures one's position within the labor market. As I explore in this chapter, immigration law generally and undocumentedness in particular expose workers to individual and systematic exploitation, which can affect not only work-ing conditions but also personal and group identities.

Currently, anyone rightfully employed in the United States must complete Form I-9 and document legal authorization to work. The form requires each employee to attest "under penalty of perjury," itself a felony, that he or she is (1) a citizen, (2) a noncitizen national, (3) a lawful per-manent resident, or (4) an alien authorized to work. Since the passage of the Immigration Reform and Control Act (IRCA) in 1986, knowingly hiring or continuing the employment of an undocumented worker is also unlawful, punishable through fines and imprisonment.[10] And yet, by current estimates, there are eight million undocumented immigrants working in the United States. They comprise over 5 percent of the total workforce and are increasingly ubiquitous in diverse industries. Once a phenomenon linked to agricultural work, unauthorized immigrants in the United States today not only retain a critical role in agriculture but also account for a disproportionately high percentage of those employed in construction, groundskeeping, building maintenance, food prepara-tion, and hospitality. In the late 2000s, undocumented workers comprised over 20 percent of private household employees.[11]

The numbers reflect global economic trends. Especially after the 1970s, because the wealth of countries such as the United States has grown and that of poor nations has shrunk (both absolutely and relatively), migra-tion out of those nations has become a matter of survival.[12] The promise of wages otherwise impossible at home outweighs the perils associated with leaving that home as well as with entering another country with-out proper authorization. The numbers also underscore how immigra-tion law, rather than curbing undocumented migrants, actually sustains a seemingly endless labor pool. By marking workers legally nonexistent and therefore relatively unprotectable, immigration law heightens their vulnerability. As it has historically, immigration law continues to work in tandem with business interests to assure a steady supply of cheap, exploit-able labor. Unsurprisingly, when the need for workers dips, as is the case with the most recent recession, levels of undocumented immigration dip as well.[13] The identity of immigrants in the United States as workers is therefore particularly reinforced.

Maid without Papers

The stories in Milcha Sánchez-Scott's *Latina*, Lisa Loomer's *Living Out*, and Octavio Solis's *Lydia* allow me to examine how the theatre pieces advocate for immigrant laborers by making visible and commenting on realities of working in undocumentedness. To borrow from Karen

Shimakawa's reading of Au Yong and Jafferis's *Stuck Elevator*, theatre has the potential in this way "to bring forth the invisible body of the neoliberal migrant laborer" and to "produce that body as a speaking subject capable of engaging in political discourse."[14] Again heeding the possibility that stories help to articulate legal consciousness (see chapter 1), I will consider domestic work here through three rather different storylines.

Sánchez-Scott's *Latina* premiered in 1980, commissioned by the New Works Division of Artists in Prison and Other Places (AIPOP, later L.A. Theatre Works). Sánchez-Scott wrote the play with director Jeremy Blahnik's input, and the original production toured California before settling into an award-winning run at the Pilot Theater in Los Angeles. The play has since been produced on regional and college stages. Set in the Felix Sanchez Domestic Agency, *Latina* introduces us to a day in the life of mostly undocumented immigrant women looking for work, their challenges in the United States, and their struggles to gain respect from inconsiderate employers. Depicting the women's contentious relationships with the agency's Guatemalan owner and with Sarita, his Chicana receptionist, and drawing distinctions between workers with papers and those without, the play also problematizes a categorical understanding of "Latina." Seen from the perspective of Sarita, a struggling actor seemingly eager to distance herself from the other women, *Latina* invites us to consider how our sense of self resides in others.

Loomer's title refers to the arrangement that Ana Hernandez, an undocumented Salvadoran immigrant, makes with Nancy Robin, an Anglo lawyer in need of a nanny for her newborn. *Living Out* thus offers a view into a domestic worker's experience both in her boss's residence as well as in her own home, to which she returns every night. Through Ana, Nancy, their husbands, and two additional employer-nanny dyads, the 2003 play explores the phenomenon of having to trust someone else to care for one's own child and the difficult bond that individuals in such a contract must forge. The Mark Taper Forum in Los Angeles commissioned the original production, which earned Loomer a Back Stage West Garland Award for Playwriting. Since its Obie Award–winning New York premiere at Second Stage, *Living Out* has been widely performed.

Lydia was commissioned by the Denver Center Theatre Company, where it premiered in 2008. The play, which continues to receive productions, invites us to observe a live-in situation and the particular dynamic established when an immigrant family, its own patriarch living without papers, brings an undocumented worker into the home. Hired predominantly to take care of Ceci, a teenager suffering from brain damage following a tragic car accident, the eponymous Lydia quickly inserts herself into the broken Flores family and compels each member to reexamine his or her own status, relationships, and dark past. A stylized, at times dream-like piece, *Lydia* urges us to consider the intimate and life-changing labor that immigrant domestic workers perform in many US households.

Sánchez-Scott, Loomer, and Solis write about workers in undocu-mentedness from their personal experiences, showcasing what research-ers confirm about domestic work. Sánchez-Scott based *Latina* on the journals she kept while working as a counselor for a domestic agency in Beverly Hills. Loomer conducted extensive interviews with domestic workers in Los Angeles, including her own employee. And Solis grounded *Lydia* in his own upbringing along the Texas border. He describes how his parents, living in undocumentedness like Claudio Flores, relied on maids from Juárez "to keep things together at home."[15] The three plays endeavor to make visible the experiences of women pushed into spaces of nonexistence and collectively draw attention to the women's exploitable and exploited positions. The plays emphasize processes of identity forma-tion located in the relationship between domestic and employer.

Importantly, the crossnational journeys of the workers depicted in *Latina*, *Living Out*, and *Lydia* all begin with a simple but crucial fact. "Why did you come here?" Misha, the Flores's 16-year-old son, asks Lydia. "'Cause I need work" (*LY* 70). The terse, honest response echoes the need described by the immigrant women in *Latina* and *Living Out*. Indeed, work means everything. David Bacon stresses in *Illegal People* that immigrant workers—legal and undocumented alike—are more than just individuals making personal choices. Rather, they are decision-makers compelled by socioeconomic and political conditions both at home and in the United States.[16] By opening *Latina* with the image of New Girl in her Peruvian village (*LA* 85), Sánchez-Scott urges us to keep in mind the home life that prompts the treacherous journey into the United States. *Living Out* also makes a home nation persistently present: With her hus-band and younger son already in Los Angeles, Ana works to bring her other son from war-ravaged El Salvador. The other two nannies we meet in Loomer's play work as well to provide for families that live elsewhere or to attempt reunification in the United States. Quite simply, people will cross the border to work, as work offers the possibility of better prospects for their families, prospects that conditions at home make impossible.

Nonetheless, the plays are careful not to traffic in American Dream tropes. In Sarita's words, the dream of a land paved with gold is "not for some piddley maid's job to keep [a] family on this side of starvation" (*LA* 119). All three plays present immigrant women who experience the possibility of a better livelihood, but at enormous costs. Solis's Lydia, for example, finds delight in a simple shopping trip. But the few toilet-ries she buys to "smell like Ali McGraw," to smell like "a rich *gringa*," cost her a full month's pay, money she can only obtain through a salary advance (*LY* 66). Lydia's sense of belonging rests here on achieving a type of Americanization through consumption (as I examine in the previous chapter). Perhaps more precisely, the shopping trip exemplifies a kind of aspirational consumption, in which goods become "bridges to displaced meaning [indicating] not who we are, but who we wish we were," to follow Grant McCracken.[17] Yet, *Lydia* makes plain that the maid's aspirations are virtually unachievable. Whatever salary a job open to an undocumented worker may command will likely not suffice to consume that which an ostensibly real gringa/o does.

The impossibility of an American Dream is not merely about consumer goods. In *Living Out*, we witness Ana's growth as an independent, self-assured woman under Nancy's influence. We also see how working to attain her goals requires indebting herself to her wealthier employer. As the playwrights make clear, work in undocumentedness generally enables only someone else's American Dream. "This country rob your soul [*sic*]," explains Solis's Claudio, who compares himself to a stone against which others can "make their own great *pinche* dreams" (*LY* 45). Paraphrasing Charles Isherwood's review of *Living Out*, we could say that all the undocumented characters at hand are doomed to miss out on the lives they seek, regardless of their hard work, because they are only accessories to the success of others.[18] The plays thus actively counter stereotypes of unauthorized immigrants, particularly female ones, as free riders. *Living Out*, *Latina*, and *Lydia* not only offer portraits that stress the role of female immigrants as hardworking laborers, as producers, but also posit employers as the real opportunists.

Indeed, all three playwrights demonstrate that it is employers who profit most from the work of undocumented workers. In this way, they position themselves in a highly contested debate over the costs and benefits of undocumented immigration. The playwrights suggest that, adapting Bosniak's language, the economic well-being of the US citizens onstage does come, or can come, at the expense of their household workers' well-being. At the end of the day, and at the end of the plays, the undocumented workers pay a much higher price for their actions than do the employers who benefit from their cheap labor.

As the playwrights explore, those without papers are placed in exploitable and vulnerable positions. Domestic labor, because it demands relatively unstructured duties from workers functioning in isolation, proves particularly prone to engendering exploitative conditions, even under the best of employers' intentions. To begin with, the work of housecleaners, nannies, and home-care workers often fails to be recognized as legitimate employment and is subsequently undervalued, underprotected, and underpaid. Loomer's Nancy well captures such attitudes when she tries to support Ana: "You should go to school and get a real job!" (*LO* 54). With her arm around the nanny, as per Loomer's stage directions, Nancy in essence diminishes to nothing the very real work that Ana has been doing. Although Nancy has been paying Ana wages to do specific labor, it is clear that the former does not consider the latter an actual employee. Hondagneu-Sotelo explains that domestic work continues to be viewed in the twenty-first century as "something other than employment" and that employers often tend to see themselves more as consumers than as law-bound employers.[19] As a result, even without taking into account immigration status, domestic work remains today essentially unregulated.

The novelty of the nation's first bill to afford domestic workers basic labor rights alerts us to the reluctance of state and federal authorities to protect domestic employment. In 2010, after a years-long period of consideration, New York State passed the Domestic Workers' Bill of Rights, requiring employers to provide paid holidays, vacation, sick leave, and overtime pay to all full-time domestic employees, dues guaranteed in other industries since the 1930s. (Hawaii and California have since passed similar measures, with Massachusetts poised to be next.) Yet, these laws protect only those employed full time, leaving hundreds of thousands others without the same basic rights. In fact, domestic work generally does not fall under the purview of federal statutes such as the Fair Labor Standards Act (FLSA), which aims to protect workers from substandard conditions. Domestic workers therefore enjoy few protections, and those protections are not easily enforced.[20]

Undocumentedness exacerbates such vulnerability, whether the work is in a domestic setting or not. Although some case law dictates that employers cannot violate FLSA on the basis of immigration status (*Patel v. Quality Inn South*), undocumented workers clearly lack basic rights accorded to others. For instance, in a 2002 Supreme Court majority opinion, Chief Justice William Rehnquist explains,

> Under the IRCA regime, it is impossible for an undocumented alien to obtain employment in the United States without some party directly contravening explicit congressional policies. Either the undocumented alien tenders fraudulent identification, which subverts the cornerstone of IRCA's enforcement mechanism, or the employer knowingly hires the undocumented alien in direct contradiction of its IRCA obligations.[21]

The decision, which held that workers in undocumentedness were not entitled to back pay after being fired for participating in union activities, exemplifies the treacherous, and thus exploitable, position that workers without documents inhabit.

In an environment in which securing a job without risking legal consequences is "impossible," holding on to a job often proves more important than calling attention to unfair or illegal conditions. The passage of New York's Domestic Workers' Bill of Rights highlights this issue. While many celebrated the possibility of adopting FLSA-like standards for an otherwise unregulated industry, many domestic workers doubt that those in undocumentedness will actually report violations to any authority. Threats of deportation and detention regularly prevent workers from taking a stand against abuse, even if those threats are not blatant or immediately palpable. One of the bill's cosponsors, State Senator Kevin Parker, agrees that the law "will not change much for [undocumented immigrants] and sadly, long after its passage, they will continue to exist beyond its reach."[22] Quite simply, domestic workers who lack immigration papers are especially vulnerable to abuse.

Latina, which out of the three plays considered here presents the most overtly exaggerated characterizations of employers, makes this abuse especially obvious. We hear explicit threats including those of the unrelenting Mrs. Camden: "She [the domestic employee] is an illegal. She is an alien. And if I wanted to, I could call immigration on her." While Sarita calls Mrs. Camden on her hypocrisy ("You talk 'legal,' you hired her because you didn't want to pay the salary a legal person gets" [*LA* 139]), the play adamantly stages the ever-present risks of undocumentedness. The characters in *Latina*, like those in *Real Women Have Curves* (chapter 2), fear a vehicle parked outside the agency; the "migra" captured their friend Hortensia just a week ago (*LA* 106). "Que Dios la bendiga y que no se encuentre con la migra," prays Sarita for Lola, who appears to be missing (*LA* 104). That sentiment—a longing for heavenly protection from immigration authorities—underscores the fragility of the women's positions as domestic workers for unbearable employers. Antagonizing an employee might well prompt the type of action Mrs. Camden threatens, and the worker could easily find herself deported. "Makes me feel hunted, like an animal," confesses La Chata (*LA* 106), crystallizing the fact that spaces of legal nonexistence are inherently marked by fear and violence. Tellingly, *Latina*, as does *Lydia*, concludes with immigration authorities onstage, with the violent sounds of a helicopter and of officers rounding up women. Despite their protests, all the women who lack papers disappear from the stage after this final raid. As the curtain falls, all but three characters—those legally allowed in the United States—remain visible to the audience (*LA* 141).

A pre-IRCA play, both in its writing and setting, *Latina* highlights the fact that the employer at hand seemingly bears little or no responsibility for what is happening. "I didn't break the law," urges the agency's owner, "I didn't bring them up here" (*LA* 141). And it is clear by play's end that Don Felix's agency will suffer little from the raid; he is confident that business will be as usual the following day. The audience will not see that next day, but the final image of the production is of another new girl and her smuggler "*creeping towards the fence*" (*LA* 141). *Latina* thus makes clear that undocumented labor will continue. The raid's only effect is personal and not systemic; the individual laborers suffer, but the structure remains unchanged.

Lydia's action takes place in the early 1970s, also pre-IRCA. The legal consequences of working without documents again fall almost exclusively on the employee. The employer is guiltless. In Solis's tragedy, much like in Arthur Miller's *A View from the Bridge* (chapter 1), a climactic betrayal of the undocumented immigrant to the authorities proves an act of purging, motivated by anger. Discovering that her husband has had sex with the maid, Rosa uses Lydia's immigration status as a means to get rid of her. After protecting her for most of the play, Rosa urges her nephew Alvaro, a border patrol officer, to "TAKE THIS *PUTA* OUT OF MY HOUSE NOW!" (*LY* 79). Rosa then rips off Lydia's shirt—a gift from the woman to the maid—and leaves the young worker screaming for mercy, "*ravaged and half-naked*" (*LY* 79). By ridding herself of Lydia, Rosa finds new power, a power she dangles over her husband in Solis's final scene:

> CLAUDIO. *¿Como que se fue?* Where is she?
> ROSA. *Con la Migra.*
> CLAUDIO. *¿Que chingados dices, mujer?* You turn her over to *La Migra*?
> ROSA. If you want her, *vete*. If you miss that fucking country so much, go.
> Let me remind you who also needs papers. (*LY* 80–81)

The play's ending is ambiguous in terms of the Flores family's well-being. We know that their lives will not be the same after Lydia, but it is difficult to evaluate the shift. What is unambiguous is Lydia's fate. Before she leaves the stage not to return again, Lydia cries, "I don't want to go back! If I go back, I'll die! I know I will. I'll die!" (*LY* 79). As does Marco in Miller's play, as do the undocumented women in Sánchez-Scott's work, Lydia disappears so that the lives of the other characters—the so-called legal ones—can continue.

By making the hiring of known undocumented workers a federal offense, IRCA sought to shift some responsibility to employers for increasing levels of illegal immigration. But the proliferation of undocumented labor after the passage of the 1986 legislation attests to IRCA's failure to curb unauthorized migration. The US economy is seemingly addicted to the cheap labor that undocumentedness affords. Moreover, as Bacon suggests, "there [is] no way to punish the employers without punishing the workers first."[23] Although both are subject to criminal penalties, it is workers, not employers, who continue to pay the highest price if they are caught working illegally.

"Nannygate" is a case and point. In 1993, President Bill Clinton nominated Zoë Baird to be the nation's first female attorney general. When it became known that Baird had hired two undocumented immigrants to work in her home, a political and media storm descended on Baird and the newly elected president. Less than a month after the nomination, Baird withdrew her name from consideration. She arguably marred her reputation and lost a prestigious appointment. Her IRCA violations resulted in a $2,900 fine, an amount not likely to have made a dent in the prominent attorney's lifestyle. It is difficult to gauge the full damages suffered by Baird: she and her husband did remain in temporary seclusion during the "exhausting ordeal."[24] Still, Baird seemed to recover. She returned to work, eventually achieved a position in the Clinton White House, and later became president of the Markle Foundation. For Victor and Lillian Cordero, the Peruvian couple whom Baird had employed, nannygate had much more pervasive consequences. The couple was generally ignored, even disregarded, by the media. However, immigration authorities did not overlook the workers as easily. Days after Baird stepped down as nominee for attorney general, the Corderos faced questioning by the Immigration and Naturalization Service (INS). First he and then she opted for so-called voluntary deportation, fearing a pending investigation. "I feel like a hunted animal," confessed Victor Cordero after INS officers descended on him, echoing La Chata's sentiments.[25] After years working in the United States, the Corderos had little option but to leave.

Like Baird and her own husband, Paul Gewirtz, Living Out's Nancy and Richard are practicing lawyers. They are well aware of the consequences of hiring an undocumented worker in a post-IRCA, post-nannygate era. But providing good, affordable care for her baby and balancing work with homemaking drive Nancy to hire Ana. Nancy begs her new employee, "Don't say anything to my husband about your, uh, situation. He doesn't need to be concerned with the legal ethics…" (LO 20). Not looking to abuse Ana in any predetermined or even conscious way, Nancy offers what she believes is a reasonable wage, a salary that apparently pleases Ana. After interviewing with Wallace and Linda, the other two employers Loomer depicts, Ana feels fortunate to have gotten a position with the saner, more understanding Nancy. As the play progresses, however, we begin to understand that this originally productive match cannot sustain itself—it depends on too many lies and a disproportionate balance of power. Both women share a need for having someone else look after their children, both struggle to balance a job outside the home and a married life, and both find support and guidance in each other. Still, as Richard confesses, he and Nancy "have options" (*LO* 62); Ana does not. The parallel structure that Loomer constructs purposefully crumbles in the concluding moments. While both women sit on the same stage bed during their final interchange, their journeys to this point have taken disproportionately different tolls. Nancy loses a trusted nanny and reevaluates her needs as a career mother; Ana loses a major source of income, the hope of legalization and family reunification, and a son.

Loomer urges us to think about the lines that divide Nancy and Ana. Ethnic and class differences clearly matter. Still, the playwright carefully depicts how legal categorization critically affects her characters' experiences. After all, Loomer juxtaposes three white mothers against three Latina nannies, but only the undocumented Ana—like the women in Sanchez's agency, like Lydia—pays an unbearably high price for taking a job. In contrast, Sandra, a nanny with whom Ana converses in the park, gets to celebrate her "happy citizenship" onstage, donuts and all (*LO* 50). Triumphantly, Sandra narrates that, with citizenship in hand, she has traveled to Texas, confronted her son's absent father, and in essence reached a breakthrough: "He thought I come for the child support, but I say—'I'm not after you! I have a happy life and I feel so proud of myself 'cause I got my citizenship now and I sent for our son!'" (*LO* 52). Sandra's pride matches La Cubana's boasts in *Latina*. "I have my green card," she loves to repeat to anyone who crosses her, "You can't push me around like the rest" (*LA* 99). Admittedly, as Linda Saborío points out, La Cubana's legal status does not afford her full control over her ability to work.[26] But her surviving the play's final raid marks her in an important way as different from her fellow *latinas*.

It is dangerous to glorify the power of a green card. It is unrealistic to believe that a change in immigration or citizenship status can immediately and utterly change one's life. Precisely because life without papers means limited access to education opportunities and to well-paying jobs, life with newly acquired papers might not bring a sudden career change or a remarkable bump in standards of living. *Living Out* and *Lydia*, especially, depict characters with blinding green-card dreams (La Chata in *Latina* also displays, in one scene, her "if I got my papers" mentality [*LA* 101]). Nonetheless, the boost in self-esteem that Sandra experiences because of her new citizenship cannot be overlooked. With papers, employees can more confidently address unfair labor practices. With papers, employees can more realistically quit and look for another position. With papers, one's work is not criminalized. So long as a job is tied to immigration concerns, the possibility for exploitation hangs heavily.

Living Out's Nancy and *Lydia's* Rosa both offer their respective domestic employees help in obtaining papers. While Nancy endeavors to secure legal counsel for Ana, Rosa connects Lydia to someone who can forge documents. Rosa seems eager to secure Lydia's status, to make her a legitimate part of the family. "She wants my name in the passport to be Flores," confesses Lydia (*LY* 68). Loomer and Solis thus examine what Judith Rollins defines as "maternalism." According to Rollins, employers of domestic workers—overwhelmingly female in the United States—tend to treat their employees—also overwhelmingly female in today's world— in a protective and nurturing manner. However, such treatment equally manages to insult and degrade; "it is not human-to-equal-human caring," explains Rollins. Along with kind offers to help with immigration, loans or salary advances, and small gifts like items of clothing also come subtly disparaging remarks and actions. Giving becomes a form of possession, and generosity a mask for control.[27] Despite the fact that she trusts Ana with her infant daughter, Nancy, for example, consistently approaches the nanny as if she were a fragile, naïve infant herself. At one point, Nancy questions Ana's ability to read (*LO* 19). Lydia is persistently referred to as a possession: "our little housekeeper" (*LY* 55). Eventually, the apparent kindness demonstrated by Nancy and Rosa surfaces as self-serving. Their concern for the well-being of their respective domestic workers rests in a need for their labor and not in a genuine desire to see Ana or Lydia succeed. Dangling the promise of a green card in front of the employees becomes a strategy to keep them in their current employ, or, at least in Nancy's case, perhaps a guilt-induced excuse for maintaining an undocumented worker. Ana's husband is more suspicious, convinced that Nancy's offers to help with immigration are simply so that Nancy won't have to "worry about hiring nobody illegal!" (*LO* 37).

Importantly, as evidenced by maternalistic practices, the dynamics of exploitation prevalent in domestic employment exceeds a strictly economic imbalance.[28] Employers gain status and elevate their sense of worth at the expense of employees, who are forced to inhabit a position defined in negative terms. The very *illegality* of the employees serves as a bolster for the employers' identity as legal and natural members of society. Rollins suggests that "any identification the employer has with the domestic is a negative identification. The menial, unintelligent, physically strong, irresponsible, weak-charactered servant provides a convenient contrast figure upon whom might be projected those aspects of herself most despised and feared." This type of symbolic violence operates to some degree because employers and employees belong to different ethnic groups. Indeed, patterns of employment in the United States today follow centuries of worldwide traditions of placing members of a different ethnic background in domestic posts; most employers of domestic workers are white and a vast majority of these employees are not.[29]

However, reducing the phenomenon of domestic work in US households strictly to questions of race and ethnicity proves difficult. In a comical scene at the park, when Ana first meets Zoila and Sandra, the latter two educate the newly hired nanny on the particularities of various employers. Ana quickly learns that "los Hindus pay the worst," the Chinese "never talk to you," and Latinos treat you like a slave (*LO* 23). The jokes prompt laughter,[30] but they also alert us to the fact that an increasing number of employers of domestic workers are not white. (I should note that Nancy's supervisor in the law firm, whom we hear about when Nancy calls the office, is named Diane Machado. Although we never see Diane, her expressly Latina/o surname further complicates a neat division along ethnic lines in the world of *Living Out*.) By making the owner of the Felix Sanchez Domestic Agency Guatemalan and by placing Lydia in a Chicana/o home, Sánchez-Scott and Solis likewise explore mono-ethnic exploitation.

In so doing, *Latina* and *Lydia* examine the way in which immigration status critically operates to maintain class divisions. By removing the issue of ethnic difference, Sánchez-Scott and Solis are able to stress how, to borrow Hondagneu-Sotelo's words, "the status of [domestic workers] as *immigrants* today serves to legitimize their social, economic, and political subordination and their disproportionate concentration in paid domestic work," and, more specifically, how "immigration *status* has clearly become an important axis of inequality, one interwoven with relations of race, class, and gender" to facilitate exploitation. It is because employers and employees occupy different legal statuses, because domestics appear "foreign and unassimilable," and because "they are 'illegal' and do not merit equal opportunities with U.S.-born American citizens" that exploitation is excused and even naturalized.[31]

The Flores family certainly lifts itself up by differentiating itself against Lydia's lack of papers. Because they occupy a treacherous and relatively low position in US society, the Floreses need a "*chavala* from *Jalisco* who just came over" to begin living "a little *mas* better" (*LY* 11, 54). The dismissive "chavala," which connotes smallness and homeliness, well captures the role that Lydia must play in the Chicana/o household. At times exoticized and at times patronized (or matronized, if we follow Rollins), Lydia must perform her job—clean, cook, tend to the brain-damaged Ceci, and in essence care for and somehow cure each family member—without being seen or treated as a legitimate employee or even person. "Mom, she makes chicken *molé* from scratch," Misha says in awe of Lydia's presumed authenticity. He then magnifies Lydia's exoticness: "She uses spices and stuff we don't even know how to pronounce. She's got recipes the Aztecs used on the damn pyramids" (*LY* 29). Predictably perhaps, Misha falls in love—or only lust—with the live-in *criada*, who is fully turned into a sexual object by the men of the house. For Claudio, himself an undocumented immigrant, "liv[ing] American" requires not only employing "our little housekeeper from Mexico-way" but also, stereotypically, sleeping with her (*LY* 6, 55). As for Rosa, she begins to feel "quasi-middle class," not because she can afford a domestic worker but because she can command and control Lydia. When she loses this control, Rosa has no option but to send Lydia back to Jalisco. In short, Lydia proves a catalyst for this family that is "all sad and wounded" (*LY* 7), because she represents something lower than what they are.

By turning Lydia into a sexualized, otherworldly being, or a lowly child in need of instruction and protection, the Flores family in essence "Mexicanizes" and "illegalizes" the maid. Borrowing from Edward Said's ideas about "orientalizing," we see how Lydia is turned into the "simple, symbolic, visible—without concern for [seeing her as] 'natural.'"[32] And these distinctions made against Lydia and her illegal status elevate the Floreses to a seemingly higher position. Thus, not only is Lydia being exploited with low wages, she is also the victim of a symbolic violence that helps the family construct a sense of self-worth, albeit a fragile one. At the expense of the *mojada*, a term regularly used in reference to Lydia, the Flores family can carve their niche in the United States.

In *Latina*, Sarita displays a similar strategy to boost her own worth, relying on the apparent distance existing between her, an Americanized Chicana, and the agency's undocumented domestic workers. She makes her feelings clear at play's opening, speaking directly to the audience:

> I hate sleezy [*sic*] Sanchez, and I hate this stupid bus bench...*(kicks bus bench)* and the illegal women who come here everyday looking for illegal jobs ...Well, I don't hate the women...it's just that...I am not one of them ...I don't want to be identified with them. [...] I am not a maid, I am a counselor. Okay! (*LA* 87)

We see in such a statement, delivered while one of the undocumented women in the background prepares to clean, the seeds for some of the 1994 election results that approved California's controversial Proposition 187. A noteworthy 27 percent of self-identified Latino voters (as did a 52 percent majority of Asian voters) opted to support the measure that would drastically impede the livelihood of undocumented immigrants in the state.[33] The road to Arizona's controversial immigration legislation has been paved with voting initiatives: in 2004, 47 percent of Latina/o voters supported Arizona's Proposition 200, seeking to make proof of citizenship mandatory

to receive government benefits, and in 2006, 48 percent of Latina/o voters supported a seemingly anti-immigrant measure to make English the
Arizona's official language.[34] Such statistics remind us that ethnic categories do not neatly apply to questions of undocumented immigration.
Like Sarita and the Floreses, many who identify as Latina/o despise immigrants in undocumentedness, a group from whom they want defiantly and
urgently to distinguish themselves. The major arc in Sánchez-Scott's play
does follow Sarita's change in perception, a change that the audience is
meant to applaud. Still, Sarita's initial approach toward "illegal women"
confirms the practice of using those in undocumentedness to construct a
sense of self.

In particular, it is domestic workers in undocumentedness who offer
employers a readily accessible and specific hue with which to paint
the backside of their mirrors. In their own homes, employers can turn
undocumented employees into objects that confer and validate status and
self-worth. "Class is a slippery concept in the United States," Hondagneu-
Sotelo tells us, "where nearly everybody, from warehouse loaders to mil-
lionaire entrepreneurs, is likely to identify as middle class."[35] With less
strictly defined class markers, the employment of a domestic worker, and
especially her evident illegality, can confirm or even bolster one's own
place on an otherwise ambiguous social ladder. We might tweak Bosniak's
tentative proposition by suggesting that first-world women's sense of class
belonging comes at the expense of their household workers' seemingly
lower status, a status often confirmed not by ethnic categorization alone,
but by immigration classification as well. Thus, although Ana escaped El
Salvador a professional dental student, Nancy imagines her as the illiter-
ate and unfortunate lower-class member against which she can pit her
own upper-middle-class position.

In fact, most undocumented immigrants in the United States do not
stem from the poorest sectors of their home countries or from the poorest countries in the world for that matter.[36] After all, there are considerable costs associated with migrating. Once in the United States, however,
their lack of papers becomes a marker of class, transforming the undocumented into a viable rung on which others can step to concretize an
elusive middle-class status. Loomer shrewdly constructs the Robins as
anxious arrivals to a new neighborhood. Worried about their mortgage
and future preschool tuition (*LO* 14), Nancy and Richard need, or want,
to resolve some of the recently experienced ambiguity. Ana provides them
with a possibility to discern their new position.

The utility of a domestic worker as a status symbol prompts her dehumanization, her conversion into an object seen only at surface level. Like
the right diaper bag or the right Mommy and Me class (both prevalent in

the conversations of Nancy and her peers), the so-called right domestic lets others know how well you do. Appearance becomes an essential element for successful job performance, as important as and at times even more so than good cleaning or caregiving. Hondagneu-Sotelo notes that employment agencies "literally groom" domestic workers by advising them how to dress and how to comport themselves physically. Employers tend to prefer 'Latina employees who are young, physically attractive, and relatively light-skinned—more mestiza than indigenous." Strikingly, employers seem most satisfied with domestic workers who appear "humble."[37] All three plays stage physical transformations, with domestic employees donning the clothes that their employers prefer. Ironically, the very illegality that makes the workers useful contrasts for their employers can diminish their value as status symbols. Thus, post-nannygate, Nancy, Wallace, and Linda adamantly assert each of their nanny's legal status, just as they affirm the generous "top dollar" that they pay (*LO* 33). But such falsehoods are only a means to project an image for their peers' benefit and, with regard to wages at least, perhaps a means to convince themselves that they are fair, reasonable employers.

Indeed, another way in which the undocumented domestic workers serve their employers is in manufacturing a benevolent sense of self. "She makes like she's doing me the big favor, letting me scrub her floors," Clara complains about her employer (*LA* 102). Precisely because undocumented immigrant workers so desperately need income, employers can begin to feel that the work they offer—regardless of salary, regardless of duties—is not only appropriate but also charitable. As the supporter of a poor, troubled, victimized maid, the employer can begin to construct an altruistic sense of self. According to Hondagneu-Sotelo, she "may get satisfaction from her intimate view of the private tribulations of a woman whose life is so unlike anything she knows that it might seem to have come from a novel—a woman who is poor, who lives in a crime-ridden neighborhood, who is raising children without the financial support of a husband, who is Latina and perhaps lacks U.S. citizenship or legal papers."[38] All three plays present employers who, believing they can empower their domestic workers, dole out unsolicited and often thoughtless advice. At the Felix Sanchez Domestic Agency, Clara complains:

> Sí, she [her "patrona"] like to talk. Eso de everybody equal. She go to meet with the other women, they talk everybody equal y de los husbands y como los hombres le tratan mal. They talk how the woman must be equal to men. Then she come to me and say, "Clara, you and me, equal." Hmmmmmph! I don't pay attention. (*Silence.*) She don't know nothing. I been taking three buses every day to clean houses for fifteen years and she...(*LA* 116)

The complaint attests to the palpable distance that employers of domestic workers create and maintain.

The domestic's immigrant status can actually serve employers as a weapon with which to demean the employees and, in turn, rationalize their hiring to tackle undesirable tasks. Mary Romero reports that many employers not only hire someone else to perform housework (clean the floor) but also demand it be done in particular ways, ways that such employers would not undertake themselves (scrub rather than mop).[39] This practice requires the construction of distance between employer and employee. Loomer suggests this process predominantly through the character of Wallace, who easily demonstrates one such distancing technique. In conversation with her peers, Wallace in essence rebukes immigrant women for leaving their own children behind in other countries—"I mean, could you do that?" Although Nancy advises Wallace to "take into consideration the political and economic situation" of their "caregivers" (LO 33), Wallace's attitude confirms in her mind that her domestic worker, Zoila, is somehow less of a woman than she is. With distance between them, Wallace can charge Zoila, who does not have a driver's license, to maneuver the children under her care through Los Angeles without access to a car. "Qué horror," sighs Ana when she learns about Zoila's plight (LO 30). Wallace can similarly use Ana's immigration status to justify her apparently unacceptable decisions. "She was illegal after all," rationalizes Wallace after learning that Ana lied about having a son in the United States and that she took Nancy's baby without notice to see the boy in the hospital. Instead of seeing a panicked mother whose son has had a life-threatening asthma attack, Wallace sees in Ana a "rather mysterious person" (LO 60). For Wallace, "illegal" becomes an adjective with which to describe Ana, with which to mark difference and conceal commonality. While Nancy is less openly offended by Ana's immigration status, she does dismiss the employee when the truths come to bear.

The dynamics at hand change an employer, regardless of her intentions. Just one day after having Ana in her home, Nancy is a different person. "Taping unsuspecting immigrants!? Who are you!?" presses her husband upon discovering that Nancy has left Ana under the gaze of a Nanny Cam hidden in a teddy bear. "Aren't you a member of the ACLU?" he asks in shock (LO 28). Nancy's political inclinations, her concern for the global socioeconomic realities that might force someone like Ana to leave her children in another country, fall by the wayside when it comes to ensuring her baby's safety. Although she feels tremendous guilt, Nancy nonetheless approaches Ana as the uneducated, untrustworthy, alien immigrant that Wallace expects. In the play's climactic moment, when Nancy arrives to an empty home and a note reading "Emergency. Gone to Hospital. Okay"

(*LO* 58), the mother's worst fears return her to a deep mistrust of Ana's foreignness and illegality. Earlier in the play, Ana had suggested giving the baby some hot tea to soothe a possible cold. At first surprised by the idea, Nancy, who has now employed Ana for months, agrees to the suggestion and adds that she fully trusts the nanny (*LO* 53). But upon finding the note, Nancy's first thought is "Oh God, maybe the tea!" (*LO* 59). By amplifying the threat of tea, Nancy betrays in the moment her misgivings about Ana's supposed difference, backward ways, and problematic decision-making. Even when the truth about Ana's having a son in Los Angeles surfaces, Nancy finds it difficult to let go of her distrust or to hire Ana back: "I mean, can you ever really know someone—who's so—different from you?" (*LO* 63).

Ana, like the majority of domestics, must tolerate such treatment. She must constantly perform a role for her employer, a part premised on the belief that employers prefer "subservient behavior and [do] not like a domestic's being too educated or intelligent, too materially well off, or too attractive," as Rollins explains.[40] Beyond mere costume changes, the domestics must fully take on theatrical roles. For instance, although Nancy seemingly convinces Ana to drop the formal "Mrs. Robin" (*LO* 36), Ana's use of "Nancy" becomes only an illusive marker of friendship. In fact, we might read it precisely as Ana's simply doing what Nancy asks. After all, Ana continues to refer to "Mrs. Robin" or to "la señora" when speaking about Nancy to others (*LO* 36, 43).[41] Even at the end, when Ana has lost a son and a job, she chooses the deferential formal address when Nancy telephones her in order to mark the distance between them (*LO* 65). Nancy, by contrast, never hails Ana as "Mrs. Hernandez." Likewise, Sarita prompts a theatrical transformation of the newly arrived Peruvian immigrant, hoping to turn her into an "*Americanized version... with a new slick hair style, make-up and SARITA's clothes*" (*LA* 133). New Girl is given a few lines of English to memorize, provided some character background, and rehearsed to appear "responsible, neat, professional" (*LA* 125). Some, like Lola, disapprove of Sarita's tactics, admonishing her for the idea that New Girl needs to be changed. Now donning New Girl's Peruvian attire, Sarita comes to agree with Lola. "She was beautiful the way she was," Sarita regrets about playing Pygmalion with New Girl (*LA* 134). However, Americanized New Girl, New Girl in-role we could say, is the only one who actually gets a job in the stage's traffic. We are left to assume that the new New Girl in the play's final montage will likewise have to take on a role in order to score some employment.

Most jobs require some sort of acting. But when undocumented workers are placed in private homes, the solo performances that are needed can prove extreme. "We lie here everyday," bluntly admits Sarita (*LA* 103). The secrecy and pretense that working without papers inevitably requires—Ana must lie about having a son in the United States to get a job, Nancy must lie to her husband about Ana's status, New Girl must use someone else's address and Social Security number, and so on—is compounded with the stress of being asked to be non-present.

Admittedly, a domestic worker can render her employer invisible. *Latina*'s Clara, for one, rejoices when her employer's daughter castigates her mother for being a bad parent, one who has let "maids do all your work" (*LA* 116). Clara's sense of purpose and self-worth comes here at the expense of her employer's, a point Sánchez-Scott further emphasizes by relegating the employers predominantly to offstage. The play urges audiences to see the domestics as more worthy of attention, as more fully developed human beings. In *Living Out*, we see Nancy's missing crucial moments in her daughter's life. Once Ana's presence allows Nancy to pursue her work, she begins to feel out of touch with her baby and husband (*LO* 49); tellingly one of the baby's first words, "Ama," is ambiguously both "Mama" and "Ana" (*LO* 43). Solis's Rosa realizes also that she does not "know everything in [her] house" (*LY* 18), that Lydia's involvement in the lives of her children and husband somehow erode the wife and mother's place in the home. Before betraying Lydia to the Border Patrol, Rosa mourns, "What does the word *madre* mean in this country? Does it mean idiot? Does it mean pretending? [...] I'm a stranger to my own children. My husband won't touch me" (*LY* 78). In the employers' seeming failures as homemakers, the domestic workers find their own sense of strength and value. As Hondagneu-Sotelo describes, domestics might be fully aware of the stigma associated with their work, but they do find reward not only in earning needed income but also in successfully caring for children and homes.[42]

But a common push into invisibility counteracts such validation. A domestic worker is often asked not to be seen working.[43] Lydia, for example, is told to "be very quiet" while she tends to the house (*LY* 21), and Nancy and her husband argue about Ana, blind to the fact that she is in the room (*LO* 48). The domestic's invisibility proves dehumanizing. She becomes another appliance, or a mere "blur," as Ceci describes Lydia (*LY* 25). Confronted by her boss after she has quit, Lola argues, "Each day you make me more nobody, more dead. [...] You take away my name, my country. You don't want a person, you want a machine" (*LA* 138–39). Forced to be both obedient and invisible, domestic workers often forge identities predicated on negative identifications. "There's no one home," answered a live-in maid when I telephoned a household not long ago. I thanked her and hung up, saddened by her self-erasure, her failure to acknowledge her own existence in the house.

Undocumentedface

If undocumented domestic workers suffer from invisibility, what kinds of remedies does performance offer to counteract such a condition? What is gained when "sensitive attention" is given to "a sector of the American workforce that is rarely examined in cultural contexts," to borrow from Isherwood's review of *Living Out*?[44] Certainly, the three plays I examine in this chapter offer compelling, sympathetic approaches toward workers in undocumentedness and make visible both their plight and their integrity. In this sense, the plays counteract prevalent portrayals of domestic workers in the media as "throwaway characters without any dignity."[45] And more positive, more considerate portrayals of undocumented workers can effect change. Theatre, especially, allows for the telling of social injustices "tal cual" (just as they are), to quote Lorena Moran, associate artistic director for Teatro Jornalero Sin Fronteras, a Los Angeles–based traveling theatre troupe comprised entirely of day laborers. In Moran's view, audiences have no choice but to confront face-to-face the humanity and emotions of the characters at hand.[46] The visibility theatre achieves can thus be quite powerful.

When she addressed the New York State senate in June 2010, State Senator Diane Savino passionately contended that, "finally allowing the invisible women to rise," the then-proposed Domestic Workers' Bill of Rights was necessary and morally imperative legislation.[47] Her phrase paid homage to a performance piece titled *Invisible Women-Rise* that she had seen a couple of weeks beforehand at a town hall meeting of the Domestic Workers United (DWU), a support organization for nannies, housekeepers, and caregivers in New York. Like *Esclavitud moderna* (Modern Slavery) by Teatro Jornalero Sin Fronteras and *Super Doméstica* by the Domestic Workers' Association (DWA) in Los Angeles, *Invisible Women-Rise* served to inspire and to raise the consciousness of friends and supporters.[48] Domestic workers were not only the proud protagonists of these pieces but also the creators and performers, providing the many audience members who were also domestics with a bold, satisfying mirror image. Presented at events that brought together a specific audience— for example, a group meeting or a workplace break—such performances celebrated the domestics' labor, combated their invisibility head-on, and energized workers and advocates to unite and fight. In short, these didactic and cheerleading performances invigorated their audiences and enhanced their groups' political efforts.

My search for more long-lived theatrical products—pieces whose trajectory demonstrate a certain resilience or viability in their cultural settings—has led me to plays like *Latina*, *Living Out*, and *Lydia*, which all maintain the commitment to keep invisible undocumented workers in view but which cater to less explicitly unified and generally more affluent audiences. *Living Out*, for instance, which premiered at the Mark Taper Forum in Los Angeles and subsequently at Second Stage Theatre in New York City, did not aim to reach audiences composed predominantly of domestic workers. Of the Taper audience, Jorge Huerta noted "a majority of the 'usual suspects,' seated around me: Anglo, middle-aged, affluent." Only through special events did a select number of domestic workers get to experience the play—a telling reminder that *Living Out* was accessible primarily to individuals such as Nancy and not Ana. When the *Los Angeles Times* invited a pair of nannies and mothers to a performance and a subsequent discussion, one of the employees, delighted, observed, "That's me on the stage... That's my life." Loomer was also able to extend an invitation to nearly 30 nannies, who otherwise might not have been able to afford the ticket to the Taper.[49] Of these women, all of whom Loomer had interviewed as part of her research process, the playwright observed that

> it is a very exciting thing to see something so close to your life up on a stage. It means your life is important. It means that people will "see" you.... The very idea that you are not a citizen, that you are "illegal" or "alien" means that society is refusing to see you as a full and equal human being. Just look at those words![50]

The stage can make the invisible both visible and compelling, thus combating the nonexistence endemic to undocumentedness. Yet, there are dangers involved in this process, particularly when the very figures being made visible are not prevalent in the audience, or in the broader theatre-making process.

First, plays about Latina domestic workers—played by Latina actors—can perpetuate rather than problematize stereotypes. Sánchez-Scott worried about *Latina* and eventually decided to stop promoting it: "This play poses problems for me because all of the women are maids and that is what we always play on television, in the movies." Indeed, many of the actors who have taken the major roles discussed in this chapter have found themselves playing a token maid or nanny elsewhere, the kind of roles the struggling Sarita feels she is forced to play as a Latina actor (*LA* 89).[51] Furthermore, casting practices, as does domestic work itself, seem to prefer conventionally beautiful, relatively light-skinned Latina actors in major roles. Therefore, while the plays themselves endeavor to paint three-dimensional figures, their productions participate in a broader system of stereotyping and reinforcing broadly held ideas about who takes or should take on domestic work. Much like hiring practices in the domestic field reproduce "a culture that systematically devalues older and over-weight women" (and we could add "darker" to the description following Hondagneu-Sotelo's own explanation of employer preferences), the casting choices onstage help to maintain hierarchies of taste that naturalize power structures and social positions.[52] Repeated images of a nonthreatening, compassionate serving class dedicated to caring for white Americans also risk perpetuating other deep-rooted notions. Investigating late-1980s and early-1990s representations of "caregivers of color," Sau-ling Wong argues that "by conceding a certain amount of spiritual or even physical dependence on people of color—as helpers, healers, guardians, mediators, educators, or advisors—without ceding actual structural privilege, the care-receiver preserves the illusion of equality and reciprocity with the caregiver."[53] By portraying domestic workers capable of helping, healing, and educating their less caring employers, the plays at hand thus play into rather than disturb certain conventions.

Lydia, in particular, perpetuates clichéd images of an immigrant domestic worker as exotic and sexualized. While this portrayal partly results from the internal dynamics between Lydia and her employers that I describe above, the efforts to turn the maid into a seductive, magical creature are not entirely grounded in the Flores men's actions and attitudes. In an interview, Solís divulges that "Lydia is really sort of a fantasy of what I wish I could have done—talked to pretty, young girls, who seemed so strange and so scared and somehow so exotic to me—and yet more real. They were like the real deal and we were imitations.... They came here to do this kind of work, and it was really kind of spooky."[54] It becomes tempting to focus strictly on what Lydia, seemingly powerful, does to the family, without regard for what the family, and by extension, the United States, does to Lydia. "It's hard to say if Lydia is a devil, an angel or some kind of witch or healer," reports an NPR review, "Clearly, she has strange powers."[55] In important ways, Lydia contradicts well-worn images of passive, meek maids She has clear effect while in the United States. Yet, it is problematic to forget that Lydia is victimized both by a home country in which she cannot exist and by a US legal system that forces her into non-existence. After all, by labeling her "illegal," the United States has strange power over Lydia. And by turning her into a magical being, Solís risks our believing she is somehow above our earthly exploitations.

I do not wish here to reargue the previous chapter's ideas, but it is worth mentioning that Solís's magical realism, among other things, serves to pin a "Latina/o" label on the work—what critics then describe as a mystical "melodrama like one might see on Spanish TV" or "the Latino cousin of *Death of a Salesman*." As such, the specific issues that the play and its productions raise about undocumented immigration can become diluted. Viewed more generally as a play about "Mexican immigrants" or "Hispanic immigration," to invoke two additional reviews, *Lydia* loses the specificity that juxtaposing US-born citizens, naturalized citizens, and undocumented immigrants bears.[56] The so-called Americanness of *Lydia*, or *Latina* for that matter (described by William Harris in his review as a "neat microcosm of Latin experience"), is partially concealed by its ostensible Latinoness. The Taper's study guide for *Lydia* attests to this phenomenon. It seeks to explain and to contextualize, among other things, *rancheras*, the *quinceañera*, and the *lotería*, but pays no attention to questions of unauthorized immigration.[57] Unlike most study guides and production-related discussions surrounding *Living Out*, these supplemental materials for *Lydia* thus focus on the play's otherness. Loomer resists such categorization in part by choosing not to highlight her own cultural background.[58] While evaluating the repercussions of such a strategy is beyond the scope of this chapter, I once again call attention to processes that push the plays, their productions, and their authors to be viewed through ethnic categorization.

Latina and, to a lesser degree, *Living Out* present a different kind of stereotyping. In their efforts to turn real-life dynamics on their feet, the plays flesh out the domestic worker characters at the expense of their employers, who can become so unlikeable that audience members might fail to see themselves onstage. Sánchez-Scott opts for a melodramatic conflict, painting her heroines with a nostalgic, buoyantly sympathetic brush and her antagonists with an equally condemning one. She romanticizes the experience that led to *Latina*: "I was working with my cousin at an employment agency for maids in Beverly Hills. It was the best job I ever had. These immigrant women, who had their feet on the ground, and their eyes on the stars, and their hearts full of love, strengthened me. It was like meeting at the river."[59] Accordingly, her immigrant characters prove positive role models for the misguided Sarita as well as for the audience. The playwright emphasizes the characters' goodness by juxtaposing them against easily detestable employers. Don Felix, who enters the stage wearing Mickey Mouse pajamas (*LA* 91), is quite brazenly a lying snake-oil salesman trafficking in impossible dreams. A buffoonish entrepreneur, he is overwhelmed running his agency in conjunction with the Felix Sanchez Wedding Chapel, the Felix Sanchez Body Shop, and the Felix Sanchez Teen Disco. The women to whom he caters prove even more loathsome. Mrs. Homes "returns" Alma to the agency (*LA* 108); Mrs. Levine's only knowledge of Spanish is the naming of household chores (*LA* 124);[60] Ms. Harris specifically wants an "illegal" maid so that she can pay less, provided she is not "one of those fat ones with the gold teeth" (*LA* 131); and, as I describe in the previous section, a belligerent Mrs. Camden threatens to report her maid to immigration (*LA* 139).

Adding to the flattening of these unlikable characters, all four women in the original production were played by the same actress, Susan Niven. The casting choice comments ironically on the attitudes of the employers, who believe domestic workers are interchangeable and easily replaceable. However, the use of a single actor to represent all the employers, especially in a play in which the other characters are so well developed, can, as evidenced by the review in *Drama-League*, prove "disconcerting": "Although it's a clever device, and Susan Niven is flawless as Mmes. Holmes, Levine, Harris and Camden, her characters become representations of *qualities* as opposed to personalities. As a result, they weaken the confrontation scenes between them and the Latinas by repetition twice too many times."[61]

More problematic is the fact that audience members might not recognize themselves in such demonized and generalized characters. Assuming a predominantly, if not entirely, immigrant-friendly public, we might expect that those watching *Latina* will or at least can congratulate themselves for attending a socially responsible event and for possessing attitudes so unlike those of Niven's cartoonish characters. These antagonists are so blatantly offensive that it becomes easy to blame the unjust situations depicted entirely on the narrow-minded. As satisfying as it might be to ridicule such employers, in so doing, the production prompts less thinking about a broader context for undocumented labor. For instance, Bill Edwards opens his review with a description of the play: "comedy dealing with the working conditions of illegal Spanish-speaking aliens in Los Angeles and exploitation at the hands of a wheeler-dealer Chicano." Immediately, we can see that he has excused the women whose demand for cheap labor allow for Don Felix's business in the first place from any participation in the system of exploitation.[62] The undocumented maids somehow exist only because of Don Felix's inherent badness, itself inspired by the employers' unmitigated greed and insensitivity. Since audience members will likely not think themselves bad, greedy, or insensitive, they can remove themselves from the exploitative system. Therefore, in raising the workers' visibility—and we should applaud such an effort, especially in a 1980 play—*Latina* simultaneously renders complex realities of an economy dependent on their labor virtually invisible.

Twenty-three years later, Loomer endeavors to present this economy in a more nuanced manner. In her "Thoughts on Production," the playwright urges her actors to focus on "good intentions as opposed to caricature," explaining that "every character in this play cares about children and is doing the best they can...in their own way" (*LO* 3). However, as foils for Nancy, the characters of Wallace and Linda can come across as one-note stereotypes of self-involved and insensitive gringas.[63] As such, like the employers in *Latina*, they become easy targets onto which we can project blame for the problems at hand. Still, the main Nancy-Ana dyad does offer a set of issues and questions to consider. Loomer admits that she wants *Living Out* to inspire "Los Americanos" to "think of the people they employ as people rather than conveniences" and to assure any domestic workers who may be in the audience that "their voices are being heard."[64] To this end, Loomer insists that "the Anglo couple" and the "Latino couple" live in the same stage space; the audience must see "overlapping and parallel worlds" (*LO* 3). By using fluid transitions between one scene and the next, the same stage furniture to indicate both Nancy's and Ana's homes, and simultaneous scenes in one same space, *Living Out* discourages identifications based on "us" and "them." The play urges thinking about the extent to which undocumented labor, especially Latina/o labor, is embroiled in the life of Los Angelinos and Americans more generally. Nancy reminds herself often, and the audience in turn, that Ana's immigration status is the result of global socioeconomic inequities and of US international policies more specifically (*LO* 62).

Through multiple productions, *Living Out* has generated meaningful dialogue. Producers of the play have often provided study guides and hosted supplementary conversations and panels. While at the Taper and during most subsequent professional productions, *Living Out* has led to discussions about immigration and domestic work in the local media. For Loomer, in fact, the "most gratifying" aspect of the play is "that people talk about it on the way home." Thus, not only does the play raise the visibility of undocumented workers but its productions can also galvanize communities to reflect on issues of domestic labor. Loomer notes that audience members have told her the play prompted them to consider how they compensate their nannies; in some cases, *Living Out* has led to salary increases.[65] We find here, then, concrete evidence for the type of "immediate effects" that Baz Kershaw terms "performance efficacy," through which a theatre production can, "however minutely," influence "the general historical evolution of wider social and political realities."[66]

Of course, a handful of raises and fleeting dialogue might not be enough to shake the structure of an economy that relies heavily on undocumented labor. Nearly a year after holding national attention, the Baird scandal and the subsequent front-page and prime-time dialogue about immigrant labor did little to alter employers' behavior.[67] Theatre can perhaps engender more meaningful conversations and even change individual practices, as evidenced by the feedback Loomer has received. But such results are necessarily limited given theatre's quantitative reach. All of the audience members who have seen professional and amateur productions of *Living Out* cannot possibly match the numbers of people Loomer reaches with a single airing of a television script. For example, nearly nine million viewers saw the premiere showing of "Beef," a 2010 episode of *Law & Order: Special Victims Unit* penned by Loomer that focuses on exploitative and unsanitary practices at a meat-packing plant. Millions more see it when the show re-airs in syndication. Loomer is optimistic about writing for television, which like theatre, allows her to explore matters of importance and to delve into what "pisses [her] off." Yet, the nature of the much more commercialized medium limits the extent to which certain issues can be scrutinized, and Loomer acknowledges that television requires more careful attention to the demands of what she calls a "broader" audience.[68]

As a stage piece, a play such as *Living Out* "enable[s] audiences to consider hard truths within their comfort zone," suggests NPR's Karen Bates.[69] Herein might lie another challenge to its efficacy. Like the employers Hondagneu-Sotelo studies, audience members, from the comfort and safety of their (expensive) theatre seats, might feel "satisfaction" from their "intimate" look into the "tribulations" of a character who ultimately proves to be so unlike them. Ana's lack of papers serves as a reminder of their own legal status, their own legitimized belonging. For as the stage picture demands parallel action and simultaneous use of space, access to the theatre creates a much different picture. On the one hand, ticket prices and marketing campaigns serve to homogenize the audience, especially in terms of class. On the other, labor practices in the professional theatre forbid the manifest employment of undocumented workers. So, everywhere but onstage, the undocumented remain invisible, if present at all. For the actor playing Ana, undocumentedness becomes a kind of mask, a defining character trait to be studied and portrayed. We could say that by impeding the undocumented from attending the event, from consuming the cultural product, and from producing or appearing in the play, the performance and the performers operate through a type of "undocumentedface." In other words, a certain ventriloquism is in operation, wherein the undocumented are representable and represented but not present in the theatre.[70] I certainly do not wish to imply here that only undocumented actors can play undocumented characters. Nor do I aim to disparage plays and productions that I believe serve an important role in engaging audiences in necessary debates and promoting immigrant rights. Rather, I question the effects of combating the invisibility of undocumented workers without an explicit, concerted effort to engage them beyond the worlds created onstage.

When AIPOP's production of *Latina* toured California in 1980, one of the ten women performing in it lived in undocumentedness (before

1986 IRCA, the theatre company was not federally mandated to check the status of its employee). But as Sánchez-Scott recalls, the actor refused to perform in places where she thought immigration authorities might be present. On those occasions, the playwright would take on the role. The very visibility inherent to stage practices—the very visibility for undocumented workers sought by the play—forced the undocumented participant back into the shadows. Post-IRCA, the professional theatre, which must abide by national labor and immigration laws, has become even less inviting for workers in undocumentedness. This does not mean undocumented workers do not participate in theatre-making processes.[71] But for professional endeavors, it does mean that those in undocumentedness might only be able to participate indirectly or under a falsified identity. The distinction is important, as professional theatre might warrant more visibility. After all, the products of professional theatre tend to dominate amateur, student, and community production. Moreover, it is more likely for professional theatre products to enjoy other types of lives, such as publications or adaptations into other media, as well as to receive critical and scholarly attention.

Once legalized, some artists have taken to the stage to share their experiences (e.g., Josefina López and Carlo Albán, discussed in previous chapters). Armed with papers, they no longer fear the visibility that the theatre affords. Albán, who has played Misha in several productions of *Lydia*, reveals that he had, since a young age, wanted to share the story of his and his family's living without papers in the United States. But, "for a lot of time I couldn't because we were illegal and those things are not told." Only with a green card in hand was Albán able to share publicly "the history, our history, my history" and ensure its continued telling.[72]

Living Out has motivated its creative teams and audiences to explore ideas about domestic and immigrant labor. What about its producing theatres? I began studying undocumentedness in the middle of my tenure at an Off-Broadway not-for-profit theatre. My research prompted me to notice an absence in the organization's staff list. Neither our website nor our programs included the individual who cleaned our space, a Dominican-born man who came in daily to ensure our small venue remained livable. I conducted some telling but unscientific research, the sample being the collection of approximately two hundred playbills collecting dust under my bed. It struck me that many of the rosters I found shared the common absence on the page or two dedicated to listing the multitude of people whose work is indirectly but significantly reflected on the stage. Often invisible to the audience members who care to read the listings are the names of the individuals who clean the theatres.[73] The current Second Stage Theatre's website, for example, offers a list of "special services" under its staff page: among them, advertising and marketing representatives, legal counsel, accountant, insurer, and technical support team. Either no one cleans the space or such effort is not deemed special enough to warrant mention. But someone vacuums, wipes, and scrubs. Perhaps, as Hondagneu-Sotelo observes, we have become accustomed to noticing or acknowledging cleaning efforts only when they are poorly accomplished.[74]

Such labor, I believe, must be taken into account, especially vis-à-vis plays focused on questions of work. As does domestic housework, the commercial cleaning industry employs a disproportionate number of undocumented workers relative to the entire US civilian workforce. Likewise, under current conditions, textiles, food manufacturing and services, farming, and construction in the United States all depend on cheap undocumented labor.[75] Thus, when costume designers buy clothing pieces at American Apparel, when casts order meals from Chipotle, when a new performance space is built or an old one renovated, when a theatre outsources its cleaning needs to local companies, when a touring company spends a night in a hotel, or when a performer relies on a nanny to look after her child—all common occurrences that involve some of the most prominent industries which employ those in undocumentedness— the ties between cultural production and undocumented labor become difficult, if not impossible, to untangle. (Both Loomer and *Living Out*'s director at the Taper, Bill Rauch, acknowledge that the nannies they hire allow them to work.[76]) I am prompted to ask: How does US theatrical production bear the imprints of undocumented labor?

Undocumented labor must be taken into account when we look at theatrical production as part of a broad capitalist system. Particular theatres, companies, and unions may take steps to verify that they are solely employing documented workers and may choose not to fundraise directly from businesses that perhaps do otherwise. Yet, the realities of theatre-making in the United States today inscribe cultural producers in a system of corporate and charitable sponsorship that benefits from the depressed wages and unfair practices that those without papers must face. A surge of undocumented workers since the mid-1980s has allowed employers and consumers in turn to reap large profits, profits that in many cases sustain both individual artists and performance art organizations. We need but follow the money to realize the intricate and often contradictory links that such a system engenders. In many cases, producers of performances seeking to combat stereotypes and to raise the visibility of workers in undocumentedness depend or have depended on financial support from businesses that implicate that very invisible and oppressive labor. These connections do not necessarily suggest hypocrisy or moral shortcomings—in fact, an argument could be made that the performances channel tainted capital into more socially responsible and productive activities—but they do call attention to the difficulty in separating today's cultural production from other sectors of the US economy and, thus, from undocumented labor.

Sánchez-Scott, Loomer, and Solis, like most major playwrights working in the United States, have received multiple grants. The three plays at the center of this chapter were developed and produced thanks also to cash awards. *Lydia*, for example, was commissioned, workshopped, and produced at the Denver Center Theatre Company, a division of the Denver Center for the Performing Arts. One of this center's donors was then and continues to be Target Stores. And Target benefits, or has benefitted, from employing undocumented labor.[77] Thus, the underpaid work of night janitors giving Target stores their taken-for-granted sheen, in part, however small, made possible the staging of *Lydia*. The links need not be direct or involve huge cash flows. But there is no escaping the reality that theatre funding and theatre artists' careers in the United States depend on profits, corporate and individual, that exist partly because of cheap, exploitable workers.

Latina, Living Out, and *Lydia* seek to personalize the struggles of undocumented domestic workers, to "look at a political issue on a very intimate level," if I may apply Loomer's words about her play to all three.[78] They tug at heartstrings and offer much-needed, specific human faces to the statistics with which the immigration debate is often waged. Yet, precisely because pity is evoked, it is perhaps difficult to notice how performances of these plays also contribute to the maintenance and reproduction of exploitative practices. The very issues the plays try to make visible are often ignored in the broader context of theatre-making. The situations onstage, isolated from the labor and financial realities in which their productions occur, can appear personal rather than systematic. And, as a review of *Latina* attests, a blind spot can develop. Sánchez-Scott and her director, *Variety* tells us, "explore the attitudes of women who degrade themselves to be debased by working for peanuts as domestics."[79] The syntax is telling. Somehow, after watching *Latina*, the reviewer (still) believes that it is the immigrant women who activate the exploitation. It is they who degrade, not the employers. Like *Living Out*'s Wallace, the reviewer can locate the women's actions in the women themselves, so that a lack of papers reflects individual decision-making rather than structural realities.

Variety's Bill Edwards is, of course, just one person reviewing a single performance of one production. His writing style may not accurately reflect his views; yet, his sentence prompts me to consider the limits of the productions discussed in this chapter. Audiences are urged to see onstage what is invisible. The domestic workers in the plays indeed rise to compelling visibility. But if the theatres' and audiences' complicity in maintaining and benefiting from an economy that relies on undocumented labor remains somehow invisible, what have we really seen? If those living in undocumentedness are not actually present in the theatre, the legal/illegal divide has remained solidly in place, and the equity projected by a curtain call like *Living Out*'s reveals itself to be largely theatrics.

4

Act § 212(a)(9)(B)(iii)(III)— Family Unity

Deporting the Divas begins with Marge McCarthy emerging from the audience to address those in attendance. She introduces herself as the Chairwoman-for-Life for the Ladies of the Church and soon-to-be mayoral candidate for San Diego. Then, she submits some basic information about the "little divertissement" about to begin. After mispronouncing the playwright's name in an exaggerated gringo accent, Marge assures us that while "Guillermo Reyes" may "sound foreign and illegal," the writer is, thankfully, a US citizen. She goes on to warn us that the play at hand traffics in issues of homosexuality and immigration, but she promises the performance will be "fun."[1] Marge makes her second and only other appearance—this time as part of the main action—when she runs into the play's protagonist, Michael, during an excursion in Tijuana. She advises the recently separated Immigration and Naturalization Service (INS) officer that "the future of this country depends on couples like you and Teresita getting back together again." The Chairwoman-for-Life suggests that heterosexual marriages are "good for the kids" and that divorce has "messed up" even Ronald Reagan's children. Since Michael is, at that moment, sharing his daytrip with a young man, Marge's sentiments take on a threatening tone. As much as she believes that "America is for Americans only"—that a nation's borders need constant protection—Marge also considers that the borders delimiting traditional marriage require careful policing (*DD* 384). Individuals and couples who do not fit inside these borders should be outlawed. Gay and immigrant stories might well serve as entertaining, titillating theatre, but in Marge's view gay and immigrant individuals need not be tolerated off the stage.

Played by a male actor, as are all the characters in *Deporting the Divas*, Marge becomes one of the tools that Reyes's self-referential theatre piece uses to comment on tensions and anxieties surrounding questions of gender, sexuality, and immigration status. The play, a response to the passing of Proposition 187 in California, "unfortunately... still resonates," Reyes tells us in his introduction to the published script (*DD* 327). It presents Michael's struggles—in his life and in his imagination—as he develops feelings for Sedicio, an unauthorized immigrant. We are intended to laugh at Marge's hardheadedness and rigid values. Reyes's humor, however, is more than cartoonish. Given that laws today very much attempt to control what "couples like you" means, a dark, uneasy undercurrent flows alongside the campy and bold-stroked characterization that *Deporting the Divas* requires.

By focusing on the endeavors of US immigration authorities to define and control personal relationships, I consider in this chapter how undocumentedness both threatens and bolsters such definitions. Moreover, I delve into the ways in which regulating immigration inevitably demands the evaluation of performances. In determining what "couples like you" and other such categorizations possibly suggest, immigration law tends to monitor not interpersonal relationships per se but rather the ways in which those relationships are put on display.

After first making a case for considering immigration law and family structures mutually, I turn in the chapter's second section to *La víctima* (The Victim), conceived and first performed by the collective Teatro de la Esperanza in 1976.[2] Through this play, I explore how immigration law generally, and undocumentedness more specifically, can rupture family structures. Teatro de la Esperanza's documentary play follows a family during nearly six decades of alternating between the United States and Mexico, their lives periodically shaken by economic downturns and immigration regulations. Ultimately comprised of individuals with different legal statuses, the play's central family highlights the power of law to shape an individual's sense of identity and belonging. *La víctima* culminates with an INS officer deporting his own mother, proving an almost mythic tale about law's power to break a family apart. Although the play stands as a fierce polemic against US immigration policies, *La víctima*'s reiteration of traditional family values and structures simultaneously sustains the categorical distinctions through which immigration law aims to function.

Janet Noble's 1989 *Away Alone* celebrates an alternate kind of family.[3] In the chapter's third section, I investigate how the difficulties prompted by a life without papers can lead to such alternatives. *Away Alone* follows a year in the life of a group of undocumented Irish immigrants in 1980s New York City, depicting the intense and intimate bonds forged by relative strangers living and working in undocumentedness. Noble stages their newfound domestic lives, small triumphs, and shared fears as they carve out a life away from Ireland. With *Away Alone*, I highlight how unauthorized immigration creates new types of families and family dynamics as it forces individuals to live in fear-producing spaces of nonexistence. As a companion to *Away Alone, Deporting the Divas* serves me to investigate the complications that arise from immigration law's interest in defining what constitutes a family and patrolling counterhegemonic lifestyles. These core concerns—defining and patrolling—promote a system in which performance plays a key role. In the chapter's final section, I reflect on the subversive, but limited, power of performance to interfere with immigration laws and the familial categories those laws seek to protect.

Constructing Kinship

We cannot understand the concept of family today without considering the legal regulations that underpin the construction of kinship. What it means to be a "child," "dependant," "husband," "wife," or "parent" depends to some degree on the legal parameters under which such categories are constructed and understood. Two seemingly unrelated debates playing out in the United States today urge us to question how the state confers labels on individuals and how those labels then grant or deny particular rights. Should pejoratively called "anchor babies," children born in the United States to undocumented parents, receive US citizenship? Should same-sex couples have the right to marry? Both debates—the first a product of political posturing during recent heated election cycles, the second a legal battle waged currently on a state-by-state basis and altered drastically by the 2013 Supreme Court decision to strike down the Defense of Marriage Act's (DOMA) federal definition of marriage as that between one man and one woman (*U.S. v. Windsor*)—remind us how definitions of family are intricately entwined with and dependent on law. One's place within family structures and, in turn, within broader social networks necessarily involves the various privileges—awarded or refused—that a legal label like "spouse"—or "citizen"—begets. By deciding what constitutes legitimate familial bonds and what fraudulent relationships are, immigration law can powerfully shape one's sense of belonging, not just to the nation but also to one's own family.

The 1965 reforms to US immigration law canonized family reunification as a keystone of the current admission system. Although protecting and respecting family units had been important before, the amended Immigration and Nationality Act (INA) officially replaced a system that prioritized immigrants based on national origin and/or skill sets with a schedule of preferences that overwhelmingly favors family relations. By the late 1980s, a vast majority of all legal immigrants to the United States arrived with visas obtained using family-based categories.[4] Despite periodic amendments, INA today continues its imperative to grant unlimited entry to "immediate relatives" of US citizens—their children, spouses, and parents—but also offers preferred access to a limited number of annually allotted visas to other family relations of US citizens and, in some cases, legal residents. These include their unmarried adult sons and daughters, married sons and daughters, and siblings. (The new legislation before Congress, BSEOIM, seeks to eliminate the sibling preference.)

Nevertheless, the law's commitment to helping relatives live together has often failed. On the one hand, the process for sponsoring non-immediate relatives to come into the United States can be lengthy and expensive, so that immigrants following legal paths to entry often suffer significant separation before a desired reunification. On the other hand, these bureaucratically complex processes are available only to relatives of US citizens or legal residents. Susan Coutin reminds us that one of the characteristics of legal nonexistence in the United States is that one's family relationships are legally inert for the purposes of immigration. The state thus regularly favors "legal definitions of belonging" over other classifications, including blood and marital ties. Moreover, one's illegal status, if discovered, can preclude legalization through categories of sponsorship altogether. In other words, a US citizen may not sponsor a relative who has been found to be present in the United States unlawfully.[5] One of immigration law's guiding principles—reuniting relatives—therefore operates alongside harsh realities of families that remain apart.

Importantly, by creating seemingly discrete categories, US immigration law frequently (re)defines the contents of each. What is a "spouse"? A "child"? A "sibling"? The apparent obviousness of the terms betrays the intricate, contested process through which they gain meaning. As Ian Haney López stresses, "Law is one of the most powerful mechanisms by which any society creates, defines, and regulates itself[, particularly] in highly legalized and bureaucratized late-industrial democracies such as the United States." Adapting Haney López's language from his study about law's integral participation in the construction of racial categories, we could say that our legal system not only determines who is a family, but also *why* someone is family.[6] Since familial relationships are critical to the immigration process, immigration law has served a meaningful role in dictating what certain relationships are and how these are manifested. In *Young v. Reno*, for instance, the Ninth Circuit Court of Appeals denied Karen Yuen Fong Young's petition to grant preferential immigration status to her "siblings" in Hong Kong. Since Young is adopted, the court reasons, her natural siblings are not eligible for immigration under her sponsorship. Before same-sex marriage was legitimated in any concrete way by a US authority, the same court ruled in *Adams v. Howerton* that

Richard Frank Adams, a US citizen, could not sponsor his chosen same-sex spouse to reside in the country. These cases showcase courts' ability to create and maintain categorical standards while failing to take into account the nature of particular relationships. Regardless of Young's ties to her siblings, regardless of Adams's shared life with his partner, the rulings in essence vacate the relationships of their effectual meaning.

In seeking to prevent purported sham marriages, immigration statutes and cases have also delineated what marital relationships might substantively entail. To ascertain the nature of bogus relationships, immigration law inevitably demarcates as well the limits of so-called real marriage. Court cases have attempted to pinpoint, among other things, a couple's specific intentions at the moment of marriage (*Bark v. INS*), the nature of a factually dead relationship (*Dabaghian v. Civiletti*), and the possible meaning of maintaining separate finances while married (*Nikrodhanondaa v. Reno*). Although courts insist that "aliens cannot be required to have more conventional or more successful marriages than citizens," immigrants who seek a visa through marriage nevertheless must often defend or prove the nature of their relationships.[7] Their cases therefore participate in the construction of those conventions through which marriage, involving immigrants or otherwise, is imagined and understood.

Likewise, immigration law has tackled the nature of parenthood. With *Fiallo v. Bell*, for example, which defended INA's constitutional right to accord preference to unwed mothers over unwed fathers, the Supreme Court in essence provided that a woman's relationship to her child is somehow more important or valid than a man's. Immigration law similarly prioritizes the relationship between fathers and their "legitimate" or "legitimated" children over that between fathers and "illegitimate" offspring.[8] Crucially, the legal fictions that result from law's determinations have clear, material effects. Whatever personal relationships the individuals involved build, it is within and against the allowances of the law that they forge connections and resulting identities. In short, through immigration law, the state imposes meaning and value on various interpersonal relations.

Unauthorized immigration, as an ostensible defiance of the law, can challenge legally imposed definitions of family and personal relationships. The "illegal alien" can surface as a subversive force that contests not only immigration law but also the familial definitions that such a law helps to (re)produce. At the same time, given the tremendous difficulties that many immigrants face to bring their loved ones into the United States, unauthorized immigration proves a necessary tactic to sustain the very reunification and familial definitions that immigration law seemingly encourages in the first place. As my previous chapters already explore, life in the United States without papers presents myriad challenges. My inquiry into *La víctima*, *Away Alone*, and *Deporting the Divas* stresses how undocumentedness complicates the maintenance and management of personal relationships.

Broken Families

In an introduction to *La víctima* published in 1989, Jorge Huerta proposes that the play's impact might wane if and when the threat of deportations in the United States fades. Still uncertain about the effects of the then newly enacted Immigration Reform and Control Act (IRCA), Huerta offers the hopeful possibility that deportations could indeed decrease.[9] The sad irony is not merely that IRCA strengthened the INS's enforcement capabilities, but that the US government increasingly has relied on deportations and detentions (see chapter 5). *La víctima* thus appears both as a document of historical realities and a forewarning of what families living in undocumentedness might continue to endure.

Prompted by the success of *Guadalupe*, Teatro de la Esperanza's first documentary theatre piece, the young theatre collective began to research the INS's spiked efforts to deport Mexican nationals in the 1970s.[10] The California-based company then expanded its investigation and crafted a play that conveys a much longer history of attacks on migrants. First performed at the University of California at San Diego in 1976 and soon after becoming a mainstay of Teatro de la Esperanza's repertoire, *La víctima* uses a fictional family to portray how immigration policies, especially as connected to economic slumps, have devastated families living in and alternating between northern Mexico and southern California. It is clear in the piece, which frequently relies on Brechtian narrators, placards, and third-person commentary set to popular music, that the story of Amparo and her children is unexceptional. Amparo's every-family thus humanizes a process by which official policies and practices rip immigrant families apart.

The ripping apart happens in different ways, but immigration procedures—subject to the caprices of a fluctuating economy—are consistently responsible for the suffering that *La víctima* stages. Narrating a decades-long struggle, the play illuminates, for instance, how the Mexican Revolution forced migrants into the United States and how the Great Depression turned those migrants into scapegoats, subject to "repatriation." These mass repatriation campaigns during the 1930s, aimed at sending back "Mexicans" to Mexico regardless of their immigration or citizenship status, were not all officially organized or funded by immigration agencies. However, immigration officials certainly promoted repatriation by fueling fears of deportation.[11] Through all of these movements, families are forced to separate. *La víctima* offers an especially harrowing separation during the "Repatriation 1935" scene. As Amparo and her two children attempt to board a train bound to Mexico, a young Sammy *"gets lost in the crowd on the platform in slow motion"* (*V* 336). Although she screams for him, and he for his mother, they fail to find each other.

Amparo and Sammy's separation underpins the remainder of the play. Sammy's participation in the Korean War, his marriage to Clara, and his work as an INS officer—an extension of his experience with the US military—are juxtaposed against Amparo's poverty-stricken life in Mexico, her other two children's return to the United States, and her own eventual illegal reentry into California. The parallel storylines come together in the final scenes, when an immigration officer arrests Amparo at a workers' strike, and the woman subsequently faces interrogation by Sammy. Her stern pleas for mercy are met only with his mechanical adherence to policy. Amparo goads Sammy, asking him whether he would like to be separated from his mother. But the INS agent only intensifies his effort to deport the professed stranger. "Take her out! Take her out!" he screams (*V* 362). The play's final scene, introduced by a placard reading "The victim," offers a distraught Sammy, haunted by the image of his mother. "I hate you!" he fires at Amparo, who appears onstage as a dreamlike figure. "She's not my mother," he repeats *"with growing intensity"* (*V* 364). The family has been completely destroyed.

The play's prologue urges the audience to consider how many Chicanas/os are victims of oppression struggling to resolve the pains caused by poverty. One of few words in Spanish that refers to both male and female individuals, "víctima" makes it difficult to single out one character as the casualty of unfair economic conditions. While Amparo certainly bears the burden of suffering, Sammy does not surface as an easy antagonist. The seeming betrayal of his mother, his blood kin, results from Sammy's own needs to survive and offer his wife and daughter a better life. He, too, is a victim of a dehumanizing system, a system that propels the "exploitation of one group for the benefit of another" (*V* 325). It is important to note that this exploitation, specific here to the Mexico-US border, operates mainly through immigration policies. Economic disadvantages may well explain the vulnerable position in which Amparo and her family find themselves. Yet, the realities of a divided family stem directly from immigration policies' compounding of poverty.

Indeed, *La víctima* reveals the power of immigration laws to mold family dynamics. For Amparo's kin, much more than geographic distance and separation are at stake, although the pressures of these cannot be discounted. The 1987 professional premiere of *La víctima* at Los Angeles Theatre Center (LATC) relied on myriad suitcases and sliding panels to suggest the train journeys marking the constant exits that keep immigrant families apart. Amparo not only loses Sammy when she returns to Mexico, but must also say goodbye to her younger children, Antonia and Meño, when the two leave for the United States in search of income. "The poor are like that, separated," bemoans Amparo, reflecting on a life marked by departures and farewells (*V* 350). Certainly, economic considerations impede regular transnational reunions. The words of Irishman Eamonn Wall well apply to all struggling immigrants seeking some time, however short, to spend together with those they love: "I commute between exile and Ireland, but it's an expensive business. I often wish I were another person; if that were the case, I wouldn't always have to be saving up my money to go 'home.'" But the challenges of "commuting" for those in undocumentedness are exacerbated by immigration policies. Coutin makes plain that the threat of detention and deportation renders the undocumented virtually "immobile." They try to stay home, avoid travel, and move about strictly as needed.[12] Leaving, reentering, and even navigating within the United States become too risky.

More critically, an immigration system that creates spaces of legal nonexistence causes individuals to disappear. The undocumented's "footprints are erased."[13] In other words, entering nonexistence, and therefore clandestinity, risks the loss of connections to people and places left behind. (*Away Alone*, to which I turn below, begins with a disappearance: the character of Seamus, whom we will never meet, "did a fade to the west" when "Immigration got wind of him" [*AA* 6].) The need to remain hidden complicates as well any efforts to find relatives and friends. Amparo and her husband Julián "tried everything" to locate Sammy. They even risked detection and returned to the United States (*V* 342). But what little they can do from within undocumentedness proves ineffective. The accidental separation from their son becomes permanent and bespeaks common realities. Immigration policies and policing have caused many to live without their mothers, fathers, children, or spouses, as the Human Rights Watch reports.[14]

La víctima illustrates the painful means that immigrant families must often undertake to be together. Through a simple theatrical convention— Antonia and Coyote sit on Amparo "*as if she were hiding under the seat of [a] vehicle*" (*V* 347)—the play stages a short, but incredibly tense border scenario. Her serving as the literal seat for Antonia and Coyote, who must bear the Border Patrol's required inquisition, strains and objectifies Amparo. We are reminded of the countless bodies that have crossed into the United States, sometimes with fatal results, crammed in cars and trucks, vans and trains, what Sasha Lewis describes as "the coffin ships of today's slave trade." Amparo will be lucky; the Border Patrol will be called away before detecting her. Huerta explains that Teatro de la Esperanza crafted the suspenseful moment with much care, looking to make a strong point about how families are often dismembered by unjust laws. He finds that audiences tend to cheer when Amparo succeeds in getting across the border.[15]

The play thus offers a most compelling case against an immigration system that often hinders reunification. Law professor Hiroshi Motomura posits that family reunification presents a "unique and sometimes irresistible rhetorical power" in immigration debates, especially in response to analyses that tend to stress a strictly economic approach. *La víctima* certainly utilizes such a tactic, opting to engage its audiences through an emotional appeal that, as Huerta describes, transcends didacticism as well as a strictly anticapitalist vocabulary.[16] In fact, the torn family that the play presents exemplifies one of the most pressing, influential kinds of arguments used by advocates of undocumented immigrants. Issues of family call attention to the complicated nature of the immigration debates; they allow for rather unexpected partnerships that problematize assumptions about how conservatives or liberals might feel about undocumented immigration. For instance, many self-identified conservative church groups, fervent advocates of so-called family values, have vehemently decried immigration laws that stand in the way of preserving family unity. The Sanctuary and New Sanctuary Movements have also sought to designate spaces of worship as safe zones for undocumented immigrants in defiance of immigration authorities.[17] Relying on melodramatic techniques, particularly during the climactic moment in which Sammy deports Amparo—emphatic screams, weeping, the reprising of Amparo's lullaby to underscore the action—*La víctima* amplifies the impact that immigration law can have on families.

Moreover, through its central family, *La víctima* shares with its audiences the uneven family dynamics that often result from members' differing legal statuses. Michael Fix and Wendy Zimmerman explain that the United States is home to a large number of families made up of both citizens and noncitizens and that these rather understudied mixed-status families can include any combination of nonimmigrants and naturalized, legal, and undocumented immigrants. The family's legal composition by play's end well reflects real-life trends.[18] It is quite common for an immigrant without papers, like Amparo, to have both US-citizen children, like Sammy and Antonia, and undocumented ones, like Meño.

Many problems and complications arise for mixed-status families. To begin with, life for undocumented immigrants is marked by increased probability of poverty and homelessness, each compounded by possible language barriers, lack of records, misinformation about US bureaucratic structures, and psychological tensions resulting from the ever-present fear of deportation. As Coutin makes clear, such fears can literally sicken the body, and health care becomes considerably less available and effective for those without papers. ("Medical repatriations," through which hospitals attempt to curb costs by sending undocumented patients to their birth countries, exacerbate these issues.[19]) Fears of inquiries about immigration status also prevent undocumented individuals from taking advantage of the few civil and economic rights guaranteed to them or of the many more guaranteed to their legal or citizen children. In essence, then, even citizen children of undocumented parents, entitled to every right and program that all US citizens enjoy, often go without the services, educational opportunities, and assistance to which they are entitled. Fix and Zimmerman's italics are adamant: *Most policies that advantage or disadvantage noncitizens are likely to have broad spillover effects on the citizen children who live in the great majority of immigrant families.*[20]

Simultaneously, because papers can at times open doors that are defiantly shut for the undocumented, mixed-status families contend also with internal imbalances of power and subsequent jealousies, resentments, and even abuse. Coutin's studies demonstrate that those without papers are inevitably "different" from relatives and peers with the legal right to live in the United States. In her investigation of four teenage girls growing up in Colorado, Helen Thorpe likewise describes the frustrations of the two who live in undocumentedness, whose access to educational opportunities, jobs, and even basic health care is inferior to that of their documented siblings and friends. Such differences place even members of the same family in different tiers of a population that is increasingly "stratified by legal status," to quote sociologists Leisy Abrego and Roberto Gonzalez.[21]

Huerta describes the actions in *La víctima* as "the ultimate repudiation of [Sammy's] history as a Mexican, a denial of who and what he really is." Others agree with this categorical conclusion. Yvonne Yarbro-Bejarano, for instance, writes that Sammy has "sold-out" by working as an immigration agent, and Sylvie Drake describes the "co-option" of Sammy by the United States as a "most pernicious" form of abuse.[22] I find in the play a more subtle critique, one that moves us away from a categorical conception of "Mexican" as a solid and easily identifiable identity. After all, Sammy is not "a Mexican," at least not legally, and the consequences of that reality alone are significant. "We're American citizens and don't you forget that!" he argues with his daughter (and, possibly, with Huerta, Yarbro-Bejarano, and Drake). We are to side with the younger Janie, who accuses her father of forgetting his heritage, of deporting "his" people

(*V* 356). Yet, the play also stresses that Sammy is a victim; he is not a deliberate traitor. Rather, a system that has uprooted and separated his family, both physically and legally, has necessarily altered him. Sammy is not the cause of the family's downfall, but rather a manifestation of a system that detrimentally categorizes differently members of the same family. "Who and what he really is" is conflicted, conscious of the fact that he and his mother are separated not only by time and space but also by law. The nation to which Sammy ostensibly belongs simultaneously denies his mother entry. Sammy therefore cannot easily be blamed for repudiating or selling out his family; he is part of a legal structure that has, from birth, stressed his difference. His actions as an agent of the US government therefore evince structural and not merely personal failings.[23]

The use of language is telling, adding another layer to the divisions that have been created within the family.[24] While Sammy interrogates Amparo entirely in his mother's Spanish during the play's penultimate scene, the final interchange between Sammy and his wife is completely in English. In an earlier time, Sammy and Clara had peppered their English with each of their family's Spanish—Sammy proposes marriage to her in Spanish (*V* 338). But, unlike Amparo's first home in the United States—where a constant alternation between Spanish and English, even within a single thought or sentence, helps to negotiate the gap between Mexican-born mother and US-born son—Sammy's adult home becomes an English-only sphere. It is not the case that Sammy disparages or rejects Spanish, to follow Marvin Carlson's ideas about codeswitching.[25] In fact, given that we have never seen Sammy speak exclusively in Spanish, his adept use of the language at play's end demonstrates a vested interest in, or at least the conscious mastery of, his mother's tongue. The shift toward the primary language of the United States could be seen as Sammy's attempt to perform his own citizenship rather than as a deliberate attempt to negate "his history."

I paraphrase Coutin to suggest that Sammy asserts his citizenship by laying claim to specific practices, such as building an English-speaking home or working for the US government. Indeed, Sammy's position as an INS agent follows the same pattern that *Lydia*'s Alvaro displays (see chapter 3): a stint with the US army paves a path for work as an immigration officer. In both cases, one's job offers an opportunity to perform a heightened type of US citizenship. Josiah Heyman finds that INS officers of Mexican ancestry, who at the time of his research comprised a significant one-third of the corps, tend not to identify with immigrants from Mexico or other Latin American countries. Rather, Heyman concludes, these officers "understand themselves as U.S. citizens who reject both domestic racism and ethnic loyalties that cross national borders."[26] In short, to expect Sammy to be, think, and act like "a Mexican" (whatever set of qualities and practices that may entail) denies concrete legal realities that compel him to see himself otherwise.

The play's depiction of Meño, Sammy's Mexican-born younger brother, in juxtaposition with the US-born Antonia, further emphasizes a concern with portraying a mixed-status family. Meño and Antonia fight "like dogs and cats" (*V* 350). Amparo urges her son and daughter to remember their shared blood when the two argue over an imminent strike at the factory where they work. Antonia is convinced that a strike—a risk—is essential to improve conditions, but her brother disagrees. To him, Antonia is merely looking for trouble. When Antonia strikes him with "Coward," the truth about Meño's feelings surfaces: "I don't have papers," he reminds his sister, a fact reiterated by Amparo (*V* 350, 358). Yarbro-Bejarano sees Antonia as Teatro de la Esperanza's purposeful attempt to create strong, active female characters.[27] But Antonia's boldness and commitment as a labor organizer stem not only from her gender but also, and crucially, from her position as a US citizen. In fact, she shares Sammy's determination to take action. While the type of action each of the siblings takes is to be judged differently by the audience, Sammy and Antonia are much more alike in their confidence, optimism, and daring than Sammy and Meño are alike in their maleness. Meño is a character defined more distinctly by his lack of papers than by his gender. His timidity in the face of conflict lies squarely in his undocumentedness. Meño, like his mother, proceeds with a caution that neither Antonia nor Sammy displays. *La víctima* thus paints a family portrait using two very different brushes, problematizing the type of solid identity that critics such as Huerta suggest Sammy fails to attain. Instead, the play offers its broken central family as an image characteristic of the mixed-status families that so commonly result when immigration law prevents legal reunifications.

In critiquing immigration policies, *La víctima* nevertheless defends the family structure so central to immigration law. In other words, the appeal that *La víctima* most vehemently makes—the nuclear family must not be separated—is also the core guiding tenet of contemporary US immigration policy. Hence, the play critiques the system's effectiveness in achieving its goals, rather than critiquing the goals themselves. In *Entry Denied*, Eithne Luibhéid compellingly describes how US immigration policies, since their earliest incarnations in the nineteenth century, have consistently constructed and reified a narrow, rather inflexible understanding of "family" centered on a model involving a husband, a wife, and their natural-born children.[28] *La víctima* similarly insists on the primacy and inevitability of heteronormative, biologically grounded family units. As archetypal Mother and Son, Amparo and Sammy become incomplete after their separation. Sammy's adoption by the Mendozas, who he admits "gave him the love of parents" (*V* 338), becomes, at least theatrically, irrelevant. Such characters are only spoken about—briefly at that—and never appear onstage. The play unapologetically pursues the notion that we somehow only belong to and with our biological parents. Likewise, *La víctima*'s attention to traditional unions and romances (we witness Amparo and Julián's first date and Sammy's proposal to Clara) perpetuates heteronormative images, unions much like those enshrined by immigration law.

Yarbro-Bejarano points out that Teatro de la Esperanza's plays generally (re)emphasize the male subject's centrality in narrative forms and fail to problematize the family structure itself. In so doing, Teatro de la Esperanza's stagework sustains hierarchies that the collective itself sought to upset offstage. (Yarbro-Bejarano praises Teatro de la Esperanza's attempts to allocate power across gender lines as well as its sensitivity to women's issues.[29]) In short, *La víctima* (re)produces narratives that, in turn, (re)produce legal structures. The play exemplifies the kind of cultural product that reinforces rather than challenges the logic behind an immigration system, a system that, like the play, naturalizes and glorifies the heteropatriarchal family structure.

Anthony Amsterdam and Jerome Bruner stress in their study of legal reasoning that

> law begins, as it were, *after* narrative. It is shaped in some measure not only by the narrative claims of contending parties in litigation, not only by "findings of fact" and "rules of law" announced by judges who have heard testimony and legal argument, but by the stock of familiar categories and story types within which all people in a culture live their lives.[30]

We can easily place *La víctima* within a web of cultural products that sustain understandings of family identical to those underpinning immigration law. The play participates in the construction of narrative models that precede the logic of law. Indeed, "family"—as conceived mutually in both legal and cultural spheres—holds a powerful grip over US immigration policies. So, while *La víctima* passionately condemns a system whose failures split families apart, the play also celebrates the unit at the base of that system's structure.

Constructing Alternatives

If immigration processes, despite their intended goals, prevent family reunification, it is important to consider how they simultaneously create alternative systems of love, support, and cohabitation. After all, "law produces its own alterities," as Coutin urges us to keep in mind.[31] Such possibilities, forged in defiance or outside the perimeters of what is legally permissible, can subvert the legal status quo. At the same time, marked as "illegal," relationships and ways of living that contradict immigration law can also serve to naturalize the so-called legal.

Precisely because post-1965 immigration law has favored particular familial ties to organize a system of preferences, circumventions of the legal system have often involved breaks with and reinventions of traditional family units. In chapter 2, I touch on ways in which fictional family ties fabricated by Chinese paper sons complicated and eventually transformed family relationships for generations. The way around exclusionary immigration laws led to the creation of kinship networks that ultimately defied the type of family structure immigration law seeks to safeguard. While different in its scope and mechanisms, the experience of Irish immigrants in the 1980s resulted in a similar need to devise new types of families not given preference by immigration law. Helena Mulkerns explains that, after emigration from Ireland lapsed during the 1960s and 1970s, Irish men and women seeking to escape an economic downturn in the 1980s no longer had immediate relatives in the United States to sponsor legal immigration. As a result, "very often, the Irish found themselves illegal," and this limitation "led to a necessary bonding among the younger Irish, the New Irish, as opposed to the established Irish Americans." Described by Brian Doyle as a group of young, relatively well-educated immigrants living predominantly in New York City, the New Irish lacked the network of family relations that had aided earlier generations of migrants.[32] The New Irish therefore had to build surrogate families in the United States.

Noble's *Away Alone*, which premiered in 1989 at the Irish Arts Center in New York City, invites us to track one young man's incorporation into such a family. Liam will learn that living among other immigrants without papers is, in the words of his neighbor Mary, "like a family situation" in which individuals away from their own homes care for one another (*AA* 74). The need for creating a support structure stems from an ever-present fear of immigration authorities. "She didn't know what would await her / Immigration left her in fear," portends one of *La víctima*'s songs about what life in California would bring for Amparo (*V* 332). Across the country, undocumented Irish immigrants must similarly live in a perpetual state of anxiety. As a reviewer of the 1989 New York City production of *Away Alone* notes, the single, most prominent, and "most painful" difference between the characters in the play and other "Americans seeking their fortunes in the big city" is their illegal status, which causes "even the most everyday activities [to] have an air of furtiveness."[33] The feeling that "the immigration's everywhere" drives Liam and his friends to "live a pretty isolated existence" (*AA* 22, 68). And the pressing, chronic awareness of legal nonexistence alters whatever sense of home or family those in undocumentedness have.

The characters' residence on Bainbridge Avenue in the Bronx, in the "Irish Mile," provides a sense of safety and belonging. Gilberto Giménez suggests that "physical 'deterritorialization'—such as that occurring through migration—does not automatically imply a deterritorialization in symbolic and subjective terms."[34] The high concentration of Irish immigrants and businesses on the Irish Mile allows Liam and other newcomers to surround themselves with peoples, foods, signs, and sounds from "home." For the play's premiere production, director Terence Lamude cast mostly Irish-born actors and enlisted Larry Kirwan to compose incidental music. A "rich... Irish tongue," to quote one critic, underscored by melodies blending traditional Irish music with urban sounds, accentuated what another describes as Noble's "ear for the language [and] rhythm of the [immigrants'] speech."[35] Sounds from a cross-Atlantic home literally reverberated throughout the space, much as they do in the corner of the Bronx depicted by the play.

However, the ever-present pressure of living in legal nonexistence transforms any feelings of belonging or solidarity. Home becomes an increasingly unstable phenomenon. We hear from local bartender and friend-to-all Mario that "New York City's the Homeless Capital of America" (*AA* 6). With this, he reassures the newly arrived Liam that he is sure to persevere, even if his only local contact has seemingly vanished. Liam quickly comes to discover that he will not be physically homeless in New York; within minutes Owen takes Liam under his wing and invites him to live in the "Irish Embassy," the apartment Owen already shares with his cousin Des and with Paddy (*AA* 12). Rather, Liam begins to learn that, as Des puts it, "there's no more home" (*AA* 66). Legal nonexistence intensifies this sense of existential homelessness. Living in an environment in which one must "watch out with the small talk," "look no one in the eye," and "keep [one's] mouth shut around strangers" (*AA* 13, 15, 22) severely complicates the forging of intimate, meaningful relationships often associated with a home.

Heightened fear and mistrust compel the undocumented immigrants to turn exclusively to one another. In so doing, they fashion bonds and connections that in essence replace the family so specifically defined by immigration law. Liam is swept into an environment in which the denizens of the Irish Embassy and their female neighbors are the entire world. Noble offers several scenes for the characters to come together in the kitchen, sit around a table, and share a meal. (*Gold in the Streets*, a film adaptation of Noble's play, emphasizes this domesticity through close-ups of food preparation and panning shots of the group at the kitchen table.) Lamude's direction further stressed familiarity and closeness through fast-paced dialogue and tightly knit movement. The domesticity staged in this kitchen, described as *"neater than the rest of the room"* (*AA* 12), transcends the anger and alienation characteristic of kitchen sink dramas by emphasizing closeness and comradeship. While Des easily surfaces as the angry young man integral to the kitchen sink naturalist critique of social realities, the play does not focus on condemning an evil United States or its laws. Instead, *Away Alone* tempers its critique of the American Dream by idealizing the power of friendship. The play depicts strangers-turned-friends into sharers of food, clothes, and shelter. They trim the Christmas tree together, share beds, and help each other get dressed. The title's "away" and "alone" aptly "connote the loneliness of exile, the alien in a strange world," writes a reviewer,[36] but also emphasize the cohesion of a group isolated in legal nonexistence. Facing doomed prospects because of their legal status, the immigrants rely on the only people they can trust—each other—and *Away Alone* boldly celebrates friendship's potential for creating new kinds of families.

In performance, the friendships can prove so effervescent that, as critic Jerry Tallmer remarks, one "ach[es] to be right up there in that room with those people on stage."[37] Newcomer Liam easily becomes "like a brother" to both Des and Mary (*AA* 71, 74). Of note, these new relationships—built in the United States and catalyzed in the first place by a shared legal consciousness, among other commonalities—temporarily sate the need for the nuclear family so cherished by US immigration law. Much like the "makeshift" furniture that characterizes the Irish Embassy (*AA* 11), the relationships forged in the apartment provide an essential, albeit provisional, function.

For example, Owen surfaces as interim parent to his roommates. His self-appointed role as cook turns Owen into a disciplinarian concerned with the health and well-being of the other men. Fearing a police raid, Owen also chides Liam when he brings black-market gadgets and appliances into the home. Owen's parental tone betrays both a fear of the authorities and a father-like disappointment with a misbehaving Liam. As he plays parent, Owen also fails his legally defined family. Admittedly in the United States to earn enough money to open a diner back in Ireland, Owen develops a close and openly sexual relationship with Mary in New York. We discover near play's end that Owen's wife in Ireland has also been unfaithful during his absence. The marriage, as well as the dream of returning a restaurateur, completely dissolves. Des explains that Owen is a man transformed; now "his wife and kids mean nothing to him"

(*AA* 65). Similarly, Mary's and Des's family ties metamorphose while in the United States. Mary comes to see that she would "rather live in Outer Mongolia" than face her relatives in Ireland ever again, and Des learns through a letter that the Irish girl he once intended to marry will marry someone else (*AA* 54, 41). Noble does not offer much to paint the lives of her characters before New York. Although we can only guess at the reasons driving them out of Ireland, it is certainly the case that their relationships to those left behind change substantially.

Simultaneously, the bonds established in New York appear to offer a psychological and emotional support system similar to those that underpin rationales for family-based immigration in the first place. After all, the law's interest in reunification stems partly from the belief that living alongside loved ones improves an individual's well-being, productivity, and stability. When the law fails to effect reunification, when economic and bureaucratic constraints make legal immigration difficult if not impossible, those in undocumentedness must resort to creating other ways of living. The grouping that *Away Alone* stages demonstrates a phenomenon characteristic of other immigrants living in legal nonexistence. As described by Ramón "Tianguis" Pérez in his *Diary of an Undocumented Immigrant*, it is often necessary to crowd multiple individuals into small residencies in order to save money, increase remittances, and importantly, create a network of support.[38]

The two characters in *Away Alone* who are living legally in the United States help to substantiate the above conclusions. A Jersey City native, barkeeper Mario appears to all intents and purposes as a loyal friend. By the end of the play, he takes Liam under his wing and offers him a job at the Old Sod Bar, a favorite hangout on the Irish Mile. Yet, from very early on, Owen's suspicions about Mario prevent us from seeing him as a full-fledged member of the makeshift family. Although Owen does not believe that Mario directly alerted the immigration authorities about the now-disappeared Seamus, he does urge Liam to dissociate from the bartender: "You don't know who Mario's friends are. You don't know who he talks to when he's not at the bar" (*AA* 13). In fact, neither do we. In performance, Mario's interactions with other bar patrons are played to the audience; as per Noble's stage directions, these customers remain invisible (*AA* 8). The most ready link to a world beyond the isolated existence at the Irish Embassy, Mario can offer help—he assists with the arrangements after Des's sudden death—but always with a question mark hovering over the repercussions of his involvement. Furthermore, appearing only in the scenes set at the bar, Mario is an obvious outsider to the group's domestic system.

Breda, a fortunate recipient of a Donnelly visa,[39] appears even more patently as an outsider. What we first hear about Breda, before she appears

onstage, is the mocking tones of the men, who dislike her apparent prud-
ishness. Yet, while Breda suffers many of the same economic struggles
her roommates and neighbors endure, it is clear that her immigration
status affords her different priorities and therefore a resented position
in the Irish Embassy. For example, Breda is able to quit a job she does
not like; her prospects of landing another one are markedly better than
her compatriots'. The mere possibility of more stability and easier travel
might help explain Breda's concern with establishing and defending traditional family. Of all the characters, she is the only one who remains
boldly attached to her family in Ireland. For instance, she invokes her
brothers as a defense mechanism when Liam challenges her (*AA* 47). She
is accustomed to their protection, and even from a distance, they retain a
functional place in Breda's life.

Moreover, Breda surfaces as the true defender of love and marriage.
Amid bachelors and a couple involved in an extramarital affair, Breda
insists that "it's natural" for "most people [to] get married." Part of her
conviction includes castigating Des for the disintegration of his relationship. According to Breda, Des's fiancée has opted to marry another man
because "you can't leave a girl to just sit and wait at home" (*AA* 49). Where
the others see a support system, Breda finds dysfunction. In her eyes, the
Irish Embassy and the apartment across the hall are not a new kind of
home but rather a hotbed for disease: "Overcrowding can actually cause
TB" (*AA* 44). Adapting a reviewer's description of David Raphel's set for
the Irish Arts Center, we might say that Breda sees only shabbiness and no
homeyness at all in her surroundings.[40] The sole legal immigrant in the
play thus echoes the trite fears of anti-immigrant advocates, who paint
pictures of immigration into the United States, especially undocumented
immigration, as an infection or infestation.

To be sure, Breda's core beliefs about marriage and family are not mocked
by Noble. Breda might be too intense, too closed-minded to allow for the
other characters' new relationships, but on the whole, *Away Alone* portrays
these interpersonal bonds as temporary or experimental. Not unlike the
"impossible subjects" described in chapter 1, the undocumented characters in Noble's work and the relationships they forge in legal nonexistence
are individually, albeit not systematically, unsustainable. Through Paddy,
Noble offers the most conventional comedic exit out of undocumentedness.
He will achieve "the pot of gold at the end of the rainbow" by marrying
a wealthy American citizen (*AA* 40). Although not a marriage of convenience, Paddy's real love conveniently affords him—through a traditional,
legally sanctioned union—both legalization and the possibility of a bina-
tional lifestyle (*AA* 79). Des's fate is more tragic. The undocumented immigrant unwilling to take just any job and the man whose heterosexuality and

masculinity come briefly into question must be sacrificed. His question-able death—Noble does not resolve whether Des is the victim of accident, malicious murder, or suicide—means that Owen and Breda will return to Ireland, the former to bring his cousin's body back "home" and the latter, "wearing black," to grieve someone she loved (*AA* 94). As mourners, Owen and Breda can return to well-established, traditional familial roles. Only Liam and Mary remain in the United States at play's end; he will continue to work at The Old Sod, eager to "chance [his] arm here for a bit," and she will take up design classes after moving to Manhattan (*AA* 94). Although their legal status remains unchanged and their prospects predominantly in fate's hands, Liam and Mary's pairing connotes a future similar to the one promised in *La víctima*'s concluding song. Whatever hope exists for a better tomorrow remains in the hands of a woman and a man, living freely in a new society as is their "right" (*V* 364).

Away Alone's final image—a young woman with a heavy backpack arrives at the bar and, like Liam in the first scene, asks for Seamus (*AA* 94)—insists on a cyclical system. The characters we have just met might eventually leave the makeshift family life they have created, vol-untarily or not, but new undocumented immigrants will necessarily continue to live in tightly built, insular, and isolated family-like groups. The play thus stages a phenomenon characteristic of undocumentedness. After all, if the law seeks to control and mold family life, then circumven-tions of the law will produce alternatives. By creating legally nonexistent, vulnerable groups, for whom resources and aid are extremely limited if not nonexistent, immigration law simultaneously encourages other types of support mechanisms and domestic life.

I must stress here that the New Irish encountered relatively fewer obsta-cles than other immigrant groups. Their European descent and perceived whiteness allowed for less contentious integration, and the play reminds us that the Irish are "lucky [to] speak English," that all they require to become "Americans" is "the passport" (*AA* 9). Still, *Away Alone*'s empha-sis on its protagonists' isolation bespeaks what Linda Bosniak sums up as the undocumented immigrants' "exceptionally marginalized" condi-tion. The focus on that isolation makes visible an unconventional kind of family life, reminding us of performance's power to bring the legally nonexistent to light. In the words of a reviewer, *Away Alone* illuminates "a niche in our city that we might not have known to exist."[41] And yet, like *La víctima*, *Away Alone* makes visible these realities without question-ing the inevitability of the family model through which immigration law prioritizes and excludes potential entrants. Noble's play thus contributes to the collection of cultural narratives that prop up immigration law's emphasis on "family" as a narrowly defined concept.

In her study of border practices that have aimed to control sexuality, Luibhéid stresses that US immigration policies have consistently marginalized "other kinds of long-term relationships that [are] not based on state-sanctioned marriage, with its implied interest in regulating blood and property." A long history of bans on the entry of prostitutes, unmarried women, homosexuals, and AIDS victims, among others, speaks to immigration authorities' role in "boundary marking... by which mainstream institutions empower and legitimize themselves, while producing diverse minoritized populations."[42] By marking marriage as the foundation of "family," immigration law simultaneously marks other types of relationships as something other than family, as something unworthy of protection and perhaps even illicit.

As late as 1990, US law denied legal immigration status to perceived or self-identified homosexuals. While the 1990 changes to immigration law were obviously important for gay men and lesbians, Luibhéid explains that they do not fully prevent immigrants from being denied citizenship under a "good moral character" requirement. For same-sex married couples and their children, the 2013 Supreme Court decision that legitimates those marriages at a federal level (*U.S. v. Windsor*) has meant immediate access to the same immigration privileges afforded to heterosexual married couples.[43] Still, with same-sex marriage banned in a majority of states (as well as a majority of nations), access to immigration benefits remains more limited for gay and lesbian couples, who cannot enter into legitimated unions as easily as their heterosexual counterparts. In short, the immigration system was and continues to be a disciplining mechanism that penalizes homosexual relationships.

We could say, then, that undocumented, homosexual immigrants occupy a doubly framed space of legal nonexistence. On the one hand, they have misused a visa or crossed the national border without proper authorization. On the other, they belong to a group that is particularly unwanted and has been actively turned away. One of a few plays that concern this twice-marginalized population, Reyes's *Deporting the Divas* offers insight into the construction of identity through and against legal categorization, especially given its emergence during a period in which no US state recognized same-sex unions and many in fact still legally criminalized consensual same-sex relationships.[44] Moreover, the play invites (re)consideration of law's power to shape family structures and police alternatives, as well as cultural products' participation in such processes. Reyes's piece premiered in 1996 at Celebration Theatre in Los Angeles, with subsequent revised premieres in Tucson (Borderlands Theater) and San Francisco (coproduced by Teatro de la Esperanza and Theatre Rhinoceros).

At the top of *Divas*'s second act, Teacher/Lecturer interrupts the play to offer the audience some thoughts on the aesthetics of Carmen Miranda and their exclusion from academia. His lesson-cum-rant includes an answer for "one of the great mysteries of sexual identity: what's the connection between the gay male and the female DIVA?" He offers his theory:

> The Diva has been battered, trashed around, used and spat out like a queer or like an illegal alien, or combinations thereof, and yet she has fought back with sweat, guts and tears and continues to occupy a space in our collective imagination. She's tough. She's grand...(*DD* 374)

The comparison between and mutual construction of queer and undocumented identities lie at the heart of Reyes's play, which presents what Beatriz Cortez describes as characters "able to negotiate a flowing hybrid identity that makes it possible for them to simultaneously belong to a variety of spaces of difference and/or to shift from one space to the other."[45] Among Reyes's nearly 15 personages are Michael, a bisexual US border patrol officer; his lover Sedicio, an openly gay, undocumented immigrant; Miss Fresno, a Guatemalan beauty queen of German descent hiding both her illegal immigration status and her male sexual organs; and Silvano, a wealthy AIDS patient from El Salvador living in San Diego without papers. *Divas*'s characters, performed through cross-gender and multiple casting techniques, well fit into Reyes's broader repertoire aiming to destabilize categorical markers of identity (his plays include, among others, *Men on the Verge of a His-panic Breakdown* and *Places to Touch Him*).

Critics regularly comment on Reyes's ability to "investigate and subvert intersections of gender, sexuality, sexual object choice, and immigrant status," as Jorge Huerta puts it, and to problematize, in Jon Rossini's words, "the concept of being defined by borders and the possibility of refusing that form of identification." Deemed an "illusion-packed fantasia on the ingeniously paired themes of immigration and homosexuality" by a reviewer of the 1996 San Francisco production, *Divas* brashly plays with undocumented status as a phenomenon in itself as well as a metaphor for sites of gender and sexual identity.[46] The danger but also the power of Michael's experimentation with homosexual desire—the core action driving *Divas*—gains additional meaning precisely because the object of his longing is quite literally illegal. Michael's role as a border agent, much like his role as a married, heterosexual man, involves making categorical choices. There are no in-betweens. The undocumented, a figure marked by legal nonexistence, surfaces as a potential means to transgress the limits of a seemingly stable, concrete identity as well as the prescribed gender roles associated with the heteronormative family. Coutin cautiously observes that "because they are placed outside the law, those who do not exist legally are strangely liberated." Without celebrating a space that is inherently violent and unsustainable, Coutin explains that "subversions...are made possible by nonexistence."[47] Michael therefore needs someone like Sedicio, a self-described "'special citizen' of the borderland" (*DD* 406), to usher him into a site where boundary markings lose some of their power. With a name that defies unity, integration, and order—the Spanish *sedición* means "sedition"—Sedicio also defies the notion that lawlessness or undocumentedness is a negative condition. "I'm undocumented and proud!" (*DD* 353), he tells the border patrol agent before their first kiss. For Sedicio, having no papers, like being gay, flouts convention(s). Sedicio, like the other divas with whom Michael interacts, therefore becomes the necessary Other through which Michael might expand, albeit perilously, his narrow notions of Self.[48]

This critical focus on Michael detracts from Sedicio's own notions of Self; viewing Sedicio as the inevitable Other merely repeats the marginalization that a lack of papers and/or homosexuality prompts. Michael might be the play's central figure, but as Sedicio himself urges after being rebuked for breaking the fourth wall to speak with the audience, Michael needs to "share [his] narrative" (*DD* 346). The original production's casting choices, imitated by several subsequent stagings, further insist on viewing Sedicio as a trustworthy narrator, one whose views merit particular consideration. *Divas*'s first director, Jorge Huerta, insists that the role of Sedicio, like that of Michael, required a more "realistic and complex" approach than that needed to play Miss Fresno or Silvano, some of the other "exaggerated characters" Rene Moreno portrayed simultaneously in the 1996 Celebration Theatre production. Less dependent on "wigs and accessories," Moreno-as-Sedicio therefore commanded an air of truth and depth.[49] I therefore propose homing in on the figure of Sedicio to consider some of the play's commentaries on family structures. In doing so, I find that *Divas* does not wholly unsettle traditional notions of family or the use of legal-like rules to protect and define relationships. After all, Sedicio, Michael's guide into "alternate families [and] other ways to live," persistently betrays his own belief that weddings are "breeder concepts" (*DD* 406, 347). Sedicio believes that the "love between two responsible adults is sacred" (*DD* 382) and desires to spend the rest of his life in a traditional, love-based, monogamous relationship. He is eager to leave a life of meaningless sex and "marry a man by the time [he is] 25," to pursue an actual relationship rather than "a series of quick insertions" (*DD* 346, 356). Throughout the play, Sedicio expresses his desire for married life. Although he claims to represent an "'open border' lifestyle," Sedicio ultimately defends a traditional notion of what a meaningful relationship should constitute. He doesn't even "believe in bisexuals" (*DD* 368).

To attain his goals, Sedicio sets up concrete, categorical regulations. When Michael expresses interest in a one-night stand, Sedicio calmly explains: "I have rules about all this, I'm going to be a teacher one day, and I believe in establishing the rules right up front. Three dates might get you a hickey" (*DD* 349). Although he succumbs to passion somewhat—"To hell with my boundaries, baby, come to mamma" (*DD* 352)—Sedicio permits Michael to go only so far. "That type of sex," the type that Michael wants to experience in order to truly "come out," remains strictly off-limits (*DD* 355–56). In a moment of desperation, fearing he is losing Michael, Sedicio holds out a condom, avers he has lost interest in "respectable" gay marriage, and offers himself to the man with whom he has fallen in love (*DD* 405). However, Sedicio ultimately fails to abandon his rules and refuses a relationship that will not be true to his desires. He remains then a staunch advocate for traditional unions and also validates an understanding of relationships as rule-bound constructs. Sedicio's rules, in turn, help to restrain performances of *Deporting the Divas*, limiting displays of nontraditional sexual desire. Huerta reminds us that, onstage, Michael and Sedicio share but one long and later one truncated kiss, hardly a transgressive display of one man's sexual desire for another.[50]

Cortez offers the view that "Michael and Sedicio challenge the stereotypical view of intimacy," that "the characters in the play do not have to subscribe to any type of predetermined ideal of what a sexual encounter should be, and they are able to try different perspectives and to participate in different types of relationships." But given that their relationship fails in the end and that Sedicio refuses to have anything but a full commitment from Michael, it becomes difficult to assert that Reyes's characters have truly challenged traditional notions of couplehood. David Foster suggests that Reyes's conclusion "queers" and "decenter[s] narrative expectations."[51] Indeed, *Divas*'s dominant comic energy—despite the play's functioning through a collage of various theatrical and dramatic styles—seems to demand a final union. However, minutes before the play concludes, Sedicio leaves Michael. Their happy ending is impossible. Like Miss Fresno before, Sedicio departs "*in a grand, fabulous manner like any other of the Divas.*" Michael, too, then "*gets to stage his own grandiose finale*" (*DD* 408, 409). The longing inherent to this sequence, like the longing of all great divas, attests to the misery and injustice of having to lose Sedicio. We are left with "this distance" between Sedicio and Michael (*DD* 408). The original casting choice of having the same actor playing Sedicio, Miss Fresno, and Silvano kept Sedicio from even appearing in Michael's fantastical finale, which featured the beauty queen instead.

With INS uniform and badge back on, Michael laments his loneliness but also celebrates the power of the divas, who will "transport [him] to that grand, fabulous world where [he] will arise, one day, ready and eager to face the music and sing along!" (DD 409).

Only two unions occur by play's end, couples that the audience never actually gets to see: Michael's sister marries his boss and Michael returns to Teresita. "We're one big INS family now," Michael confesses (DD 408). It seems he has dutifully followed his boss's advice ("The family comes first" [DD 394]) and resigned himself to continue married life despite feeling that "marriage is overrated" (DD 380). In short, only heterosexual, legally married couples such as Michael and Teresita remain together. Chairwoman-for-Life Marge McCarthy, the mayoral candidate with a keen interest in Michael's personal affairs and an express dislike for border crossers of all types, would be pleased. This ending does not necessarily decenter expectations. The belief that a protagonist couple must emerge at play's end remains quite prevalent, albeit unmet. Michael simply ends up with the wrong partner. Sedicio, and not the unseen Teresita, is Michael's proper dramatic love interest. By keeping them apart, Divas does not urge its audience to demand something other than a couple as a satisfying conclusion but stresses instead the need for a less limiting definition of such a couple. The play urges a more inclusive type of narrative, one that may help usher in more inclusive legal thinking.

Existing laws (both immigration and family laws) mark the homosexual union that Sedicio demands from Michael as not only unconventional but also illegal. When Sedicio suggests running away, Michael reminds him that the "type of things [he] like[s] to do are illegal in Arizona" (DD 378). In this sense, Sedicio is very much minoritized, to evoke Luibhéid's language, and necessarily pushed into legal nonexistence. But if he lives "near the Gay Center on Normal Street" (DD 349), Sedicio surely is more interested in making the Gay Center a bit more like Normal than in changing the structures underpinning Normal. He wishes Normal were a more inclusive category. Arguably the play's most reasonable character, Sedicio thus offers a critique of a system that denies him full existence based on its exclusivity rather than on its inner logic.

In an introduction to Reyes's work, Foster posits two types of nonexistence plaguing homosexual individuals in heterosexist contexts. The first is an outright denial of gay identities. The second variety of nonexistence, more prevalent in popular discourses, is "the acceptance of a 'homosexual type,' but concomitantly a rhetorical exercise by which every possible attribute of identity is shown to be nothing more than a distortion of the master narrative of the patriarchy, and therefore, if not inconsequential... at least existentially invalid."[52] Sedicio's ideal society, it seems, endeavors to un-distort and to realign his identity—at least his identity as one half of a loving couple—with the standards espoused by the master narrative, without much change to the standards themselves. In short, Sedicio does not really seek an alternate way of living but rather a place of full existence at the table that has already been set.

The fight for marriage equality epitomizes this kind of approach. Some critics worry that the inclusion of same-sex couples in the tradition of marriage limits the potential for upending heteronormative, patriarchal power structures. In the words of William Eskridge and Darren Spedale, "Formal access to oppressive institutions such as marriage would only strengthen them; gay liberation must seek to transform the status quo rather than join it."[53] Indeed, the legal recognition of same-sex marriage, by various states as well as by federal agencies, reinforces the belief that only certain kinds of interpersonal relationships merit protection. Although the recognition of same-sex marriages by US immigration authorities will undoubtedly improve the lives of many, we must also consider how queered notions of family and partnership are simultaneously jettisoned from privilege when institutional marriage is deemed the sole standard for evaluating relationships. In this way, immigration law continues to police the definition and content of "family," and, in turn, of "normal."

While Sedicio expresses his desire for a traditional, so-called normal personal relationship, he is less specific about fitting into a "normal" national citizenry. He is supposedly "proud" of his lack of papers. Yet, Sedicio does not reveal his immigration status until long after divulging that he is "openly gay" (*DD* 353, 343). There is much more at stake, it seems, in embracing one's illegal status than one's homosexuality. After all, this is a universe in which even the staunchest of conservative voices, Marge McCarthy, opines that "having a gay son these days is not as tragic as having an immigrant in the family" and in which immigrating is more "shocking [and] immoral" than sodomy (*DD* 329, 354). At the moment in which Sedicio finally offers himself to Michael, a tempted Michael still hesitates. The immigration officer cautiously broaches the subject of Sedicio's undocumentedness, a topic that has seldom arisen between them. Sedicio remains defiant:

> Maybe I don't mind passing for something I'm not. Yes, most of us learn how to hide it, learn English correctly, get the right false id's, try to "look white."
>
> But I don't need to lecture you on the art of hiding, Miguel Angel. You're the expert. (*DD* 405)

Undocumentedness surfaces as a metaphor for the closet. But *Deporting the Divas* carefully stages the limits of the analogy.

The need for concealing undocumentedness proves much more pressing than the need to pass as heterosexual. In the play's world, in which,
as Cortez tells us, there exists "a range of possibilities for the negotiation
of a hybrid identity through which an individual can be part of different
spaces at the same time, even spaces that are contradictory or incompatible among themselves,"[54] the space of legal nonexistence still surfaces as the most (potentially) violent. It is the most difficult space from
within which one may negotiate. Deportation, or the threat of deportation, becomes a prevalent strategy to keep those without papers in check.
Marge, for example, threatens to call the immigration authorities on
Sedicio's roommate, Leonel, unless he ceases to impersonate her in a drag
act. Although Leonel claims that he is "disgusted with everything that's
going on" (DD 386), it is obvious that his decision to return to Costa Rica
and to leave his friend Sedicio stems directly from Marge's intimida-
tions. In Michael's "Tango Fantasy," a femme fatale named Sirena also
finds herself left vulnerable by her lack of papers and threatened with
deportation by a sergeant (the same actor playing Michael) involved in
a murder investigation. And in what is "perhaps the most moving scene
in the play," as Huerta describes it, Michael deports the AIDS patient
and diva extraordinaire Silvano. The Salvadoran native claims that he
"could have gotten [his] papers straightened out by marrying a senator's
daughter," that he has "those types of connections" (DD 388–89). What
becomes clear is that Silvano's fabulousness masks how his family shuns
him because of his homosexuality.[55] The deportation thus forces Silvano
out of the safety and comfort he has created in the United States and back
into a dangerous space.

A media frenzy over deportations makes the threat within nonexistence all the more palpable. Even within Divas's highly theatrical world,
where everyone performs roles, deportations become intensely watched
performances. The "glare of a news camera" accentuates Silvano's deportation; he is "blinded by the lights" as Michael escorts him out of the hospital room and into the street (DD 392). The diva's final exit marks the
beginning of what will surely become a most-watched event; he leaves the
stage ready to answer questions for the press, so we know the spotlight
will follow. A few minutes later, Michael gets paged for a work emergency.
Miss Fresno has been "caught" just as she was about to be crowned the
new Miss USA. "Marge McCarthy denounced her in front of the cameras," Michael explains, adding that "now Marge is up twenty points in
the polls" (DD 399). Together, the instances of deportations that are part
of the play's action bespeak a culture that broadcasts and consistently
reiterates images of captured undocumented immigrants: handcuffed,
heads down, marshaled by some uniformed officer. Although Silvano

attempts to maintain his dignity during the deportation ordeal, his exit is also quite distressing, marked by "the pain, the struggle, the essence of all diva-dom" (*DD* 391).

Given that Michael cares deeply for him, the threats made against Sedicio prove most troubling within his space of nonexistence. Facing the possibility of consummating their relationship, Michael attempts to normalize, or naturalize, Sedicio. "Maybe we can get you a lawyer and—," Michael pleads before Sedicio interrupts him. When Sedicio says he might not be "that interested in 'legality,'" Michael fumes: "How can you live the way you do? [...] Tell that to the INS. I'm just warning you—we've got your file—" (*DD* 405–6). The warning proves especially menacing within the context of performances that abide by the original cast breakdown. We have already seen Michael deport a body just like Sedicio's—Silvano's. The prospect becomes not only imaginable but, in some ways, already lived. Although Michael condemns Sedicio's desire for an open homosexual relationship as much as his lack of papers, attacking his vulnerable immigration status becomes the only way for Michael to control the situation. Sedicio gets a preview of the possible life he ultimately rejects, a life in which a relationship marked by uneven immigration status opens the door for easy manipulation and even abuse. Indeed, statistics reveal that immigrant spouses of citizens and permanent residents are made more vulnerable by a system that makes their immigration status contingent on their partners' demonstrated support.[56] In short, the metaphor aligning undocumentedness with minoritized sexualities falls slightly apart once we consider the power dynamics at play between those with papers and those without. Much like the central family in *La víctima*, the central relationship in *Deporting the Divas* crumbles in part because immigration policies place individuals in decidedly different positions.

Performing Family

As I discuss in chapter 2, immigrating into the United States requires a performance of sorts. Especially for immigrants seeking to enter without papers, the process necessitates a performance of credibility or invisibility during the border scenario. Issues of immigration law and family alert us to a related, longer-term performance. Using Judith Butler's notions from *Bodies that Matter*, Luibhéid describes immigration policies in the United States that "compel the formation of families in particular ways, or else compel the performance of being a family within parameters that are designed to satisfy immigration officials." Importantly, because immigration authorities can choose to investigate a particular case beyond the moment and site of entry, the performances required of immigrants can last extended periods of time and actively change their experiences while living in the United States. Additionally, immigrants may rightly come to see, as Owen's misgivings about Mario attest in *Away Alone*, that non-official encounters extend and intensify this need to perform. Luibhéid confirms that "inspection at the border is not a one-time experience but is rather, as Foucault's image of the carceral archipelago suggests, a process that situates immigrants within lifelong networks of surveillance and disciplinary relations."[57] One's immigration status as well as the validity of the familial relationship underpinning it can come under scrutiny at countless points. We could rework Foucault's language from *Discipline & Punish* to say that bureaucrat–immigration judges, teacher–immigration judges, doctor–immigration judges, social worker–immigration judges, neighbor–immigration judges, and even relative–immigration judges supplement the ever-present threat of checks and inquiries by official immigration authorities.[58]

Bosniak explains that all immigrants—documented or not—must live in "the shadow of immigration law," their identities and experiences profoundly affected by the ever-present threat of deportation. Of immigrants living without or in violation of their papers, Bosniak adds that the "collateral effects" of always-looming and oft-enforced deportation policies "arguably structure their experience in this country more than any other single factor."[59] Immigration authorities can conduct unscheduled, surprise visits to couples suspected of marriage fraud, and increasingly, non-immigration authorities as well as everyday citizens are indoctrinated to say something if they see something. As I introduce in chapter 2 and as I continue to describe in chapter 5, the task of policing the border and checking a person's right to be in the United States has spread beyond official federal channels. Tellingly, in several of the plays that I discuss in this book, undocumented migrants have been betrayed to immigration authorities or threatened with such action by nonofficial agents. Living in the shadow of immigration law, then, can come quite close to living under the "perfect eye" that Foucault proposes in *Discipline & Punish*. Immigration control, or the threat of control, becomes a type of "perfect disciplinary apparatus" seeking "to see everything constantly." The legal border, it follows, functions just as much to expel so-called undesirable entrants as to compel them to *be* the border, wherever and whenever, as Shahram Khosravi compellingly describes.[60] And immigration law's shadow is increasingly cast on immigrants at times and places that are unpredictable and pervasive. The border then ceases to be an edge and becomes a panopticon.

While performing evident heterosexuality or real marriage might well carve an initial passage through immigration authorities, immigrants need—or might feel compelled—to maintain such performances vis-à-vis a system that deems their residence within the nation's borders a tenuous privilege rather than a right. Ironically, those living in a space of nonexistence, marked as invisible in so many areas, thus can simultaneously become hyperv sible. Adapting Foucault's ideas about the ideal prison, we might say that the ubiquitous possibility of coming under investigation and facing detention and deportation places those living without papers—and possibly all noncitizens—in "small theatres," where successful performances of "normal" might deflect the spotlights. If the "[immigration] judges of normality are present everywhere," then immigrants in fear of immigration authorities understandably erase, disavow, or mask alternate lifestyles and family structures. The "art" of immigration authorities "*normalizes.*"[61]

Luibhéid focuses a large portion of her study to the ways in which immigration authorities construct and then police (homo)sexual identities, a normalizing phenomenon she tells us is understudied. In a system structured around examination—of "immigrants' bodies, documents, biographies, and appearances"—as well as one with a built-in "inducement to speak," immigrants before 1990 were made, if not coerced, to perform a gendered identity in order to satisfy officials. For example, many men and women undertook a process of "straightening up," seeking to appear more so-called masculine or feminine, respectively. They did so to face immigration officials conducting "monitoring based on visual appearance[, which] operated around the notion of gender inversion—that is, homosexuals could be visually identified by the fact that gay men looked effeminate or lesbians looked masculine."[62] Given that even after 1990 gay and lesbian immigrants continue to face legal challenges, many entrants still ensure that immigration authorities remain unaware of their sexuality, or put more bluntly, that authorities assume their heterosexuality. We could say that such efforts to adjust markers conventionally or stereotypically associated with homosexuality in order to pass through the border constitute a hybrid performance of credibility and invisibility. After all, potential entrants seek to have immigration officials believe their heterosexuality by making invisible any traces of perceived homosexuality. Through such performances, then, border crossers are able to subvert a system that otherwise seeks to exclude them.

Immigration requirements for married couples can lead to similarly coerced but also subversive performances. In order to prevent ostensible marriage fraud, Congress amended INA in 1986 to curb and more severely punish green-card weddings, a phenomenon that lives strongly in the nation's shared legal consciousness. (Indeed, green-card weddings have become a staple in our storytelling, from television sitcoms to romance novels.) The Immigration Marriage Fraud Amendments of 1986

(IMFA) thus created a system of conditional status for immigrant spouses. Through IMFA, INA bolstered its policing efforts against marriages entered for the "purpose of procuring an alien's admission as an immigrant," those that have been "judicially annulled or terminated," and those involving "a fee or other consideration."[63] Couples seeking to circumvent immigration laws often resort to elaborate performances to appear married. The *Immigration Marriage Fraud, Hearing Before the Subcommittee on Immigration and Refugee Policy of the Committee of the Judiciary* offers some insight into the "folkloric" proportions that staged ceremonies aiming to convince immigration officials that a legitimate wedding has taken place have reached: "everything from happy-looking witnesses at bogus marriage ceremonies to reusable cardboard and paste wedding cakes that appear in wedding photo after wedding photo." The report concludes that "marriage fraud appears to be a 'growth industry.'"[64]

Of course, the line between "real" and "fraudulent" marriage can be difficult to detect, and many an immigration hearing or trial has attempted to assign one or the other label to a couple. Thus, immigrants are forced to perform versions of so-called true marriage to avoid deportation. Luibhéid reveals that such legal processes have inherited tactics used by interrogators working to uncover Chinese paper sons in the early 1900s, including invasively personal interrogations and separate, isolated interviews for individuals in a couple. The proceedings often rely on questions "eliciting details about sexual practices," which Luibhéid understandably reads as a state inspection of heterosexuality.[65] I would add that the proceedings and the many other types of questions seeking to assign meaning to a personal relationship also simultaneously attempt to inspect and define marriage. In seeking a public demonstration or confirmation of private relationships, such proceedings make visible the kinds of limits around which "marriage" is to be understood. Those under scrutiny need to perform "married" solely for the satisfaction of observers, regardless of the particular meaning that "husband" or "wife" may have for the individuals involved in the actual relationship.

Deporting the Divas repeatedly plays with the ruptures and limits of a system that predicates inclusion on performances of identity. Reyes's use of cross-gender and multiple casting, as well as his play's self-awareness as a performance, urge a consideration of all categorical identities as problematic constructions. Rossini well encapsulates *Divas*'s concern with rigid understandings of gender, sexual, ethnic, national, or legal identity: "At stake in this play is the concept of being defined by borders and the possibility of refusing that form of identification." Because all forms of identification are but constructs, Rossini continues, minoritized categories—such as illegal—can only be policed at their "most visible moments."⁶⁶ It would follow that the possibility of manipulating subversive behaviors' (in)visibility, more than the behaviors themselves, truly threatens a disciplinary system like immigration control. Several of Reyes's characters, including Sedicio, Miss Fresno, and Sirena, infiltrate spheres arguably prohibited to them because of their gender, ethnicity, and/or legal status by masking visible markers of difference. "We all learn to show the face that's most convenient," Michael acknowledges (*DD* 339).

Reyes's characters are well aware that they can transcend categorizations, but I think it is the actors' portrayals of these characters that truly illuminate performance's deep power to subvert visibility. Although an analysis of acting techniques is beyond the scope of my work, I pause here to consider briefly the actors' work in productions of the plays at hand. Reyes's directions call for male actors to transcend "*camp impersonation[s] of womanhood*" (*DD* 359). Huerta insists that audiences should be led to perceive a character such as Sirena as a "real woman." And indeed, audience members can come to accept characters such as Marge as "definitely" female, to quote just one reviewer. Huerta recalls that "many audience members would tell [him] after the show that they thought 'she' was a she." Similarly, heterosexual actors can purportedly convince audiences of a homo- or bisexual identity. Huerta reveals that Rene Moreno, the actor who played Sedicio and Miss Fresno in Los Angeles, is heterosexual.⁶⁷ The actor's sexuality is supposed to make his portrayals all the more impressive. I do not wish to engage here in the long and ongoing debate over actors, their sexualities, and their roles. Rather, I call attention to the possibility that the actors somehow "fooled" their audiences and to an obvious parallel—that immigrants can fool immigration authorities as well.

Reviews of *La víctima* and *Away Alone* alert us to the playability, and thus visibility, of emotional bonds. Performers can convincingly manufacture "family," even in anti-illusionistic pieces such as *La víctima*. Onstage, actors can create a "poignant portrait" and make visible the "genuine tenderness" existing between a mother and her children (or between spouses). And, borrowing representative language from several of its reviewers, we find that *Away Alone* can craft a "ring of authenticity," "natural ease," "palpable sense" of relationships, and "flawless" interactions; "we feel that these people really know each other, really live together."⁶⁸ The praise for the actors' abilities to persuade audiences reminds us of the potential that exists for immigrants to actualize familial roles and gender and sexual categories through performance. If immigration authorities construct categories during and through the process of examination, immigrants themselves can potentially control some of what they make (in)visible. In so doing, they may subvert policing efforts.

Thorpe's investigation into the lives of two undocumented teenage girls provides insight into the power that performance holds for them. Thorpe marvels at one of the young women's ability to "get by" in the face of roadblocks. "Whenever [Marisela] didn't have the right documents, she just turned up the brightness of her smile and usually people were charmed," Thorpe explains. Always aware of her illegal status, Marisela understands, for instance, the potency of a "sorority sweatshirt" and a "high-wattage smile" to convince a police officer of her fake Mexican license's validity.[69] While the stakes may be different for a couple trying to convince an immigration investigator of their relationship's validity, Marisela's anecdote attests to the possibility of bypassing obstacles by manipulating what is observed.

But performance has its subversive limits, especially given the US immigration system's vested interest in policing the content of the categories it creates. Subversion in this case "marks out an area where the identity [the immigration system] is trying to contain and expel is also reestablished and reinforced," explains Luibhéid.[70] *Nikrodhanondha v. Reno*, a 2000 decision by the Board of Immigration Appeals (BIA), is quite telling. Pairoj Nikrodhanondha and Darlene Sincere—her maiden name is an unfortunate irony—were unable to convince the BIA that their marriage was real. Inconsistent stories about their courtship, separate finances, and separate residences proved the visible markers of a sham. But the couple had two children. In this regard, they performed their expected heteronormative reproduction quite perfectly, manifestly demonstrating their heterosexuality, their commitment to a joint enterprise, and perhaps, their onetime love for one another. *Nikrodhanondha v. Reno* reminds us that in determining what "couples like you" means, to return to Marge McCarthy's sentiments, US law can define, quite meticulously, the type of personal relationships that its immigration system will support. Individual performances that conform to the multiple visible markers that immigration law sets might well avoid the state's scrutiny, but, collectively, they also reify and naturalize the legal categories. Couples—and families—"unlike you" then become more and more unwanted, more and more illegal. Marge gets her way.

5

Act § 331—Alien Enemies

When the residents of Fuente Ovejuna collectively claimed responsibility for the 1476 murder of Knight Commander Fernán Gómez de Guzmán, they successfully thwarted the process aimed at pinpointing and punishing the culprit. The account of these events inspired Lope de Vega to write *Fuente Ovejuna*, whose characters withstand great torture but steadfastly protect Frondoso's identity. After all, in killing the commander, Frondoso saves the town from a cruel tyrant. One by one, they audaciously tell the inquiring judge, who will later report to the Spanish monarchs, that 'Fuente Ovejuna" is responsible for Fernán Gómez's death. In so doing, the oppressed villagers—a unified collective—defy the logic of the legal procedures. The "innocent" insist on their guilt to ensure that the "guilty" retains his innocence. By blurring these distinctions, Fuente Ovejuna's residents achieve a type of justice unforeseen by the legal system. Their solidarity leads to the crowd-pleasing denouement characteristic of Lope's *comedias* (King Ferdinand and Queen Isabella pardon all). But more critically for the purposes of my project, the villagers' feat attests to their ability to manipulate a legal system and alter its categorical definitions.

Michael John Garcés's *Los Illegals*, first produced in 2007 by Cornerstone Theater Company in Los Angeles, relies on *Fuente Ovejuna* as a model.[1] Garcés's play offers a group of mostly undocumented day laborers as twenty-first-century versions of Fuente Ovejuna's exploited inhabitants. At "the Center," a day-labor work site located on the parking lot of a Giant Hardware franchise, the group endeavors to facilitate a more productive system for securing jobs. They face multipronged pressure: from migrant workers who do not want to abide by the group's rules, from a friendly but concerned store manager, and from nearby protesters whose loud voices constitute a persistent hounding. Although their oppressor is less clearly an individual tyrant, the group nevertheless confronts systematic criminalization and dehumanization. After all, immigration violations, pursued and punished by the government with intensified rigor, effectively stigmatize individuals. Immigration status becomes a defining trait, one that serves both official and private actors to debase those without papers. (The staging of two gruesome border-crossing stories alongside the main action heightens the intensity of the workers' struggle.) When an employer, encouraged by the lead protestor, accuses a worker of assault, tensions erupt and Giant attempts to banish the laborers from its premises. Gloria, the employer, claims the man threatened to attack her; we later learn from Ernesto that he hit a wall with a hammer when she refused to pay him for his labor. But the group of laborers collectively claims responsibility for the "assault" and, in so doing, saves Ernesto from detention and deportation. Their victory is sure to be short-lived; they will be forced to fight again the "same battle as always. Forever" (*LI* 116). For a moment, however, the workers' triumph reasserts their right to justice and demonstrates their ability to break the constraints of legal labels imposed by increasingly intolerant laws.

In this chapter, I focus on questions of criminal labels and rights. Drawing from David Engel and Frank Munger's *Rights of Inclusion*, a study of disability that approaches identity through the lens of legal consciousness, I evaluate how the increasing criminalization of undocumentedness dehumanizes not only those without papers but also all US residents and citizens. In the chapter's first two sections, I study Garcés's *Los Illegals* and Ntare Mwine's *Biro*.[2] The plays offer insight into ways individuals contend with labels such as "criminal" and live under the disciplining gaze of US immigration law. Simultaneously, the works of Garcés and Mwine illuminate processes of activating rights. In the chapter's third section, I move to Yussef El Guindi's *Back of the Throat*, a dark vision of post-9/11 antiterrorist strategies, to examine how federal laws have largely recast immigrants as terrorists and relied on already existing spaces of legal nonexistence to justify dehumanizing Homeland Security policies.[3] Inspired by the kind of collectivity forged by productions of *Los Illegals* and *Biro*, I dedicate the chapter's final section to the role that performance can play to counteract such processes of dehumanization.

I focus on *Los Illegals*, *Biro*, and *Back of the Throat* for several reasons. First, as products of post-9/11 sensitivities, the pieces evidence practices that punish immigrants with a severity and scope arguably unmatched in US history. Second, by bringing together stories centered around distinct immigrant populations—of Latin American origin in *Los Illegals*, Ugandan origin in *Biro*, and Arab/Muslim origin in *Back of the Throat*[4]—I advocate for the joint consideration of struggles that often receive isolated attention. Together, the three plays stress how it is predominantly nonwhite individuals that continue in the twenty-first century to be marked "illegal" by US immigration law. More critically, the law has served effectively to foment divisions among marginalized populations, as I hope my analysis can illuminate. Finally, because each of the plays tells a story about and puts on display a legal procedure in action—a trial, a prisoner-lawyer meeting, and an interrogation—I find in their juxtaposition a productive entry into a discussion about law's presence in the lives of immigrants both as a palpable threat and as a forum for action.

An Unforgiving Gaze

Writing in 1971, sociologist Julian Samora proposed that the struggles of undocumentedness were akin to a "game." Although he described many difficulties for those in legal nonexistence, Samora asserted that immigrant workers and their employers "happily break the law time and time again, the only serious consequence being an inconvenience to one or another or both." Such language fails to capture the force with which the United States pursues and punishes noncitizens today. Although "illegal presence" in the United States does not officially violate the US criminal code (it is a civil offense), the means for penalizing those in undocumentedness increasingly function otherwise. Persistent criminalization—what legal scholar Stephen Legomsky sums up as the introduction of criminal justice techniques into civil regulation—has, since the late 1980s and then again after 2001, radically altered undocumentedness.[5] The monitoring of physical borders has intensified, everyday spaces have become sites for expanded policing, legislation has stripped immigrants of rights and protections, and violators of immigration law have encountered increasingly harsher penalties. Simultaneously, debates about and representations of undocumentedness, especially in mass media, have concentrated more and more on conflict between lawbreakers and law enforcers. Throughout this chapter, I rely on a language of "criminality" to highlight these shifts.

One need look only at how immigration control has transitioned from one governmental agency to another to note fluctuating attitudes about the state's relationship to immigrants. The first federal office charged with immigrant-related matters actually sought to promote immigration and operated under the Treasury Department. Responsibility for monitoring immigration in the early twentieth century moved to the now-defunct Department of Commerce and Labor and then to the Department of Labor. Bringing together the duties of two separate bureaus, the Immigration and Naturalization Service (INS) was established as part of the Department of Labor in 1933. In 1940, the INS became part of the

Department of Justice. The Homeland Security Act of 2002 (HSA), a response to the September 11 attacks, eliminated the INS and shifted its responsibilities to the newly created Department of Homeland Security (DHS). In short, the magnitude and understanding of immigration law infringements have clearly changed. What were once fiscal or employment-related transgressions came to be seen as defiance of federal law and, today, breaches of national security. In the process, the relationship between those in undocumentedness and a more general US population has also altered.

Mwine's one-man biographical play, based on the life of his uncle, premiered in 2003 at the National Theatre in Kampala, Uganda, with subsequent noteworthy productions at the Drill Hall Theatre in London and the Public Theater in New York City. From the opening, *Biro* stresses how US immigration law has transformed its protagonist into a criminal. When the play begins, a man wearing a state-issued orange prison suit—an immediate, iconic mark of criminality—walks downstage to a tight center spotlight. On either side of him is a projected sign: "VISITOR RULES & REGULATIONS" on his left, "NO TRESPASSING PRISON PROPERTY" on his right. The amplified sound of metal bars sliding marks the man's move from his cell to a new location. Biro begins to address his listener, a lawyer or some other legal advisor. For the remainder of the play, Biro tells his life story in a desperate plea for help—living under Idi Amin's and Milton Obote's violent regimes, joining Uganda's National Resistance Army and training in Cuba, returning to Africa upon discovering he is HIV-positive, grappling with AIDS, and coming to the United States in search of medicine and work. The tale transports the audience to Uganda and to Cuba; projections showcase images of Africa and the Caribbean. But the bright orange uniform remains throughout the entirety of the play a stark reminder of the man's present situation: Biro has been "under [immigration's] cuffs without trial," "two years in a Texas jail for a misdemeanor" (*BI* 110, 908). Despite quite distressing experiences as a victim of war and of disease, Biro confesses that "so far in my life this jail is the biggest nightmare I have gone through" (*BI* 910).

A captive awaiting deportation, a misdemeanant punished more severely than a felon, Biro remains in legal limbo. His situation is telling. Unauthorized immigrants are entitled to only some of the rights given to US citizens or legal immigrants. To begin with, US law allows for the categorical distinction between citizens and noncitizens. The federal government can operate through discriminatory practices that affect noncitizens negatively, be they in the United States legally or not. Even if the government cannot deny any immigrant the rights to "life, liberty, or property without due process," as the Supreme Court affirmed in *Mathews v. Diaz*, Congress can implement rules for immigrants that "would be unacceptable if applied to citizens."[6] Not only can the federal government discriminate in its allotment of benefits, as was the question in *Mathews*, but federal policies can also weaken a noncitizen's claim to certain procedural rights. Federal agents, for example, have broad power to stop, interrogate, and search noncitizens. The fourth amendment does not limit evidence that can be used against immigrants in deportation hearings, and noncitizens are not necessarily entitled to appointed counsel during deportation proceedings. In fact, because immigration law views deportation—or "removal," as it is now officially called—as a civil, administrative proceeding rather than as a criminal punishment, deportation processes can circumvent certain rights, such as those afforded by the sixth amendment to ensure speedy and public trials. Noncitizens can be detained without right to a bail bond hearing.[7]

Undocumentedness exacerbates these legal disadvantages. *Mathews* stresses that noncitizens do not belong to "a single homogeneous legal classification" and instead comprise a "heterogeneous multitude of persons with a wide-ranging variety of ties to this country." Those in undocumentedness easily fall into one of the least protected and most severely punished sectors of the population. Judy Rabinovitz, deputy director of the ACLU's Immigrants Rights Project, points to a current crisis for those in undocumentedness: their missing right—the right to be in the United States—leads to Kafkaesque situations in which those without papers are often unable to exercise even the basic constitutional rights *Mathews* supposedly guarantees. After all, if citizenship is "the right to have rights," in Chief Justice Earl Warren's words, then unauthorized immigrants are fundamentally right-less.[8]

In addition to having to contend with fewer and often suspended rights, those in undocumentedness simultaneously have become, since the 1990s, the targets of harsh penalization and vitriol.[9] The very term "removal"—which as Susan Coutin indicates suggests a calculated process of eradicating something dangerous, something ugly—attests to the undesirable position unauthorized immigrants must inhabit in the national imaginary. Joseph Nevins underscores that they have emerged from relative invisibility to become "a category of social identity" marked as "a threat to the socio-territorial fabric of the United States." He identifies the detrimental results for those living in undocumentedness. First, the intense criminalization of undocumented immigrants has led to a heightened "distinction between 'us' and 'them,' between citizens and 'aliens,' placing so-called aliens on the wrong side of the social boundary that distinguishes law and order from criminality." Second, this increasingly "illegal" status forces migrants "into the proverbial shadows of society, thus necessitating that the migrant break other laws in order to survive." And finally, transformed into a criminal, into an alien enemy of the state, the undocumented immigrant more easily becomes, for citizens, "someone whose supposed criminal activity (in violating the law) is independent of [the citizens'] own actions and thus is someone for whom [they] need not accept any responsibility." The systematic erasure of crimes committed *on* undocumented immigrants compounds these three interrelated trends, which insist on distance between supposedly criminal outsiders and guiltless insiders.[10]

With Engel and Munger's approach toward identity in mind, I find in the stories of *Biro* and *Los Illegals* strong evidence to support the proposition that legal rights and social and cultural settings are mutually constitutive. One's sense of inclusion or exclusion from a system of legal rights and entitlements shapes a sense of individual identity as well as the relationships underpinning sociocultural dynamics. When legal rights or social and cultural settings change, individuals' perceptions about themselves and their sense of belonging necessarily shift as well. Engel and Munger explain that "rights can transform the sense of self simply by increasing individuals' perceptions of their own worth," even when those legal rights are not directly asserted.[11] I examine this type of transformation in the chapter's next section. But first, I consider the contrary implication and inspect how an actual or merely perceived lack of legal rights detrimentally affects one's sense of social worth.

Garcés and Mwine both stress the dehumanizing consequences of feeling right-less. *Los Illegals*'s Lalo, a migrant worker who distrusts the Center's organizing efforts, despairs when a member of the local community job center suggests he join a protest: "No one in this country cares, ain't nobody going to listen to us." Like many of Garcés's undocumented characters, Lalo reflects on a sociocultural context that devalues the life of those in undocumentedness: "Ramón almost got runned over yesterday by some crazy guy who didn't want to stop, like he was aiming at him or something, and George [the Giant store manager] was all like it was our fault" (*LI* 84). Absorbing the blame for their own disenfranchisement becomes part of the dehumanization process. Nevins makes clear that the "illegal" label urges those who are "legal" to believe that the undocumented immigrant "deserves nothing from the United States, regardless of what his or her contributions to the society might be and of what his or her rights are as outlined in the U.S. Constitution, in the wide body of American law, or in various international human rights covenants."[12] The undocumented therefore exist in a context that proves, at almost every juncture, palpably unjust. At a moment of crisis, when one of their fellow workers is charged with the assault, Yolanda speaks for the group of undocumented day laborers, "They [Gloria and the nearby protesters] can say what they want, and the police and the papers and everyone will believe them." Jimmy agrees, "Who are they going to believe, the one who has papers, or the one who doesn't?" (*LI* 89), thus revealing the lowly social place he knows those without papers occupy.

Biro similarly comes to believe that he is no more than a lab rat in the United States. Obtaining basic necessities proves difficult without a visa, so Biro is actually surprised by how easy it is to find medicine, even while in jail: "Apparently my immigration status did not prevent me from being put on federal funded AIDS research" (*BI* 758).[13] He is quite aware that others can volunteer to be human subjects (human objects seems more fitting) for experimentation and that many will get paid to participate in such tests. But as an "illegal immigrant," Biro knows he has no choice but to "cooperate" (*BI* 756–57). While his health improves, it is only within the context of imprisonment, literally as well as psychologically. Like a guinea pig, he is caged, tested, and under constant watch. Coutin describes how practices of detention and removal serve to transform individuals into "animal-like, 'lower,' people who could be denied hygiene, food, physical comfort, information, and rights." She reveals that US immigration authorities at times rely on hollow bullets, designed originally to hunt wild game, to impede and capture avowedly threatening border crossers. Anti-immigrant rhetoric in current discourse periodically debases those in undocumentedness with comparisons to animals.[14]

Issues of dehumanization return us to the disciplinary mechanisms proposed in the previous chapter in relationship to family and gender roles. Immigrants generally, and those without papers more specifically, must exist in a space of increasing vigilance and subjugation. Throughout this book, I have discussed the repercussions of living under the constant threat of deportation. At the risk of redundancy, I point out that alienage, by definition, entails the always-present possibility of removal. But, as Linda Bosniak explains, US immigration law today threatens deportation for actions that are often ungermane to immigration regulation per se. The law applies higher standards of personal conduct for those whose presence in the United States is deemed a privilege rather than a right. Under increasingly intolerant legislation—set predominantly by the Illegal Immigration Reform and Immigrant Responsibility Act of 1996 (IIRIRA) and the Antiterrorism and Effective Death Penalty Act of 1996 (AEDPA) and enforced with much more diligence since September 11, 2001—and under a system in which immigration judges have lost much of their discretionary power, immigrants can find themselves detained and deported for offenses that, for citizens, mean just a nominal fine or days-long detention. Minor convictions such as petty theft and public urinating can well result in automatic deportation in this draconian system.[15] Although a 2010 Supreme Court decision (*Carachuri-Rosendo v. Holder*) offers some hope that *legal* noncitizens charged with minor drug offenses may avoid mandatory removal through the discretion of the attorney general (and thus through extensive, expensive legal battles), the Court makes clear that such noncitizens remain "removable" in the eyes of the law.

Those in undocumentedness remain subject to an unforgiving gaze. As the number of behaviors and professed infringements for which unauthorized immigrants can face detention and deportation rises, that gaze becomes ever more powerful. In the words of Shahram Khosravi, "There is a risk that the 'illegal' migrant, subjected to a gaze and treatment that divest him or her of humanity, will internalize the shame—as I did—and understand the lack of travel documents and documentation as personal deficiencies and inadequacies."[16] This risk, of a disciplining gaze degrading self-identity, is magnified with the expanding power of local and private authorities to police immigration. Examples of this trend include the DHS's growing 287(g) program, which allocates federal authority over immigration to state and local agencies; E-Verify, an Internet-based system designed for businesses to determine the citizenship/immigration status of employees; and Secure Communities, which relies on information-sharing networks between local police, the FBI, and federal authorities to detect unauthorized immigrants through the use of fingerprints. As epitomized by efforts like California's Proposition 187, Arizona's SB 1070, and Alabama's HB 56, individual states have endeavored also to turn everyday encounters and interactions into inquiries over immigration status. Enrolling a child in school, renting an apartment, and arranging for water service potentially become actions through which undocumentedness can be revealed and reported. Many of these practices have ultimately proven unworkable, if not outright unconstitutional. HB 56, the harshest of all state initiatives waged against those in undocumentedness, has by now been essentially repealed.[17] Some of their techniques, however, remain legally in place. After *Arizona v. U.S.*, for example, a state cannot criminalize the act of applying for a job or soliciting work. But the decision for now permits local police in certain circumstances to ascertain the immigration status of persons detained or arrested on other legitimate bases. And the fear these techniques engender, fueled further by efforts to inure a whole US population to say something if they see something, makes those without papers hypervisible. Tram Nguyen concludes, "There's very little room left, within a national climate of fear and growing intolerance, for any infraction by someone without the legal status to be here, for immigrants to do more than play a role, to be more than cardboard cutouts."[18]

As the first of six plays in Cornerstone's Justice Cycle, *Los Illegals* seeks to explore the role that law plays in shaping and disrupting communities. Specifically, it shows how the threat of deportation compels intensified levels of self-restraint from its protagonists. Garcés explains that conversations among Cornerstone's members about ways in which bodies are legislated served to inspire the cycle.[19] *Los Illegals* thus presents the physical controls that immigration law can place under its shadow (a variation on the kind of geographic immobility I introduce in the previous chapter in relation to family reunification). Taking a hammer to a wall, standing on Giant Hardware's sidewalk, and littering all come under scrutiny during the play. It is clear that those without papers endeavor to avoid demonstrating any "single blemish" (*LI* 111) lest they call undue attention to themselves.

The character of Brenda, who in the play leads the fervent anti-immigrant protests, becomes a potent reminder of the persistent gaze placed on those in undocumentedness. Hers is a scornful, acid gaze made all the more prevalent in Cornerstone's production through the use of projections. Huge slides with photographs of protesters such as Brenda loomed over the playing area, adding to the offstage yelling that occasionally underscored the action. We constantly see and hear mantras like "Illegal is illegal," "Hire a citizen," and "You are breaking the law." (Periodic helicopter flybys during Cornerstone's outdoor performances of *Los Illegals* inadvertently helped to magnify hypervisibility.[20]) And such hypervisibility helps to underscore how a disciplinary apparatus operates constantly and thoroughly on those in undocumentedness.

The targets of such vitriol endeavor to restrain themselves. More accurately, those in undocumentedness are disciplined to control their anger. Even their friends and supporters mandate particular behaviors. Nathan, a lawyer from United Day Laborers defending the accused Ernesto, cautions the group to avoid confrontation at all costs. Likewise, Kim, an advocate from Acción para Inmigrantes, is uncompromising when it comes to the workers' deportment. When Mauricio rationalizes Ernesto's so-called crime, insisting on the injustice of being cheated of wages, Kim forcefully puts an end to the debate: "He shouldn't have done that. [...] No buts. It's unacceptable. It's that kind of thing that hurts everyone" (*LI* 110). Those in undocumentedness are repeatedly told throughout the play what not to do, where not to stand, where not to sit, where not to be. They are compelled to act, as Nguyen describes, like nothing more than cardboard cutouts. *Biro* likewise stages the power of the immigration system to control individual behavior. Biro's incarceration is first prompted by an arrest for drunk and disorderly conduct during a misunderstanding with the police (*BI* 102). Biro suggests that his detrimental arrest has resulted from the devil's "working on" him, tempting him with alcohol (*BI* 67). He thus underscores the possibility that a perfectly behaved individual, one with superhuman self-restraint, could have gone undetected.

For immigration law to exert such power on the individual body, its presence and consequences must be readily perceived. Following Sally Merry's assertion that the "law looks different" to individuals occupying various socioeconomic positions, I concentrate now on how those without papers might come to "see" immigration law, especially beyond the confines of border scenarios (see chapter 2). Nevins, for one, describes the necessarily theatrical nature of immigration enforcement. He writes that the 1990s security escalations at the US-Mexico border were, among many things,

> a political sideshow designed for public consumption to demonstrate the Clinton administration's seriousness about cracking down on unauthorized immigration. Efforts by the White House and the INS to maximize coverage of the implementation of the operation demonstrate that Washington, DC, was acutely aware of the importance of the operation for purposes of public consumption. In this regard, the U.S.–Mexico boundary became a stage with a national audience.

The sideshow is also for the undocumented to consume. Nevins explains that boundary policing has "a lot to do with performance in addition to particular tasks."[21] I will rephrase his words to emphasize that it is *through* particular tasks that performances can be perceived. Through the interchanges prompted by the Border Patrol at entry points, through immigration raids at worksites, through the driving of vans in immigrant-heavy neighborhoods, the state performs its power. And through trials, regardless of their outcome, the state also performs its power.

When *Los Illegals* becomes a courtroom drama, we witness the force with which the ritual structure of the proceedings alters behavior. "Mr. Huerta, yes or no," the judge twice demands a categorical response from Ernesto, now dressed up for his court appearance (*LI* 113–14). Did he argue with Gloria over payments? Did he take a hammer to her wall? As soon as Ernesto tries to explain himself, filtered through the actions of an official translator, the judge—her very robes a marker of her authority, a US flag prominently placed by her chair—disciplines him into admitting the required "yes." She also disciplines his narrative, producing an artificial (from Ernesto's perspective) reality and knowledge of the events under question.[22] The judge manages to control Nathan as well, admonishing him for "grandstanding" in her courtroom (*LI* 112). Through the ritual of the trial, the judge simultaneously disavows the legitimacy of

Ernesto and Nathan's more subtle argument. She resolves that an angry Ernesto has indeed caused damage to Gloria's property, as opposed to acknowledging, say, that Ernesto has taken back the labor for which he did not get paid Complementing the judge's clout, a DHS officer is present at and participates in the proceedings.

Foucault argues that shifts away from torture as a public spectacle and into more private systems of punishment such as the carceral system have meant the "downgrade" of "theatrical elements" in the art of punishing and disciplining. He writes that punishment shifts "to become the most hidden part of the penal process" and that "publicity [shifts] to the trial, and to the sentence."[23] For many of the undocumented immigrants within the fiction of *Los Illegals*, Ernesto's trial indeed proves a very public performance. After all, they are in attendance. Therefore, while the proceedings aim to determine Ernesto's fate, the trial simultaneously serves as an exercise of power over the entire group (as well as an opportunity for them to exercise their own power, as I will explore below). A trial, as a *"performance of the laws,"* can therefore become a "singularly powerful locus of social control, . . . the very means by which the members of the community know who they are" and by which an audience larger than the individuals directly involved in the proceedings can be engaged, as Robert Hariman tells us.[24] Those at Ernesto's trial can visualize themselves in his shoes and gauge the state's actions toward anyone lacking papers. Audiences for *Los Illegals*, in turn, watching a dramatized trial, also experience a legal proceeding, albeit a fictional one. Trials are, in fact, ubiquitous elements of US cultural narratives and omnipresent in most media, allowing us to extend Foucault's evaluation of their publicity to the context at hand. In stories, fictionalized trials encourage their audiences to position themselves in relation to the law. Stories about the law are therefore integral to examining the production of legal identities.

Both *Biro* and *Los Illegals* stage the power of stories to drive individual choices and actions. The experiences and, more importantly, the anecdotes of and related by others become key guideposts for managing legal nonexistence. Biro pursues a "new identity," for example, based on what he "was told," on what "this West African guy I had met" related (*BI* 816, 820). Although she is quickly cut off in the hectic environment, Teresa, a new arrival to Giant's lot, begins to tell a story about finding her way to the job center: "A man told me that . . ." (*LI* 74). The plays, moreover, themselves represent the kinds of narratives through which anecdote, myth, and life all merge. The plays stage and become stories about law. As such, they are critical to understanding legal consciousness. Engel and Munger stress that "the role of law in everyday life—and its effect on identity—cannot be measured only by the frequency of recourse to lawyers and official legal institutions or remedy systems."[25] Within the stories in the plays and through their stagings, we engage with the power of narrative to help construct one's legal consciousness. I stress again, as I do in chapter 1, the important role of stories in shaping attitudes and ideas about law, especially when individuals do not have direct contact with official legal agents or institutions.

Biro concerns another narrative related to that of the trial: the narrative of incarceration. While it is certainly the case that, inside the Texas prison, Biro is concealed from the public, the play itself seems to make visible that "most hidden" aspect of the disciplining system. A story about an immigrant in prison, the piece exemplifies the kind of narrative that participates in the fabrication of law's palpable presence. Outside the jail, Biro's absence will become a tale about disappearance, a rumor about immigration authorities. For a moment, I return to other plays I have considered in this study, plays whose action did not feature as direct an involvement with legal institutions or agents. The women in *Real Women Have Curves*, for instance, fear a van parked outside their factory partly because of a story they hear on the radio and because of gossip about a missing neighbor. Likewise, using the story of Hortensia's deportation, the women in *Latina* assume another colleague, Lola, has met the same fate when she fails to show up to work. In short, the invisibility inherent to carceral punishment or deportation is far from invisible. In fact, the state produces a new kind of theatrical element to complement the public spectacle of a trial by engaging in what we may call performances of removal.[26] By creating absences, immigration authorities amplify fears of deportation and detention, fears fueled further by stories circulating among undocumented populations.

The particular task of deporting or detaining an immigrant becomes a performance that can communicate law and order to some viewers but simultaneously make others shudder. The "penalty" imposed, to draw from Foucault's ideas about disciplining technologies, is in the case of undocumented immigration communicated to a broader community by creating a conspicuous absence. Thus, such penalty potentially has "most intense effects on those who have not [yet been caught for] the crime." It is not enough to place those in undocumentedness under a seemingly constant, panoptical gaze; additionally, the consequences of being caught need to feel persistently real. Coutin acknowledges that, although the risk of apprehension and removal remains statistically low for the millions of unauthorized immigrants living in the United States today, the *perception* of potential deportation persists and indeed grows.[27] While Biro's actual punishment is certainly hidden from most, the *idea* of similar punishment remains quite prevalent for those outside the prison.

Importantly, the removal of Biros and Hortensias has communicated punishment more potently since the late 1980s because the nature of such punishment has changed drastically. The federal government continues to view deportation as an administrative solution to the civil offense of "illegal presence." Even setting aside the fact that deportation proceedings reflect judgments on the "moral worth of individual conduct" and carry potentially dire consequences, deportations are not criminal prosecutions in the eyes of the law.[28] In fact, detention associated with immigration procedures, as a matter of law, is meant to be different from and less severe than criminal incarceration. Yet, if removal used to mean "only" deportation, it has increasingly come to mean prolonged detention as well. As made clear by Dora Schriro in a 2009 report to the DHS, immigration detention and criminal incarceration have actually come to be viewed by the public as akin to one another. More crucially, both types of confinement are now managed similarly. Immigration detention regularly involves containment in a secure facility far removed from detainees' counsel and communities. Today, the "design, construction, staffing plans, and population management strategies" of current Immigration and Customs Enforcement (ICE) detention facilities "are based largely upon the principles of command and control." The average period of detention is a month, though much shorter for those who choose voluntary removal and, in some cases, years long.[29] Whether classified as civil or criminal punishments, such realities can hardly be described as a game.

Furthermore, the federal government has stepped up efforts to prosecute other immigration-related activities, many of which are legally classified as crimes. Thus, "improper" entry and reentry, Social Security fraud, identity theft, and other tactics often made necessary by undocumentedness become a means through which unauthorized immigrants are criminalized and "warehoused in federal prisons," in the words of Jonathan Inda and Julie Dowling. Since 2005, a zero-tolerance approach toward illegal entry and reentry—a collection of enforcement strategies known as Operation Streamline—has brought especially dramatic increases in apprehensions. The result has been a veritable explosion of immigration-related detention and imprisonment in the United States with unmistakable consequences: immigration-related "criminals" make up a significant (and growing) portion of the nonviolent incarcerated population in the United States, and the percentage of Latina/o prisoners in the country has skyrocketed since the 1990s.[30] Ironically, the ostensible need for removal from the United States now entails prolonged periods of enforced captivity within its borders.

These shifts are part of broader trends. Since the 1970s, the United States has witnessed extraordinary growth in its prison populations, with a resilient prison-industrial complex fueling a culture of mass incarceration. While the Obama administration seems interested in reducing the number of federal prisoners charged with nonviolent drug offenses, unauthorized border crossers remain in the meantime "valuable commodities whose worth lies in being placed and kept behind bars," to quote Inda and Dowling. We can easily pinpoint today a well-protected immigration industrial complex designed to benefit government bureaucracies, corporate and media interests, and politicians. The business of jailing immigrants, and thus the need to criminalize them, has become quite lucrative for both the public and private sectors.[31] As they are turned into profit-making opportunities, unauthorized immigrants in detention inevitably suffer. Deportation in itself can mean a death sentence, as Biro desperately explains (*BI* 114, 916–17), but imprisonment for undocumented men, women, and children can mean additional and undue torment. "Just deport us. It would be a lot more dignified than having to go to jail," protests one of the unauthorized immigrants depicted in Moustafa Bayoumi's study of Arab and Muslim Americans in a post–9/11 United States. As Bayoumi summarizes, prison "terrifies."[32] It follows that terrifying stories about prison and the regular removal of individuals from their communities serve to concretize immigration law.

Jean and John Comaroff propose that narratives and images of policing—the "spectacle of policing"—have become more prevalent under neoliberal, post–Cold War conditions. They urge us to consider how the logic of Foucauldian discipline has inverted itself: new types of "theatrics" now reveal the state's "desire to condense dispersed power in order to make it visible, tangible, accountable, effective." Certainly, the disappearance of bodies caused by immigration enforcement becomes a kind of public spectacle that "allows the performance of power to reach very different audiences," in Diana Taylor's language.[33] It is a spectacle that urges its viewers to consider, at once, the might of the state and the consequences of breaking immigration laws. I return to Merry's proposition: How does the law "look" to Biro and others in undocumentedness? And how does the law look to their friends, their neighbors, or their coworkers who one day face the sudden absence created by a removal? It is a spectacularly omnipresent law, a spectacularly cruel law. It is a law whose gaze one is desperate to avoid and, therefore, a successfully disciplining law.

It is also a self-upholding law. US immigration law sustains its own legitimacy and naturalizes itself through the use of the very categories it produces. Labels such as "illegal" compel impassiveness and scorn from the "legal." It follows, as Nevins explores, that debates over the rights of unauthorized immigrants generally ignore the complexities of present-day immigration.[34] "Illegal" serves to portray the decision to live in undocumentedness as an individual's nefarious choice. "Illegal" serves to displace blame from the capitalist interests that benefit from the production of an exploitable, unprotected source of labor. "Illegal" serves to mask the US and global policies that compel immigration in the first place. A prime example of symbolic violence, the label of "illegal" serves quite literally to legitimize the distance between those with papers and those without. The label becomes a weapon of domination that at once naturalizes the rights of those who are "legal" and the crimes of those who are not.[35]

Los Illegals attempts to call attention to these processes of symbolic violence. In Cornerstone's production, a large sign reading "GIANT"—an unmistakable allusion in its design to Home Depot, where day laborers in the Los Angeles area regularly congregate—loomed over the playing area throughout the performance. Marking the site of the action as the store parking lot, the sign made ever-present the corporate interests that exploit immigrant labor. Giant Hardware becomes an unmistakable Goliath, but one whose very largeness and nonpersonhood help to conceal its active participation in the creation of undocumented immigration. After all, the major conflict in the play surfaces as that between individuals, and especially between protesters and laborers. Although Giant remains a presence, it is dramatically inactive.

Likewise, Los Illegals points to the effectiveness of legal labels to foment intra–working class antagonisms by creating a readily identifiable scapegoat for social ills. During a particularly touching moment, in which Kim and Brenda find themselves talking over a cup of coffee, the workers' advocate urges the anti-immigrant protester to consider the commonality of their causes. Both want the same thing: "Good jobs. Good wages. Opportunity" (LI 102). Kim suggests that a united front against capitalist and political interests is the only way to achieve such things. However, Brenda's commitment to ridding the United States of all "illegals" betrays the efficacy of legal categorization to conceal how governments and corporations create unjust working conditions and instead pit exploited groups against one another. David Bacon stresses that current political machinations, fueled by portrayals in the media, pit African Americans against Latina/o immigrants by suggesting that victories for one community can only come as losses for the other. This racial division then blinds workers from pinpointing their actual exploiters and prevents productive alliances from forming.[36]

The division is not so patently organized around racial categories. Seeing it as such reinforces some of the very ruptures among potential allies. Brenda, for example, explicitly campaigns for her "black brothers and sisters" (LI 82). Would she support a black man like Biro? Rather, the state-produced legal/illegal divide, which Nevins explains is increasingly normalized, has successfully convinced "the vast majority of Americans—*including Latinos*—[that] the wrongness of illegal immigration is simply beyond question." As a result, many have come to see an enduring struggle for civil rights in the United States as a fight that should be reserved for citizens only.[37] Even as Brenda preaches that she "stand[s] against the government, the corporations, the special interest groups that are at war with us," her protest and her acrimony aim strictly at another enemy: the undocumented. It is by attacking those without papers—an action that in itself helps to naturalize them as loathsome—that Brenda believes she can regain her country (*LI* 82). At the same time, Brenda and the other protesters become the most visible and accessible antagonist for some of the immigrant workers. They become "esa gente," "those people" at whom workers such as Lalo and Ramón can direct their anger (*LI* 84). As *Los Illegals* makes clear, in both cases the resentment is ultimately misguided and certainly unproductive. No change can result from those in the margins fighting with each other rather than with the marginalizing system itself.

Given the power of the legal/illegal divide, the need to distinguish oneself as "legal" prompts ruptures within mono-ethnic communities as well. Garcés counterposes characters such as Juan, Giant's security guard, and Police Officer Hernandez to the immigrant laborers in order to problematize pat understandings of racial or ethnic allegiances. Almost in reflex, Juan distances himself from the undocumented workers when they press for sympathy: "I never broke the law" to get a job, he insists (*LI* 87). Garcés challenges further the assumption that a Pan-Latinidad somehow unites his characters by having Lalo retort to Juan's statement, "Look, I'm Mexican too you know," with a flat "Psss, I don't care, man, I'm Salvadorean, yo" (*LI* 87). The playwright confesses that the rehearsal process for Cornerstone's production attested to the divisions that exist within the local Latina/o community, some stemming from citizens' and legal immigrants' struggle with the idea of working side-by-side with undocumented individuals. Garcés told me during an interview that while the process of working together allowed the cast and crew to build a sense of cohesion, individuals did not come to any easy agreements over the issues. We thus must heed Sonja Kuftinec's caution in using terms such as "community" to mean an erasure of difference.[38] Paying close attention to how legal categorization maintains divisions among different as well as within single communities seems an important step in understanding and perhaps altering undocumentedness.

Post-1965 state-sponsored campaigns to penalize undocumented immigration generally have come hand-in-hand with strong defenses of legal immigration, serving to magnify rifts within mono-ethnic communities. While current immigration policies undoubtedly bear the imprints of centuries-long racism and continue to marginalize predominantly nonwhite populations,[39] we must avoid the easy assumption that "illegal" serves strictly to obfuscate racist judgments. Rather, in producing legal and illegal immigrants, the law manages to protect business interests and shift attention away from commonalities around which seemingly different communities could unite. Brenda's, Ramón's, and Lalo's fury—seen at a most surface level in terms of us/them, black/brown—obscures the power of legal categorization to divide the US working class, (re)produce racial and ethnic difference, and sustain capitalist structures.

Mwine's Biro bluntly tells his audience, "What you don't realize until you come to America is that capitalism is pursued with more fervor than religion" (*BI* 811–12). While such fervor can create opportunity— Biro thanks capitalism for encouraging a clinic to test him in order to receive funds and for inspiring an immigration officer to receive bribes (*BI* 816)—it is also responsible for perpetuating what Nevins terms the "two-tiered system of humanity" that neoliberal pursuits necessitate in their globalized spread of capitalism. Capitalist interests not only drive the need for exploitable, immigrant labor (see chapter 3), but also compel the criminalization and penalization processes.[40] *Los Illegals* attempts to stage the sheer force with which capitalism consumes us all, problematizing any obvious dismantling of the two-tiered system. When Kim argues with Brenda over workers' rights, she does so while the two share Starbucks drinks—"Grande nonfat latte with extra foam" for the immigrants' advocate, "triple cappuchino with a shot of caramel and three sugars" for the protester (*LI* 100). Garcés thus posits that even an awareness of capitalism's injustices does not alone remove one from the capitalist system. Kim fights to correct some of the consequences of capitalist greed, dedicating herself to bettering the lives of undocumented workers and to finding ways to change immigration laws. But, at the same time, she exists as a consumer, serving as a driving force to maintain structures solidly in place. Like the Starbucks cup that she and others hold onstage, the character of Kim simultaneously suggests a "liberal reputation" together with the "ills of globalization."[41] When asked if he will be at Starbucks, George replies, "Where else?" (*LI* 86). Where else indeed—in *Los Illegals*, there is no identifiable outside. The play alerts us that the fight for immigrant rights in the United States must happen within and not only against capitalism.

Offering no easy answers and pointing to many lacunae instead, Garcés does propose that all his characters—whether one of "los illegals" or "the happy legals" (*LI* 89)—are victims of a single, dehumanizing system. All are seeking a better life; many are mostly blind to the reasons behind their hardships. It becomes easier to blame an "other," and in this case, the law neatly demarcates that difference. In Biro's words, US capitalism "bulldoze[s] you" (*BI* 505). We are left with Brendas on one side, convinced that the undocumented have made her country a lawless place, and Lalos on another, firm in their hatred against seemingly bigoted US citizens, with a majority of characters struggling to negotiate a position somewhere between the two extremes. Legal divisions, then, in combination with criminalizing efforts, successfully encourage antagonisms that displace frustrations. Legal divisions, as they become naturalized, prevent us from seeing alternatives and leave us paralyzed. "Nothing I can do," meekly confesses George as the workers face expulsion from the lot and a man faces criminal charges for standing up to an injustice (*LI* 103). Yet, Foucault stresses that no disciplining mechanism is exhaustive; "there always remain the possibilities of resistance, disobedience, and oppositional groupings."[42] Paralysis is, or should be, breakable. Of interest here is how a claim to rights serves as a form of resistance and how performance activates such claims.

An Invocation of Rights

In chapter 3, I discuss how undocumented immigrants and their advocates often endeavor to portray those without papers as hard workers seeking to improve their lot. In this mold, Biro pleads with his audience to understand his actions: "The main reason I came to the United States was for medicine / That was the primary goal along with taking care of my son" (*BI* 29–30). Juan José Mangandi, who played Ernesto in Cornerstone's *Los Illegals* and directed Spanish-language excerpts of the play for a convention at the National Labor College, praises Garcés's work precisely because it allows the undocumented to "break the mistrust" that seemingly keeps a general public from understanding the realities of unauthorized immigration.[43]

Fighting the criminalizing label of "illegal" with justifications for actions taken surfaces as an important but often insufficient strategy toward recognition and inclusion. It becomes important also to attack the logic sustaining criminalization. Biro's emphatic "I did not / I did not steal $300 / No no / I did not" (*BI* 108–9), a categorical denial of an accusation waged against him when he is first arrested, refutes all the levels of criminality with which he is charged. Mwine's impassioned portrayal at that moment bespeaks Biro's frustrations. Biro needs desperately to make the lawyer whom he is addressing—us—understand that nothing he has done in the United States should be deemed criminal. "Are we guilty just because they say so?" is how one of the migrant workers poses the question in *Los Illegals* (*LI* 89). It is the anti-immigration demonstrators who are criminal, Lalo points out: "They're not here to protest, man, they're here to stop me from working. They're attacking me" (*LI* 83). Kim offers a related argument, criminalizing the law itself: "If the law keeps families from eating, people from working, then the law is wrong" (*LI* 101).

To insert themselves differently into the immigration debate and change the logic of their opponents' arguments, those in undocumentedness need to assert their rights, however limited, more forcefully. Generally, invoking rights becomes a key tactic through which the characters in *Los Illegals* effect some agency within legal nonexistence. Learning about and fighting for the few protections to which they are entitled bolster their social position. For instance, the simple act of stepping off Giant Hardware's parking lot and onto the sidewalk provides the workers some leverage with which to confront the store's manager and guard. "Public property, ¿qué no?" charges Jimmy, emphasizing his legal right to be on the sidewalk (*LI* 85). Such a right becomes a dear cause, one that is constantly cited and defended in the play. Jimmy, otherwise rejected and ostracized by the laws of the land, thus relies on those very laws in order to defend himself. In so doing, he shines new light on the shadow of nonexistence.

Leisy Abrego has examined the effects of a law that gives undocumented university students in California the right to in-state tuition rates. Her conclusions support the idea that exercising a right can have transformative consequences exceeding the express intent of the law. Abrego finds that students who took advantage of their right not only gained access to education but also achieved an increased sense of self-value and belonging. Although their immigration status per se did not change, the students generally shifted their perspective toward law and carved a space of legitimacy within legal nonexistence. They found new ways to mobilize in order to demand additional rights beyond those accorded by the law.[44] While Abrego reminds us that marginalized groups do not always make direct use of rights-granting laws, her study reaffirms Engel and Munger's proposition that even unexercised rights can improve self-esteem, raise aspirations, and alter expectations from others and from social institutions. The assertion of the right to be on a sidewalk—or a story of such assertion—can therefore claim a legitimate presence and inspire others to experience nonexistence differently.

Judith Butler offers a stimulating example of immigrants in undocumentedness claiming a public space. She analyzes a 2006 street demonstration in Los Angeles, where participants sang the US national anthem in Spanish translation, and points to the "performative contradiction" that allows the singers at once to demand the freedom denied to them and to begin its exercise. In other words, by congregating, making themselves visible, and singing *somos iguales*, demonstrators not only call attention to their nonexistence but simultaneously begin to counteract it. Butler clarifies that asserting one's rights will not alone accomplish enfranchisement. But such an assertion when rights do not exist becomes a critical initial step in making them possible. Butler's argument needs some finessing, as Noa Ben-Asher points out. The legal scholar notes that Butler fails to take into account the constitutional right to assembly and free speech undocumented immigrants do indeed have. Yet, Ben-Asher ultimately agrees with Butler, underscoring that the fear of deportation easily invalidates such constitutional rights, as I have explored above.[45]

Mwine's and Garcés's stories suggest another context for observing the performative contradiction in play. We might approach Biro's or Ernesto's use of US law through Butler's lens, even if their performances in a more traditional legal sphere are differently prompted than the street protest Butler describes. Butler highlights the importance of action that exposes, calls attention to, and enacts disenfranchisement. She ponders how asking for legitimation "is to also announce the gap between [freedom's] exercise and its realization and to put both into public discourse in a way so that that gap is seen, so that that gap can mobilize."[46] Finding themselves accused of wrongdoing, both Biro and Ernesto seek to turn the legal system that denies them the right to be in the United States into a tool with which to activate their rights in the United States.

Biro's entire soliloquy is framed as a plea to a lawyer. Dire as his situation is, Biro has not resigned himself to it. The very legal system that crushes him offers the possibility of a victory needed to motivate his ongoing struggle. Biro has an urgent need to tell his story because a part of him believes that The Law will somehow understand, pardon, and perhaps even help him. Biro retains some hope that the US legal system will recognize his humanity; he asserts what he believes is his right to be heard. Biro thus begins to break through the dehumanizing discipline prompted by immigration law by sharing his narrative.

Narrative indeed functions to dispute the law. Peter Brooks proposes that telling stories

> serves to convey meanings excluded or marginalized by mainstream legal thinking and rhetoric. Narrative has a unique ability to embody the concrete experience of individuals and communities, to make other voices heard, to contest the very assumptions of legal judgment. Narrative is thus a form of countermajoritarian argument, a genre for oppositionists intent

on showing up the exclusions that occur in legal business-as-usual—a way of saying, you cannot understand until you have listened to our story.

Biro places his trust in a lawyer to fight for the right to make his story public, just as Ernesto does with his attorney, Nathan. In pursuing such a right, Biro and Ernesto stake claims for inclusion. They boldly step outside nonexistence and reposition themselves in relation to the state. Doing so is not only an affirmation of rights but also a critical step in the ever-changing process of identity formation. As Engel and Munger write, "The perception of boundaries wrongly marked is inseparable from the sense of self."[47] By insisting on having their stories heard, Ernesto and Biro maintain their innocence and simultaneously affirm a presence that the law denies. Made to perform the role of defendant or claimant in a US court, each man, who theoretically does not have the right to be in the United States, exercises a right to be seen, to be heard, and hence to be present while still in the United States.

In this manner, Biro and Ernesto work toward performances that can "puncture" disciplining mechanisms, to reference Foucault. We might approach Nathan or Biro's soon-to-be lawyer as directors or acting coaches who can empower performers by stressing their rights, urging them to transcend the "small theatres, in which each actor is alone, perfectly individualized and constantly visible," that a disciplining system seeks to construct.[48] In *Los Illegals*, characters such as Kim and Carmen, respectively an immigrant rights advocate and a manager at the workers' center, play similar directorial roles. By making the undocumented workers aware of their accorded rights, Kim and Carmen encourage a different kind of performance from those without papers, one that cannot so easily be conducted by immigration authorities. For example, when the police arrive to make the first arrests in connection with the alleged assault at Gloria's home, Carmen and Kim immediately intervene. The former adamantly avers that the police will "need to provide a translator," as the latter adds that no interrogation can take place "without a lawyer present" (*LI* 95). By calling attention to rights and entitlements, Carmen and Kim alter the landscape of legal nonexistence, pointing to the inconsistencies and limits of exclusion.

Importantly, *Los Illegals* and *Biro*, as cultural products, can also serve to direct alternate types of performances from within spaces of nonexistence. Just as narratives of punishment and disappearance share in making law's power tangible, so can stories contribute to broadcasting rights. Like the other plays I have examined, *Biro* and *Los Illegals* participate in what Coutin identifies as a critical project of challenging characterizations of the undocumented as undesirable and as erasures. More positive visibility, Coutin concludes, enables those without papers to claim legal rights. The growing phenomenon of young men and women living in undocumentedness "coming out" attests to the power of coordinated, affirmative visibility.[49] From award-winning journalist Jose Antonio Vargas disclosing his undocumented status in a *New York Times* column to "DREAMer" Benita Veliz speaking prominently during the 2012 Democratic National Convention, from Dulce Matuz appearing as one of *Time* magazine's "100 most influential people" to Jose Luis Zelaya's headline-grabbing run for Texas A&M University student body president, the stories of perseverance and achievement within undocumentedness prove a key tool with which to counter stereotypes of criminality.

There is, however, a paradox inherent in assertions of rights. By invoking legal rights and equality, individuals in essence summon the authority of the law as protection. (The demonstrators Butler describes likewise call upon the "Star Spangled Banner" as "nuestro himno" [our anthem], so that the paradox haunts Butler's performative contradiction). While they empower themselves, these individuals at once cede control to the very legal system that would seek to disenfranchise them. Biro and Ernesto, entrusting lawyers to represent and defend their rights within the court system, simultaneously validate the legitimacy of US law. Merry makes clear that "resistance within law is available only to already disciplined subjects. As resistance moves inside the law instead of outside of it, the law itself, as a privileged arena of contest over power, is strengthened."[50] Moreover, by activating their legal rights, Biro and Ernesto exemplify a logic that (dis)places the responsibility of change onto them. It is those in undocumentedness, assisted and encouraged by advocates, who must find a way to better the injustices they face. Citizens, employers, governments, and consumers, in other words, are not liable for modifying a system that creates nonexistence. Only *after* those who are legally nonexistent demand their rights of inclusion, to borrow Engel and Munger's title, should adjustments to that system be made. And given the myriad difficulties associated with legal nonexistence, demanding that change come from within such a space prolongs the status quo.

Laws do change. Three years after *Los Illegals* premiered, the US Court of Appeals for the Ninth Circuit decided with *Comite de Jornaleros de Redondo Beach v. Redondo Beach* that municipalities can block day laborers from soliciting work on certain public sidewalks and streets. Under new local ordinances, the claims to rightful presence on the sidewalk that *Los Illegals* stages cease to mean as much. The ruling neatly fits into the pattern of increased criminalization. Yet, as Coutin's studies indicate, the US immigration system creates its own disjunctures. The judge's ruling in *Los Illegals* exemplifies this point. After the group of laborers claims collective responsibility for Gloria's damaged wall, the judge dismisses the assault charge against Ernesto and Gloria pays the worker his due. Despite its disciplining power, the court ultimately legitimizes Ernesto's purported illegal labor as well as his unauthorized presence in the United States. "I'm here' is Ernesto's final line (*LI* 118). The endpoint in Mwine's play is considerably less hopeful. But Biro's closing plea for help contains the slim possibility that he, too, might be—or at least can be—legitimized. Coutin emphasizes that US immigration law regularly redraws its own limits "so that activities and persons that were once in the domain of the illegal are now (and therefore always were) on the road to legality."[51] The line between legal and illegal is often indistinct and unstable. Showcasing such instability surfaces as a strategy with which to resist and perhaps transcend nonexistence. Before considering how *Los Illegals* and *Biro* imagine tools for this kind of resistance, it is crucial to address how the erosion of one group's rights wears away the rights of all. Such a context makes the need for resistance all the more pressing.

Fine Lines

Although *Los Illegals* and *Biro* are post-9/11 plays, neither focuses great attention on the terrorist attacks themselves. (Briefly, Biro underscores that his plans to bribe an immigration officer collapsed along with the Twin Towers [*BI* 829–30].) But it is important to heed the mutual constructions of "illegal immigrant" and "terrorist" in order to grasp how divisions between citizens and noncitizens become increasingly concretized and naturalized. To that end, I want to bring into my discussion Yussef El Guindi's *Back of the Throat*, which premiered in 2005 as a coproduction of Thick Description and Golden Thread Productions in San Francisco and has since been staged regularly in the United States and abroad.

El Guindi stages an encounter between two government officials, Bartlett and Carl, and Khaled, an Arab/Muslim American writer. Through the course of the play, whose title refers to the initial sound required to pronounce "Khaled," we discover the agents believe the writer has some connection to Asfoor, an infamously savage terrorist. Khaled maintains his innocence. What begins as a polite, almost friendly exchange morphs into a violent, demeaning ordeal that leaves Khaled stripped and debilitated. Early on, the writer alerts the two federal agents that he is a US citizen (*BT* 14). *Back of the Throat*, unlike the other plays I analyze in this book, does not in fact present undocumented characters or reference immigrating without proper papers. Yet, it is vital to my study because El Guindi's reflection on post–9/11 realities for Arab/Muslim Americans evocatively stages the increasingly blurry and blurred limits of legal nonexistence. The violence and dehumanization experienced by the workers in *Los Illegals* and by the imprisoned Biro must be understood in relation to the violence and dehumanization to which Khaled is subjected. Likewise, we can more productively approach the seemingly extraordinary measures undertaken by the US government in the name of Homeland Security when we connect them with pre–9/11 approaches to undocumented immigration.

Analyzing US policies after September 11, particularly the treatment of noncitizen detainees, Giorgio Agamben suggests that measures such as the Patriot Act and the Enhanced Border Security and Visa Entry Reform Act (EBSVERA) have ushered in a new order, one that "radically erases any legal status of the individual, thus producing a legally unnamable and unclassifiable being." A "state of exception," justified by the US government to prevent other terrorist attacks, has created "an anomic space in which what is at stake is a force of law without law." Such space legitimizes "a legal civil war that allows for the physical elimination not only of political adversaries but of entire categories of citizens who for some reason cannot be integrated into the political system."[52] Indeed, as reported by Amnesty International in 2002 (and as later admitted by the Department of Justice), post–9/11 state procedures gravely infringed on basic rights guaranteed under international law, violating, among others, "the right to humane treatment, as well as rights which are essential to protection from arbitrary detention, such as the right of anyone deprived of their liberty to be informed of the reasons for the detention; to be able to challenge the lawfulness of the detention; to have prompt access to and assistance from a lawyer; and to the presumption of innocence."[53]

The seeming exceptionality of post–9/11 policies aids in the construction of other ostensibly extraordinary phenomena. Bayoumi describes the astonishing manner in which Arab and Muslim were instantly constructed as a new "identity under siege," pushed into a discourse of criminality "with a bang." He proposes that since the planes hit, Arabs and Muslims, transformed from being "virtually unknown to most Americans" to being "the first new communities of suspicion after the hard-won victories of the civil-rights era." Dalia Basiouny similarly posits that the "formation of a new identity for Arab Americans" began on September 11, 2001. A relatively "invisible" minority pre–9/11, Arab/Muslim Americans suddenly found themselves "thrust into blatant 'negative' visibility," a new "face of the enemy."[54]

It is certainly the case, as Nguyen carefully documents, that post–9/11 security efforts shepherded palpable, almost instantaneous changes.

Government agencies shifted to more blatant profiling techniques based on ethnicity, race, nationality, gender, and religion. It is also the case that post–9/11 operations targeted, at least initially, Arab/Muslim Americans and Arab nationals much more forcefully than other groups or communities. But it is important to remember that the state of exception appears less exceptional once we consider the spaces of legal nonexistence into which undocumented immigrants were placed *before* September 11, 2001. Neither Bayoumi nor Basiouny, for example, considers the construction of a "new" identity in conjunction with categories seemingly reserved for groups other than Arab/Muslim Americans. Nor does Allan Havis contemplate the subject of undocumented immigration as part of post–9/11 theatre that "reverberate[s] in the wake of our nation's ordeal."[55] Still, a model for erasing legal statuses, producing impossible subjects, and eliminating those deemed unintegrable into the political system was already very much in place before the attacks. Throughout the post–Civil Rights 1990s, many communities were already the targets of suspicion and criminalization under the lenses of border security and illegal immigration. Undocumented immigrants had, in the decade before 9/11, also moved from relative invisibility to negative visibility, perhaps with less of a bang but nonetheless as a result of government persecution.

The logic of policies collapsing unauthorized immigration and terrorism falls apart when confronted with hard evidence (so does the logic of collapsing unauthorized immigration with violent crime). Targeting immigrants has not led to the capture of terrorists, immigration-related efforts have drained resources from more productive intelligence operations, and anti-immigrant policies have prevented cooperation during investigations. These approaches have actually fomented anti–United States sentiments both at home and abroad.[56] But the muddling of the two phenomena served the state well to achieve many of its post–9/11 objectives. After all, the federal government already had exceptionally broad regulatory power over immigrants, legal or not. Nguyen details how George W. Bush's administration took advantage of immigration laws in order to hold suspects "in a system where officials had almost absolute discretion, instead of charging them in the criminal justice system, where they would have more legal rights, including access to a free lawyer." Through the use of laws and precedents that divide citizens and noncitizens, the US government already had mechanisms in place to make "individuals vulnerable to abduction, to being pulled through the hole that illegal personhood creates within legal jurisdictions," in the words of Coutin.[57] What we might deem "exceptional," then, is not so much the actual techniques undertaken by the state, but rather its manipulation of legal categories. The attacks of September 11 reenergized, but did not create, the growing criminalization of immigrants. They facilitated a collapse in categories, mobilized the use of racialized anti-illegal immigration, anticrime, antiterrorism rhetoric against *all* noncitizens, and superimposed the (il)logic of a legal/illegal divide into a broader citizen/noncitizen split.[58] In short, the nightmarish world of *Back of the Throat* is less the product of exceptions than of continuations and rejustifications.

El Guindi explains that his play emerged originally as a "paranoid thought game." He admits that, after the passage of the Patriot Act, stories about Arab/Muslim Americans coming under scrutiny led him to lose his grasp on his own rights: "In this climate, where one feared officials needing to look and act tough and avoid allowing more terrorists through the net, I personally, on a visceral level, found myself fearing a knock at the door." He began to wonder what his own apartment would reveal to federal agents, which of his possessions "might alarm" officials conducting inquiries.[59] In the play, Khaled at first complies, eagerly even, with the surprise search of his apartment. But as Bartlett and Carl construct a blameworthy portrait based on various objects around the home, Khaled begins to resist. Such resistance only fuels the agents' misgivings and, eventually, their violence.

I want to emphasize here three points regarding *Back of the Throat*. First, El Guindi's work draws attention to the frailty of legal categorizations. Second, it suggests the possibilities that exist when the state extends the aforementioned disciplinary mechanisms to new limits. And finally, the play prompts us to consider further the role that performance has in navigating post–9/11 procedures.

Early in the play, Khaled mentions his US citizenship and begins to assert what he believes are his rights. He defends his pornographic magazines as "legal," requests to call a lawyer, and then more generally begins to affirm that he has "rights" (*BT* 16, 20, 22, 25). Khaled voices that he has a right to privacy, a right to know why he is under investigation, and a right to refuse to cooperate with the agents. His invocation of rights, "*quiet*" at first (*BT* 22), culminates with more emphatic declarations: "This is my country too, you know. This is my country! It's my fucking country! [. . .] This is still America and I will not be treated this way!" (*BT* 25). Bartlett's retort railroads Khaled: "*This* is your fucking country. Right here, right now, in this room with us. You left the U.S. when you crossed the line, you piece of shit" (*BT* 26). But Khaled's claims to rights are invalidated because the arguably unjustified behavior of the agents is, as Agamben might describe it, a "perfectly 'juridical and constitutional' measure . . . realized in the production of new norms (or of a new juridical order)."[60] Bartlett seems to suggest that the new rule is that there are few or no rules. He asks Khaled, "What is more important: Inconveniencing you with accusations of having broken the law or ensuring the safety of everyone?" (*BT* 24). In the name of securing the nation, Bartlett insists that Khaled does not have the right to a lawyer. In fact, the only right Khaled holds is 'the right to cooperate with [his] intelligence and do the right thing" (*BT* 20).

Reminiscent of Kafka's *The Trial*, in which K.'s (Khaled's?) guilt is pre-supposed before there is even a trial, *Back of the Throat* projects a para-noid worldview. El Guindi admits to a certain absurdity.[61] But the play, sadly, stages anything but a farfetched encounter. Nguyen stresses the secrecy and intensity characteristic of post–9/11 detentions, the ways in which "closed hearings, combined with the Justice Department's refusal to release any names, meant that the detainees had entered a twilight zone where their families had no idea where they were, no idea of how long they would be held or what charges were being brought against them." Bayoumi likewise chronicles stories of Arab/Muslim Americans whisked from their daily lives into prisons without even hearing a formal charge, confronted by robotic government employees, and challenged by unpre-dictable, bureaucratically overwhelming procedures. Several of the sub-jects in Bayoumi's study describe their experiences as surreal, as works of fiction. El Guindi's paranoid thought game therefore proves especially frightening; as one reviewer admits, "it doesn't seem nearly as *implausible* as it ought to."[62]

Ultimately, Khaled's citizenship would have mattered, especially if he had had access to a lawyer. After all, it was precisely the precarious position of *non*citizens and the exploitation of immigration laws that provided the US government a pretext for persecuting individuals after September 11. Access to legal counsel—denied to Khaled in the play as it is to many noncitizens—is often critical to surpassing the many challenges posed by the tangle of immigration and DHS structures. Indeed, Khaled's almost instinctual request for a lawyer attests to a particularly privileged legal consciousness (or at least the performance of one). In invoking the right to counsel, Khaled at once assumes that the legal system will actually help him, that the services of a lawyer will be available to him, and that he will be able to afford legal representation. Effective, trustworthy lawyers are oftentimes unobtainable for those struggling in a space of nonexistence.

But as a foreign-born US citizen, as a *naturalized* rather than a *natural* citizen, Khaled's allegiance to the United States comes under the agents' scrutiny. When Khaled appeals to the Constitution as one of the reasons for his becoming a US citizen, Bartlett again snaps: "You became a citizen so you could indulge in your perverted little fantasies, you sick little prick. Come here, wrap the flag around you and whack off. *(He picks up a porn magazine.)* Well I don't particularly want your cum over everything I hold dear!" (*BT* 26). It has been noncitizens, both legal and not, who have suffered most under post–9/11 investigations, detentions, and deportations. Yet, *Back of the Throat* alerts us to the paradoxically thin line that separates noncitizens from citizens, particularly when profiling becomes institutionalized. Such a dividing line can be severe, as attested to in Bayoumi's account of citizens avoiding the nightmarish detention their noncitizen siblings could not. At the same time, when surface traits—skin tone, accent, religious garb, name—become the markers of "noncitizen," even citizens fall victim to the disciplining that the persecution of immigrants sets in place. Arizona's SB 1070 law, to offer one notable example, has solidified the notion that "looking Latino" means "appearing suspicious," regardless of citizenship or immigration status.[63]

A brief account from El Guindi's own life exemplifies the erosion of his citizenship. The story illuminates how governmental targeting of a vulnerable group jeopardizes everyone's freedoms. In an instance of what Bayoumi describes as "flying while brown," El Guindi confesses:

> I had to fly to San Francisco from Seattle...after take-off I was sitting there wanting to get up and go to the restroom. And I thought: I better not. I had better not go to the restroom, because people might get a little nervous. I remember sitting there and thinking: "This is insane. I want to go to the restroom, but I'm not getting up because I'm worried that I might unsettle my fellow passengers." Generally, after 9/11, I began to feel a bit outside the pale, a bit alienated, because my ethnic group was being scrutinized. It was like a spotlight being turned on one for all the wrong reasons. People were just very suspicious.[64]

Petrified of calling attention to himself, El Guindi demonstrates the power of state authority to discipline even basic biological needs. His paralysis results from a combined awareness of law (the Patriot Act), stories about law (others' encounters with government agents), and mistrust of those around him (his fellow passengers). Khaled similarly feels an overdetermined pressure to perform "normal" (*BT* 19) and thus avoid undue suspicion. It is not only the two agents scavenging through his apartment that produce this pressure, although they are its clearest manifestation. Surrounded by rumors about other investigations, Khaled fears also the possibility that anyone and everyone around him is a potential informant.

We find here a seamless extension of the disciplinary system set in place by immigration law. Not only does the play illustrate how the power struggle between immigration authorities and individuals now takes place at unpredictable moments and in everyday spaces, much like Khaled's apartment. *Back of the Throat* also proposes that such a struggle now involves individuals seemingly outside immigration law's reach: citizens. What constitutes noncitizenship becomes murky in El Guindi's cautionary tale. Khaled desperately tries to establish himself as a "patriotic" US citizen with minimal ties to the Arab world. He dismisses the Koran in his apartment as merely "a present from [his] mother" (*BT* 12), for instance, and avers he does not speak Arabic (*BT* 16). The September 11 attacks, El Guindi believes, urged an intensified consideration over "who counts as a real American." "But what were the criteria? It wasn't quite understood," he explains. Khaled's need to prove his belonging to the United States, to maintain his innocence by claiming so-called normalcy, points to broader disciplinary practices intended to prevent the attention of immigration authorities and a policing citizenry. Speaking English in public, changing names, wearing particular articles of clothing, reducing so-called accents, all of these performative practices must be understood as part of a broader disciplinary system underpinned by immigration law and its power to deport. (Alongside the criminalization detailed in this chapter, English-only rules have also increased since the 1990s, with new public regulations seeking to control not only what language can be used in certain locations and situations but also the accent and syntax of speakers in fields such as education).[65] Managing racial and ethnic differences certainly plays a key role in the disciplining process, though we must avoid too-easy conclusions about what this means. Many Arab/Muslim Americans, for example, in attempts to "pass as other-than-Arab" in a post–9/11 United States have adopted Latino names,[66] urging a more subtle approach to categorical assumptions about who "counts" as American.

Questions about "real Americans," in addition to anchoring issues of discipline, allude to the role that performance plays in practices of distinction. Regardless of Khaled's guilt or innocence, the agents' strategy requires that he be stripped not only of legal rights but also of his humanity. To this end, the agents must take on an almost theatrical role, a mask, through which they can distance themselves from Khaled. I would thus argue with critics that fault a production of *Back of the Throat* for offering "cardboard" agents, as Neil Genzlinger does in his review.[67] The flatness of the characters is critical in understanding the mutually dehumanizing process that is at play. Throughout the play, agents Bartlett and Carl draw attention to their performance. At one point Bartlett calmly explains, "We're switching from being civil and congenial to being hard-nosed and focused. It will have the effect of taking away from your humanity and it doesn't do much for ours" (*BT* 24). They arrange furniture in Khaled's apartment with theatrical precision and rely on a sort of script, a "*small guidebook*," for the necessary directions with which to "bring the full weight of our authority" (*BT* 41). Khaled understands what is happening and accuses the agents of "*acting* like" thugs (*BT* 25, my emphasis). But it becomes clear that Khaled has little control over a performance that has precast him both as criminal in and author of the drama.

El Guindi explains his interest in showing how an individual can easily be "forced, kicking and screaming, into someone else's narrative... and then find himself unable to extricate himself from these stories."[68] This is precisely what happens in *Back of the Throat*, as the agents' interviews with different women in Khaled's life take over the stage and implicate him in meetings and conversations that might or might not have ever taken place. Unwilling to concede any of the accusations, Khaled nonetheless ends up participating in the reconstructed encounters. With Khaled playing himself in the flashbacks or memories or fictionalized accounts, it becomes difficult, if not impossible, to determine what is real. "I don't know who you're talking about anymore; it's not me," he insists (*BT* 35).

Yet, Bartlett and Carl quite efficiently attribute their performances to Khaled, assigning him authorship of the narrative. Carl insists:

> If you were innocent, why would I have kicked you? Something you've done has given me good cause to assume the worst. The responsibility for that kick lies with your unwillingness to assume responsibility for the part we know you played. We need to know what that was. It might have been a bit part, but never think that makes you a bit player. (*BT* 41–42)

The roles that Carl and Bartlett understand themselves to be playing become, in their eyes, Khaled's manufacture. By play's end, the logic of the performance that the agents initiated flips, so that responsibility lies entirely in Khaled's hands. "You know what I really resent?" Carl asks rhetorically to a beaten-up Khaled, "What you force us to become" (*BT* 43). *Back of the Throat* thus presents, at an intimate level, the same kind of spectacularity required of large-scale immigration enforcement efforts. On the one hand, the government officials portray undaunted, dehumanized seriousness in their efforts to maintain so-called law and order. On the other, that very performance criminalizes its targets, precasting individuals into already established, legally categorized roles in order to justify and exonerate itself from wrongdoing.

Agamben warns that inherent to the state of exception is a "vicious circle": emergency measures instituted in the name of securing a democracy inevitably lead to a state's demise.[69] *Back of the Throat* serves as a warning. The play not only stages Khaled's state-enforced dehumanization. It ominously admonishes against such a vicious cycle. Bartlett and Carl, after all, force Khaled into a specific blameworthy narrative but simultaneously foreshadow another use for that narrative. "You really give a bad name to immigrants, you know that," Carl throws in Khaled's face. The agent continues, "Because of you we have to pass tougher laws that stop people who might actually be good for us" (*BT* 42–43). Khaled, pushed into the role of alien enemy, legitimizes and naturalizes the government's policing efforts while displacing the production of criminality onto the so-called criminal. In the play's present, such a process is clearly directed against Arab/Muslim Americans, even an Arab/Muslim American citizen, but El Guindi does not let such process exist in a vacuum. As Bartlett rationalizes, "Yesterday the Irish and the Poles, today it's you. Tomorrow it might be the Dutch" (*BT* 23). When the state pushes some into spaces of nonexistence, where individuals can be "disappeared into little atom-sized pieces of nothingness" (*BT* 29), its entire population—citizen and noncitizen; legal and illegal; Latina/o, Muslim, Ugandan, or Dutch—risks finding itself in the dark shadow of the law.

The Power of Performance

Mangandi, who besides playing Ernesto in Cornerstone's *Los Illegals* has served as artistic director for Teatro Jornalero Sin Fronteras, admits that no play or theatre company will change the world. With assured optimism however, he acknowledges that the kind of dialogue a play might prompt as well as the nuances it can reveal become critical to advancing a particular cause. Mwine likewise concedes that it is difficult to measure the effects his work may prompt, but he is confident that his play has "opened up dialogue on a number of issues that had been swept under the rug."[70] To date, *Biro* has surfaced more actively as a tool to promote conversations about HIV/AIDS than about immigration issues, especially as Mwine has toured and performed the play alongside AIDS-prevention workshops. Nevertheless, based on live audience responses and on correspondence he has received, Mwine believes his performances also draw attention to the harsh circumstances immigrants encounter in the United States and to the ways in which "we tend to oversimplify" conversations about immigration.[71] *Los Illegals*, *Biro*, and *Back of the Throat*, like other plays I have discussed in this study, attest to the power of theatre to spur dialogue and advance ideas that rise above the reduced sound bites often surrounding immigration debates.

The unlikely production processes for *Los Illegals* and *Biro* perhaps have allowed for particularly silenced points of view to emerge as well as for broader access to performances. For example, Cornerstone's community-based focus allows for a theatre-making and consumption process that transcends the kind of "undocumentedface" I discuss in chapter 3.

By providing a small honorarium but not directly employing certain per-formers and crew members, and by offering productions to audiences at a pay-what-you-can rate, Cornerstone encourages a kind of participation other professional endeavors do not. Anne García-Romero, who served as a dramaturg in Cornerstone's Justice Cycle, considers the company's commitment to including members of the community in every step of the production, from development to performance, to be unique. In the case of Los Illegals, this meant the deliberate inclusion of actors living in undocumentedness.[72] Mwine defied his agents in Los Angeles, who believed Biro's subject matter was unmarketable. He took out a loan, sold some of his photographic work, and premiered the production in Uganda.[73] Mwine then toured extensively with the show, bringing Biro to a varied range of performance venues in the United States and abroad. But, Biro and Los Illegals, especially, reveal other ways in which theatre and performance can intervene in the (un)making of legal/illegal catego-ries and thus problematize Back of the Throat's doomed, but plausible, vision.

In chapter 2, I propose that Real Women Have Curves exemplifies a type of performance that asserts a way of being. I would like to fine-tune my proposition and underscore that performance can become a means to assert rights. Kuftinec allows that, beyond the collaborative nature of theatre-making, the very act of public performance can prove empower-ing for those under the limelight. Some of the actors in Cornerstone's Los Illegals (the cast consisted of 10 professional actors and 20 local laborers) indeed found the performance an occasion to defy disenfranchisement and abuse. "How many people dream of standing up to bosses who take advantage of us but never do it?" asks María Refugio Jacinto (Yolanda). The play offers just that opportunity. Cornerstone artist Lorena Moreno proposes a related perspective, explaining that theatre can change an audience by first changing a participant's consciousness. She believes that creating theatre provides day laborers like herself "un aliento" (courage) to persevere.[74] Studying undocumented workers and unions, Bacon mar-vels at the efficacy of theatrical practice to alter its participants. He quotes labor organizer and theatre-maker Juan Carrillo: "If you can demand your rights from an employer in a play, then you can do it in life." Recalling Engel and Munger's conception of identity and rights, we can see how the shifts in consciousness precipitated by performance, however slight, must necessarily alter the performers' self-perceptions as well as their relation-ships to others. A play about immigrant rights not only "become[s] buffer and balm" against harsh realities, as a critic at the National Labor College convention observes.[75] It also surfaces as a means to alter those realities.

Nevins cautions that meaningful change will come if and when we escape the "prison that is the national imagination." Only then can we create a "transnational integrationist vision" that "puts humanity above national citizenry." *Los Illegals* and *Biro* suggest a possible course for activating Nevins's charge. In performance, Garcés's and Mwine's works attempt to forge, at least momentarily, an integrated community. They strive to build the kind of "we" that Butler insists might "not suffice as efficacious action but that constitutes one of its minimally necessary conditions."[76] For example, Mwine chooses to have Biro speak straight to the audience and casts spectators not only as lawyers but as his last hope. In so doing, Mwine insists on making us all part of Biro's plight. There is no outside, as reviewers seem to agree: "In one stroke, we become part of the play," "the audience has no choice but to be rapt," and the performance therefore has the potential to "move anyone without a heart of stone," to get "under your skin and stay there."[77] Addressed to and not just for the audience, the play's final "Please / Help me" (*BI* 922) encourages spectators to imagine what they can or cannot do for Biro. Either way, Biro's struggles and his illegal status become, for a moment, ours as well.

Similarly, reviewer Catherine Wall notes of Cornerstone's *Los Illegals* that she felt "as if we [the audience] too were laborers waiting for work, surrounded, in effect, by the conflicted voices of the 'los illegals' issue."[78] Director Shishir Kurup encouraged this reaction with an environmental staging in the actual parking lot at the Armory Center for the Arts in Pasadena. He asked audience members to sit alongside actors at several picnic tables suggesting the workers' meeting space and literally to occupy a middle space through which the various disagreeing viewpoints traversed. The audience watched amid the action, with little choice but to let the play occur, not in front of, but all around them. The play itself demands a certain engagement, particularly the scene immediately prior to the court proceedings. When Jimmy first suggests that all the laborers have committed Ernesto's alleged crime—"Who hasn't felt in his breast the desire, the need, to scream? [...] we did it! Every one of us!"—he charges the group to take collective responsibility. Compellingly, he shifts from "we did it" to "even you" (*LI* 111), addressing both his fellow workers and the audience at once. Kurup staged Jimmy to weave through the various tables, pointing directly at audience members with several repetitions of "even you." And that involvement, of the *you* as opposed to only the *we*, insists on countering the belief that immigration issues are only about immigrants and immigration authorities. Indeed, by pointing out how the *you* is part of the whole, the play makes it more difficult to differentiate an *us* from a *them*.

I return to the way in which the workers disrupt Ernesto's legal proceeding. The judge pushes Ernesto to admit his guilt. But before Ernesto
has a chance to answer, Omar stands up from among the spectators and
claims responsibility. The judge asks for order; a crescendo of voices and
bodies comes forth with "Yes! I did it!" in both English and Spanish.
Garcés's script carefully layers the buildup, asking Omar, Translator/
Jimmy/Omar, the workers in the courtroom, all workers, and finally
"todo el mundo" (everyone) to come forth, their voices "HUGE" (LI 114).
Kurup had each additional confessor stand proudly, raising a hand to call
attention to his or her guilt. Although the moment came to a quick end,
perhaps preventing willing audience members from rising as well, many
of the same bodies who earlier sat among and were at one point indis-
tinguishable from the audience now took a defiant stand in support of
Ernesto. Before the scene shifts, the judge simply says, "Well, this is a new
one" (LI 114). Were she familiar with Spanish Golden Age theatre, the
judge would know there is nothing new about the spectacle. Garcés draws
directly from Fuente Ovejuna to empower his characters to take charge of
Ernesto's trial. The unusual display, we will soon learn, leads to the man's
release. While this denouement perhaps ignores certain legal realities, the
moment does propose an alternative to the "status quo [that is] seemingly
not even imaginable given how profoundly national territory and its ideological and material expressions have become embedded in our ways of
seeing the world," in Nevins's words.[79]

The proposal is not strictly a theatrical happy ending. A brief example
might well illustrate how the legal/illegal divide can crumble in the face of
such collective performance: The College Republicans club of New York
University sponsored a "Catch the Illegal Immigrant" game in February
2007. The controversial event, conceived originally in 2006 by a College
Republican National Committee field representative in Michigan and
still staged in various campuses around the United States, was purportedly intended to prompt dialogue and debate. The game was simple in
its design. Interested students signed up to "be" immigration enforcement agents at a table in Washington Square Park; at an appointed hour,
a member of the club would circulate through campus wearing an "illegal immigrant" sign; whichever agent spotted the sign-bearer first would
win a $50 gift card. But hundreds of protesters wearing signs flooded the
area, many donning the same label of "illegal immigrant."[80] In so marking themselves, the protestors therefore disrupted and nullified the seemingly clear lines established by the club. The few agents trying to spot
the illegal immigrant were forced to navigate an ocean of marked bodies
performing "illegality." Much like the thwarted trials in Los Illegals and
Fuente Ovejuna, the hunt thus proved nearly impossible.

Together, such events suggest how a performance that showcases a shared humanity by making individuals visible and present can defy, at least theoretically, the marks of illegality. And the techniques through which *Los Illegals* and *Biro* engage their audiences point to the possibility of forging, even if just for a moment, a sense of collective responsibility for the violence inherent to spaces of legal nonexistence. Even if the law remains, the line between "citizen" and "noncitizen," between "guilty" and "innocent," between "legal" and "illegal" fades in the face of these performances.

6

Act § 505—Appeals

The plays I examine in this book span several decades and attest to varied production contexts. Together, they have offered a window into undocumentedness. More than that, they have illuminated for me connections among law, performance, and identity. I hope my analysis serves to underscore the power of legal labels vis-a-vis processes of identity formation, both at individual and collective levels. Furthermore, I hope it points to the role that performance plays in both resisting and in policing the limits of those labels. I have found that theatre, as exemplified by many of the works I discuss, has the potential to confront audiences with complex questions that often go unasked in other media. Theatre can offer visibility and dignity to a depressingly large population that is dismissed in so many ways. Spaces that other scholars describe in terms of "shadows," "darkness," "invisibility" become, onstage, spaces to spotlight flesh-and-blood human beings. Throughout my study, I have looked for the ways in which turning nonexistence and invisibility into stageworthy performances can puncture nonexistence. While I therefore celebrate theatre that calls attention to and advocates for those in undocumentedness, I have also questioned how theatre production and scholarship perpetuate certain forms of exploitation.

In lieu of offering neat conclusions or answers, I would like to use the final pages of this study to crack open my own approach. Let us leave the space of professional theatres and consider another type of performance. Let us also reconsider the proposition that US law shapes individual identities and contemplate instead how individuals marked "illegal" reshape the United States. To these ends, let us travel to present-day Times Square.

With annual visitors approaching a staggering 40 million, Times Square in New York City is perhaps the world's most-visited tourist attraction. Its nickname—the Crossroads of the World—is perhaps an appropriate characterization for the iconic location. The Times Square Alliance wears the moniker with pride and promotes the densely packed piece of Manhattan real estate as not only a crossroads but also an undeniable center of power. The "world's most dynamic public space" "can be neither replicated nor subdued," as touted by the Alliance in its website.[1] Issues of immigration law and performance point to alternate ways with which to approach this alleged dynamism. This is because, alongside an increasingly globalized commercial theatre industry so central to the Times Square experience, there exists a growing form of immigrant street performances. These performances alter not only the physical space of Times Square but also the events and exchanges that happen at the crossroads. In so doing, the street performances transform Times Square, from a place of intersections to a site of collisions. Indeed, multiple realities collide at Times Square causing its centrality—and by extension, that of the United States—to budge, however slightly.

Following its so-called Disneyfication, which started in the 1990s, as well as its more recent transformation by Mayor Michael Bloomberg's administration into a pedestrian plaza, Times Square is now witness to a new strain of Disneyfication. Street performers have propagated in the area. One man donning an Elmo costume and posing with tourists soon led to a growing cast of Mickeys, Minnies, Grovers, and other Elmos populating the streets. Other performers, including the well-known Naked Cowboy, had claimed the new Times Square as a performance space over a decade ago. But the increase in pedestrian traffic as well as the economic downturn of 2008 have led to a sharp increase in the number of street performers. Although there are Hello Kittys, Smurfs, and SpongeBob SquarePants as well, one can observe that the bulk of the characters currently appearing in Times Square are part of the Disney family. As they pose for photographs with passersby, the characters expand the theatrical space that is so inherently linked to Times Square. In fact, tiered bleachers above the TKTS Discount Booth at the core of the plaza plainly transform the outdoor space into a theatre of sorts, what the *New York Times* describes as "the best seats on Broadway."[2] Giant screens projecting live video feed and photographs from the streets reinforce the notion that what is happening at street level merits our spectatorship.

It is important to view the work that the Mickeys do as a performance, not simply because their interactions with passersby occur in a theatricalized space. The Mickeys of Times Square use their bodies to attract attention. Their goal is to invite people to wave, stop, and pose for photos in exchange for cash tips. While the full-body costumes garner notice, it is the individuals underneath who must activate presence. Drawing from Eugenio Barba's ideas about actors, we might say that the Mickeys are "decided bodies" which seek extra-daily attention.[3] Their success, measured by the crowds they attract as well as by the tips they receive, depends on their expert portrayal of beloved, well-known characters.

More crucially, when seen as performers, the Mickeys gain some measure of legal protection. The City of New York can regulate a few aspects of the performances, including bans for certain locations and times. Performers can be cited for blocking traffic or for disorderly conduct. Since money is being collected in the form of tips, the police can ask performers for (expensive) vendor licenses or tax IDs. Critically however, the First Amendment allows the performers some level of freedom to continue their work. Constitutionally, anyone can don a costume and express him or herself publicly. This means that many of the shows happening at street level in Times Square cannot be easily controlled. In fact, the New York City Police Department (NYPD) has deliberately slowed its active pursuit of street performers. Even the companies that own the trademarks for the characters have little incentive to stop performances that arguably help rather than hinder their business. Given that the performers are "not really harming anyone," as Russell Novack from Legal Aid explains, "no one seems interested in seriously prosecuting" them.[4] Accordingly, most legal charges levied against street performers often do not prove sustainable. This does not necessarily mean that the performers feel secure taking to the streets. Caramelito, a performer hailing from Peru whom I interviewed in September 2012, continues to be weary of the police, who have on occasion asked him for identification and warned him that his costume could be confiscated.[5] Nonetheless, the proliferation of street performers and the express assertion from the police that ticketing will slow down confirm that the practice for now is generally accepted and legitimate.

But other laws are being tested: many of the Mickeys are unauthorized immigrants.[6] They come predominantly from Peru, from Guatemala, from Mexico, from Colombia. While they have a right to free speech, they do not have the right to be in the United States. While they demand attention in order to earn tips, their undocumented status urges them to remain undetected. While they embody symbols of US capitalism and global culture, their own bodies are officially unrecognized by the United States. These are some of the contradictions that stem from a system that attracts and demands migrants and their labor but denies them legal personhood. Caught in the crux of these contradictions, the undocumented Mickeys of Times Square simultaneously bolster and undermine a world order that places the United States at its center.

To live and work in the United States without the legal right to do so, immigrants who lack authorization must work actively to erase their presence. Any undue attention carries with it the potential for destructive detention and deportation. Therefore, there are deep connections between undocumentedness and invisibility. The Mickeys of Times Square perform under transformative full-body costumes that aid in the process of erasure. A report in the *Wall Street Journal* depicts their process of changing into costume as a full metamorphosis, "from an undocumented immigrant from Peru whose grasp of English is tenuous to perhaps the most iconic American character of all time, Mickey Mouse."[7] Caramelito similarly refers to the transformative qualities of his costume. He feels an excitement when he puts the Mickey suit on, an excitement that helps him combat shyness and fear. "The costume hides me," he explains. We could approach the work that these immigrants do as part of the broader system of performances of disappearance made necessary by US immigration laws (see chapter 2).

However, the process of erasure here is complicated by the hypervisibility that the work itself demands. First, the performances in Times Square can potentially interrupt some of the damage caused to the individual by invisibility. As Mickey Mouse, José Luis Vásquez finds that "people come close to me, they hug me, they kiss me, smile at me." Such affection counters realities of living in undocumentedness. "When I don't have my costume on, people don't talk to me" confesses Vásquez, "They don't see you."[8] The work is grueling, especially because the furry suits prove tremendously hot, but the possibility for recognition and warmth can motivate performers to continue. Caramelito agrees that handling the heat is perhaps the most difficult aspect to the job. Yet, for him, the opportunity to bring joy to others and to receive a warm reception in return lets him overcome such a challenge. Second, the performances in Times Square defy conventional and stereotypical notions of undocumentedness that drive individuals to work unseen (e.g., cleaning private homes, washing dishes in restaurant kitchens, tending agricultural fields). Tourists and other passersby might not know or care who is inside the Mickey costume, but authorities are well aware that many of the performers lack proper immigration papers. While city authorities might not have the power or desire to enforce immigration law (and a post–*Arizona v. U.S.* regime may complicate this question), immigrants who place themselves so boldly on a public stage risk legal complications and apprehension. In so doing, the performers begin to claim a space in the United States by asserting rather than erasing their presence.

Reactions to the performers in Times Square seem to revolve more often on the quality of the performance than on the immigration status of the performers. It is only when the performers break character that they garner unwanted attention and perhaps punishment, both official and unofficial. A recent police intervention involving the street performers centered on a troublemaking Elmo whose anti-immigrant and anti-Semitic rants led to an apprehension. This particular Elmo liked to shout, among other offensive slurs, that other performers in Times Square are "all illegal immigrants" and therefore unworthy of photographs. The NYPD took the troublemaking Elmo into custody and ordered a psychological evaluation as onlookers applauded. The apprehension was much appreciated by other street performers, who continued to garner attention through character-appropriate presentations. After a Mario Brother groped a woman and a Cookie Monster shoved a toddler, City Councilman Peter Vallone introduced legislation that would ban or at least regulate these street performers.[9] But legal action might not be entirely necessary. Those who do not fully create a convincingly lovable character are shunned by their peers. "Overly aggressive characters" taint the work of those working hard to "put a smile on kids' faces." And potential audiences can be equally disciplining. A tourist stresses to a reporter investigating the Elmo incident that bad behavior from the characters is unlikely to be tolerated: "If they grabbed someone inappropriately, they'd be beaten half to death, at least where I come from they would."[10]

Although we see a version of the disciplinary system that I describe in chapters 4 and 5 very much in place in Times Square, it is important to note a palpable shift toward rewarding good work. Indeed, authorities prefer not to "lock up Elmo," in the words of Novack. What we could call *ticket*-me-Elmos draw undue attention and sympathy from onlookers, making interactions with the police more challenging. Videos posted on YouTube by tourists illustrate occasions in which a character's interacting with police generates palpable sympathy. "I feel so bad for Elmo. He's getting a ticket," bemoans a young woman watching two policemen interview an individual donning the furry red suit.[11]

Caramelito speaks with pride about his ability to stay in role. "From the moment I put on the costume, I feel within me, within my heart, that I am the character," he explains. Caramelito usually plays Mickey Mouse, although he has also donned the Minnie and the SpongeBob costumes. He underscores that anyone doing the work that he does "must feel the character." He loves to bring joy to children; their applause and smiles inspire him. "All summer is happiness for me," Caramelito shared with me. Breaking character would not earn him such *cariño* from young spectators. Caramelito is careful not to be seen out of costume. As do most of the street performers as well as their counterparts in Disney-owned settings like Disneyland and Disney World, Caramelito does not speak with his audiences. He relies on a CD player to incorporate children's songs into his routine. In role, the street performers communicate through and with the costume, endeavoring to express emotion physically. One reporter describes the "acting chops" developed by a Minnie Mouse to convince audience members to take photos. Another explains how the performers, deemed "impersonators," "hang their oversized heads in mock dismay" when a tip does not follow a photo.[12]

The act of placing themselves on display and, importantly, of claiming a First Amendment right as protection exemplifies what Judith Butler calls a "performative contradiction" (see chapter 5). Many of the men and women under the costumes do not have the right to be in the United States. The law prohibits them from being in Times Square. Yet, their performances not only claim but also flaunt their *here*-ness: look at us, photograph us, hug us. To paraphrase Butler, the performers are exercising a right they do not have. This exercise becomes a demand in incipient form, one that asserts equality in relation to an authority that precludes equality. This exercise announces and puts into public discourse an existing gap in rights, "so that that gap can mobilize."[13]

I do not wish to romanticize what is happening in Times Square. Like millions of other unauthorized immigrants, the performers are endeavoring to make a living and help support families in the United States and abroad. The work is arduous and the pay unpredictable; the dangers are many (Caramelito reveals that he is weary not only of police but also of passersby, notably teenagers, whose taunts he finds threatening). It is not difficult to see the performers as the products of neoliberalism's triumph. Nevertheless, it is also crucial to view the performances in Times Square as part of a broader web of performances of assertion that combat invisibility. We find this tactic increasingly in use. I return to the questions raised by journalist Jose Antonio Vargas that I introduce in chapter 1. Vargas insists that coming out as undocumented becomes a "game changer" for the immigration debate: "What happens when even more of us step forward? How will the U.S. government and American citizens react then?"[14]

While Vargas's questions are provocative and point to the critical importance of asserting existence, the street performers in Times Square become a pointed reminder of how difficult it is to gain meaningful visibility. They work in the epicenter of an industry that revolves around placing bodies and stories on display, an industry that arguably stages the United States to itself and to the rest of the world. Yet, the commercial theatre of Broadway has been reticent in recent decades to stage the struggles, or even the existence, of undocumentedness. Despite the great loudness with which immigration laws have been debated publicly since the late 1980s, there has been mostly silence around such issues on the Great White Way. With the exception of a handful of author/performer–devised shows (*Mambo Mouth, Bridge and Tunnel, Latinologues*), traditional Broadway fare has not highlighted unauthorized immigrants in its storylines since the 1950s, when *A View from the Bridge* and *Flower Drum Song* tackled the topic directly, if unrealistically (see chapter 1). As I argue in chapter 3, even off the stage, commercial theatre in the United States is an inhospitable arena for unauthorized immigrant workers. Perhaps unsurprisingly, when the television series *30 Rock* set a scene in midtown and featured the now ubiquitous street performers, the bodies under Elmo, Oscar the Grouch, and Cookie Monster turned to be ostensibly nonimmigrant (at least their speech was unmarked by any seemingly foreign accent).[15] Precisely because they are omitted from narratives, those living in undocumentedness must strive to make their presence felt.

The assertions to existence disrupt the dehumanization and violence that accompany the ever-increasing criminalization and punishment of immigration law violations. Moreover, such assertions endeavor to redefine undocumentedness by pointing to its ordinariness, indeed its essentiality, in increasingly globalized economies. Unauthorized immigrants are in the United States not only because they need to provide for their families, but also arguably because the United States requires their cheap labor and because their countries of origin require their remittances. Susan Coutin urges us to consider how a system of remittances complicates understandings of immigration patterns. Remittances prove at once a recognized alternative to foreign aid, an addictive source of income for sending countries, and a phenomenon that strengthens national allegiances while simultaneously fostering distance and separation.[16] The Mickeys of Times Square exemplify the intricate networks of exchange that turn the Crossroads of the World into a veritable vortex of resources. Like the performers themselves, the costumes worn often come from other countries; a significant percentage of the money earned returns to those countries. Earning an income to support her children in Peru, Isabel-as-Minnie carries a photo of her daughter in a dangling bracelet that becomes part of the costume. She interacts with little girls on the street who become a painful reminder of her six-year absence and a welcome source of surrogate affection. Her yearning for Peru has grown.[17]

On the one hand, the performer is swallowed whole by her costume. Consumed by and turned into a walking advertisement for Disney, she is unabashedly erased by global corporate interests and US law. On the other hand, wearing a costume not licensed by Disney in view of one of its flagship stores, generating income in a place that does not allow her to work, and transferring moneys across national borders, the performer defies, however slightly, a system designed to deny her agency. On the one hand, Isabel is clearly absent from her life in Peru. On the other hand, her links to Peru are bolstered when her so-called illegal presence in the United States becomes a recognized form of participation in Peruvian life. In 2010, remittances to Peru grew to $2.53 billion, making it the third biggest recipient in South America of moneys earned abroad. Clearly, the Peruvian government understands that much of this income is earned by immigrants living abroad without authorization. Its current official guide for immigrants includes help on how to manage undocumented-ness in the United States.[18] Such trends are not unique to Peru.

The Walt Disney Company has itself wielded tremendous influence to shape international flows of capital and of individuals. In a fascinating article, Kit Johnson traces the ways in which the company in essence penned its own chapter of US immigration law—the Q visa today is used for so-called cultural exchange workers and is known as the "Disney visa"—and subsequently reinvented such a visa program for increased profits.[19] As immigration control, Disney transforms into an entity that (re)defines nations. On a much smaller scale, Isabel likewise forges a personal immigration policy that helps her to increase her family's—and by extension, her homeland's—profits. Of course, Isabel must contend with the label of "illegal" that the US government does not pin on the Walt Disney Company. But it is important to see that in entering the United States without authorization and in sending money earned in one nation to another, Isabel, just like Disney, responds to, participates in, and reshapes the flow of resources across national borders.

Crucially, the performer therefore not only comes from but *becomes* Peru in such a process. Coutin proposes that the presence of unauthorized immigrants "transforms the places through which they travel." Because they "*displace* legal space," unauthorized immigrants in essence move with them the national borders that they have crossed. Coutin describes the journeys undertaken by unauthorized immigrants as incomplete. Because they are not legally allowed to occupy the space that they do, migrants living in the United States without proper authorization are not fully present. A part of them—their legal selves—remains elsewhere. Whereas tourists from outside the United States exist fully, if temporarily, in New York City when they visit, unauthorized immigrants are neither fully present in the United States (the law denies them such a possibility) nor fully gone from their nations of origin. We can conceive then, as Coutin does, unauthorized immigrants as sites at which "nations leak." It is worth quoting her fully:

> In that they embody both law and illegality, unauthorized migrants may disrupt and extend the bodies of various nations. Thus, unauthorized migrants "enter" national territories where they allegedly do not belong,

but, as beings rendered wholly alien, they also extend their own national territories.[20]

Mickeys and Minnies in Times Square might transform from immigrants to iconic American characters. But their performances resist full erasure and make present their countries of origin in New York City. This presence is not token or symbolic but material. Peru, Colombia, Mexico are *there*, in the *here* that the performers demand and in the exchanges of moneys that result from their labor. Precisely because the United States denies the performers full presence, their nations of origin appear in Times Square and demand involvement in the crossroads.

Once again, I do not mean to romanticize what is happening. By bringing their countries with them, the immigrant performers become absences. The girl whose photograph dangles from Minnie's wrist lives without her mother at home. The billions of dollars that Peru receives annually in remittances from abroad arguably do not fully alter its position within a US-dominated world system. Nonetheless, when we heed Coutin and see the performers not only as individuals but as nations in flux, we can conceive of their so-called illegality differently. It is Times Square that transforms. In this bowtie-shaped area—it is not a square—the world is not merely crossing paths, it is fully rupturing and folding into itself. Therein lies its true dynamism. Those sitting at the TKTS booth might catch sight of multiple Mickeys and Minnies urging passersby to take photos. Such performances easily go unnoticed as part of Times Square's celebrated energy. But it is an undeniably complicated show. With each tip, Minnie shapes international flows. With each photo, tourists unknowingly take with them not just a part of New York City but a part of Peru, of Ecuador, of Guatemala as well. And with each wave, Mickey asserts a right to exist where he is persistently denied existence.

Notes

1 Act § 237(a)(1)(B)—Present in Violation of Law

1. Mae M. Ngai, *Impossible Subjects: Illegal Aliens and the Making of Modern America* (Princeton: Princeton University Press, 2004), 5.
2. 8 U.S.C. § 1101(a)(3) (2013).
3. *The Associated Press Stylebook and Briefing on Media Law, 2013* (New York: Basic Books, 2013), 132–33; Deirdre Edgar, "L.A. Times Updates Guidelines for Covering Immigration," *Los Angeles Times*, Readers' Rep, 1 May 2013, latimes.com/news/local/readers-rep/la-me-rr-la-times-guidelines-immigration -20130501,0,5876110.story (accessed 17 May 2013); and Margaret Hartmann, "John McCain Isn't the Only Immigration Reformer Sticking with the 'I-Word,'" *New York* online, 29 March 2013, nymag.com/daily/intelligencer /2013/03/mccain-isnt-the-only-senator-using-the-i-word.html (accessed 8 April 2013).
4. I cite Albán's unpublished script for the INTAR production. References are noted parenthetically and abbreviated *I*.
5. Susan Bibler Coutin, *Legalizing Moves: Salvadoran Immigrants' Struggle for U.S. Residency* (Ann Arbor: University of Michigan Press, 2000), 34; Susan Bibler Coutin, *Nations of Emigrants: Shifting Boundaries of Citizenship in El Salvador and the United States* (Ithaca: Cornell University Press, 2007), 5.
6. Coutin, *Nations of Emigrants*, 197.
7. Coutin, *Legalizing Moves*, 41.
8. Michel Foucault, *Discipline & Punish: The Birth of the Prison*, trans. Alan Sheridan (New York: Vintage, 1977); Coutin, *Legalizing Moves*, 43–46.
9. Josefina López, "Playwright's Notes," *Real Women Have Curves* (Woodstock, IL: Dramatic Publishing, 1996), 5 (boldface in original); John Leguizamo, *Mambo Mouth*, in *The Works of John Leguizamo* (New York: Harper, 2008), 217–18.
10. Harold Fernandez, *Undocumented* (Mustang, OK: Tate Publishing, 2012), 61; Ramón "Tianguis" Pérez, *Diary of an Undocumented Immigrant*, trans. Dick J. Reavis (Houston: Arte Público Press, 1991), 47; and Helen Thorpe, *Just Like Us: The True Story of Four Mexican Girls Coming of Age in America* (New York: Scribner, 2009), 45–46.
11. Joseph Nevins, *Operation Gatekeeper and Beyond: The War on "Illegals" and the Remaking of the U.S.-Mexico Boundary* (New York: Routledge, 2010), 8.

12. See, for example, Rebecca Fuentes's interview with Albán, Palabras Acentuadas home page, 22 May 2009, palabrasacentuadas.wordpress. com/2009/05/23/entrevista-con-carlo-alban-interview-with-carlo-alban/ (accessed 27 September 2013).

13. Bob Verini, review of *Intríngulis*, *Variety*, 15–21 November 2010, 57; Theodore P. Mahne, "Child Star Reveals Struggle as Illegal Immigrant in Powerful One-Man Show 'Intringulis,'" *Times-Picayune* (New Orleans), 15 March 2011, www.nola.com/arts/index.ssf/2011/03/child_star_reveals _struggle_as.html (accessed 27 September 2013); and Karen White, review of *Intríngulis* at INTAR Theatre in New York City, Off-Broadway Reviews, n.d., artsandleisurenews.com/off-broadway.html (accessed 18 July 2012).

14. Review of *Intríngulis* at Atlantic Fringe Festival, *Twisi: The Way I See It Theatre Blog*, 3 September 2011, www.twisitheatreblog.com/archives/933 (accessed 27 September 2013); and Mahne, "Child Star Reveals Struggle."

15. "Excerpt of Intringulis by Carlo Alban," posted on DREAM Act Union website, 10 March 2012, dreamactunion.org/?p=184 (accessed 27 September 2013). Albán serves on the organization's advisory board.

16. Jose Antonio Vargas, "Not Legal, Not Leaving," *Time*, 25 June 2012, 36 (italics in original). For Vargas's initial "coming out," see his "Outlaw," *New York Times*, 26 June 2011, MM22.

17. The DREAM Act, originally drafted by Republican Orrin Hatch and Democrat Dick Durbin, seeks to provide a path to citizenship for individuals who (1) were brought to the United States before the age of 16, (2) have been present in the United States continuously for a minimum period of time, (3) have achieved a certain level of education, (4) are of a certain age at the time of application, and (5) have no criminal record. The bill ties the legal adjustment in immigration status to either college attendance or military service. As of this writing, the bill has yet to be signed into federal law. Hundreds of thousands of young men and women took advantage of Obama's Deferred Action for Childhood Arrivals (DACA) program in its first year (Kirk Semple, "Study Offers a Picture of Young Immigrants Seeking a Reprieve From Deportation," *New York Times*, 14 August 2013, A13).

18. White House official website, "Issues—Immigration," whitehouse.gov/issues /immigration (accessed 1 June 2013).

19. Karen Shimakawa, *National Abjection: The Asian American Body Onstage* (Durham: Duke University Press, 2002), 3 (italics in original).

20. Linda S. Bosniak, *The Citizen and the Alien: Dilemmas of Contemporary Membership* (Princeton: Princeton University Press, 2006), 116.

21. Bosniak, *Citizen and Alien*, 10, 70; Shannon Gleeson, "Labor Rights for All? The Role of Undocumented Immigrant Status for Worker Claims Making," *Law & Social Inquiry* 35, no. 3 (Summer 2010): 563.

22. Joshua Takano Chambers-Letson, *A Race So Different: Performance and Law in Asian America* (New York: New York University Press, 2013), 214; Bosniak, *Citizen and Alien*, 134.

23. For studies about immigration law and legal consciousness, see Leisy Abrego, "Legitimacy, Social Identity, and the Mobilization of Law: The Effects of

Assembly Bill 540 on Undocumented Students in California," *Law & Social Inquiry* 33, no. 3 (Summer 2008): 709–34; and Gleeson, "Labor Rights for All?".

24. Sally Engle Merry, *Getting Justice and Getting Even: Legal Consciousness among Working-Class Americans* (Chicago: University of Chicago Press, 1990), 5.

25. Patricia Ewick and Susan S. Silbey, *The Common Place of Law: Stories from Everyday Life* (Chicago: University of Chicago Press, 1998), 20. Some examples of texts informing my work include Rosie Harding, *Regulating Sexuality: Legal Consciousness in Lesbian and Gay Lives* (New York: Routledge, 2011); Nancy Levit, *The Gender Line: Men, Women, and the Law* (New York: New York University Press, 1998); Ian F. Haney López, *White by Law: The Legal Construction of Race* (New York: New York University Press, 1996); Suzanne Oboler, *Ethnic Labels, Latino Lives: Identity and the Politics of (Re)Presentation in the United States* (Minneapolis University of Minnesota Press, 1995); and Shonna L. Trinch, *Latinas' Narratives of Domestic Abuse: Discrepant Versions of Violence* (Amsterdam: John Benjamins, 2003).

26. David M. Engel and Frank W. Munger, *Rights of Inclusion: Law and Identity in the Life Stories of Americans with Disabilities* (Chicago: University of Chicago Press, 2003), 41.

27. Gad Guterman, "Field Tripping: The Power of *Inherit the Wind*," *Theatre Journal* 60, no. 4 (December 2008): 563–83.

28. Ewick and Silbey, *Common Place of Law*, 16.

29. Harding, *Regulating Sexuality*, 11.

30. Joseph Roach, *Cities of the Dead: Circum-Atlantic Performance* (New York: Columbia University Press, 1996), esp. 2–4.

31. Martin Puchner, *Poetry of the Revolution: Marx, Manifestos, and the Avant-Gardes* (Princeton: Princeton University Press, 2005), 26.

32. Ewick and Silbey, *Common Place of Law*, 29; Patricia Ewick and Susan S. Silbey, "Narrating Social Structure: Stories of Resistance to Legal Authority," *American Journal of Sociology* 108, no. 6 (May 2003): 1332.

33. Dave Williams, introduction to *The Chinese Other, 1850–1925: An Anthology of Plays*, ed. Williams (Lanham, MD: University Press of America, 1997), xii–xiii.

34. Frank Powers, *The First Born*, in Williams, *Chinese Other*, 168.

35. Sean Metzger, "Charles Parsloe's Chinese Fetish: An Example of Yellowface Performance in Nineteenth-Century American Melodrama," *Theatre Journal* 56, no. 4 (December 2004): 627–51.

36. Julian Samora, with the assistance of Jorge A. Bustamante F. and Gilbert Cardenas, *Los Mojados: The Wetback Story* (Notre Dame: University of Notre Dame Press, 1971), 34, 6.

37. Peter H. Schuck, *Citizens, Strangers, and In-Betweens: Essays on Immigration and Citizenship* (Boulder: Westview Press, 1998), 24.

38. Nicolás Kanellos, *A History of Hispanic Theatre in the United States: Origins to 1940* (Austin: University of Texas Press, 1990), 46–57.

39. Esther Kim Lee, *A History of Asian American Theatre* (Cambridge: Cambridge University Press, 2006), 14.

40. Ngai, *Impossible Subjects*, 58, 149.

41. Arthur Miller, *A View from the Bridge*, in *Arthur Miller: Collected Plays 1944–1961* (New York: Library of America, 2006), 569–636; Richard Rodgers (music), Oscar Hammerstein II (lyrics), and Joseph Fields (book), *Flower Drum Song* (New York: Farrar, Straus and Cudahy, 1959). References to these works will be noted parenthetically and abbreviated *VB* and *FDS*, respectively.

42. The fetishized portrayal of San Francisco's Chinatown complicates my reading of Mei Li's effortless inclusion. She is accepted only into an exoticized version of the United States. Nonetheless, her acceptance, like Rodolpho's, suggests the relative ease with which unauthorized immigrants could join communities in the United States. For more on *Flower Drum Song*'s exoticism, see Lee, *History of Asian American Theatre*, ch. 2; Robert G. Lee, *Orientals: Asian Americans in Popular Culture* (Philadelphia: Temple University Press, 1999), ch. 5; David Palumbo-Liu, *Asian/American: Historical Crossings of a Racial Frontier* (Stanford: Stanford University Press, 1999), 156–70; and Karen Wada, afterword to Richard Rodgers, Oscar Hammerstein II, and David Henry Hwang, *Flower Drum Song* (New York: Theatre Communications Group, 2003), 99–115.

43. Miller, interviewed by Christopher Bigsby, in *Arthur Miller: A Critical Study* (Cambridge: Cambridge University Press, 2005), 192.

44. Palumbo-Liu suggests that Mei Li's "*doubly* efficacious" identification with the television character allows her a clean break from Sammy and a promise of erasure of her illegality. As with *A View from the Bridge*, a romantic union offers here the "ideal process for the socialization and reproduction of Americans." Mei Li and Wang Ta "present the ideal balance of 'Chinese tradition' and American individualism, which will stand as a model for both Asian Americans and Americans in general" (Palumbo-Liu, *Asian/American*, 166 [italics in original], 159, 165). The 1986 Immigration Marriage Fraud Amendments severely alter Alfieri's description of the situation in the 1950s (see chapter 4).

45. Bosley Crowther, "The Screen: 'East of Eden' Has Debut," *New York Times*, 10 March 1955, 33.

46. Copies of various programs, both for the production's out-of-town and Broadway engagements, can be found in the clippings files for the play and for the actors in the New York Public Library for the Performing Arts.

47. Press Release from Michel Mok, 4 August 1958, in "Flower Drum Song" Clippings File, New York Public Library for the Performing Arts. There is much to say about the casting of a Japanese actor to play the "Chinese" role, but my point here is to call attention to the nonthreatening nature of Mei Li, as played by Umeki.

48. Since the 1970s, undocumented immigrants have come predominantly from Mexico and other Latin American countries. Immigrants from Asia comprise the next largest—although significantly smaller—group. In 2010, for instance, Mexican nationals made up approximately 58 percent of the total undocumented immigrants entering the United States, with individuals from

other Latin American countries comprising 23 percent. About 11 percent are from Asia, 4 percent from Europe and Canada, and the remaining 3 percent from African nations and other countries (Jeffrey S. Passel and D'Vera Cohn, *Unauthorized Immigrant Population: National and State Trends, 2010,* Pew Research Center Report, 1 February 2011, pewhispanic.org/2011/02/01 /unauthorized-immigrant-population-brnational-and-state-trends-2010/ [accessed 19 July 2013]).

49. Leguizamo, *Mambo Mouth,* 220.
50. Barbara Crossette, "From a Chinese Bridge," *New York Times,* 7 July 1978; and *CAAC: Chinese American Art News* 3, no. 8 (August 1978); both in "View from the Bridge" clippings file at the New York Public Library for the Performing Arts. Enoch Brater, "A Dominican View: An Interview with Darryl V. Jones," in *Arthur Miller's Global Theater,* ed. Brater (Ann Arbor: University of Michigan Press, 2007), 87–95.
51. Arthur Miller, accepting Finley Award in December 2001, quoted in City College website, www1.cuny.edu/events/cunymatters/2001_december/miller8 .html (accessed 9 July 2013).
52. David Henry Hwang and Laurence Maslon, interviewed in "A Classic Evolves: From Print to Stage to Screen," DVD release of *Flower Drum Song* film (1961), music by Richard Rodgers, lyrics by Oscar Hammerstein II, and screenplay by Joseph Fields (Universal City, CA: Universal Studios Home Entertainment. 2006).
53. Rodgers, Hammerstein, and Hwang, *Flower Drum Song,* 60.
54. Universal Studios Entertainment website, www.universalstudiosentertainment .com/flower-drum-song/ (accessed 1 September 2013).
55. Brooks Atkinson, "Theatre: 'A View from the Bridge,'" *New York Times,* 30 September 1955, 21; Richard L. Coe, "Revised 'Bridge' Given in Capital," *New York Times,* 9 November 1956, 34; Howard Taubman, "Theater: Miller Revival," *New York Times,* 29 January 1965, 24; Mel Gussow, "Stage: Miller's 'A View from Bridge' Revived," *New York Times,* 28 December 1981, C16; Frank Rich, "Theater: Arthur Miller's 'View from the Bridge,'" *New York Times,* 4 February 1983, C3; Ben Brantley, "Incestuous Longings on the Waterfront," *New York Times,* 15 December 1997, E1; and Ben Brantley, "View from Brooklyn of Tragedy Most Classic," *New York Times,* 25 January 2010, C1.

2 Act § 275(a)—Improper Entry by Alien

1. Culture Clash, *Bordertown,* in *Culture Clash in Americca* (New York: Theatre Communications Group, 1997), 20. Subsequent references to *Bordertown* will be noted parenthetically and abbreviated *B* (all italics are in the original).
2. Sophie Nield, "On the Border as Theatrical Space: Appearance, Dis-Location and the Production of the Refugee," in *Contemporary Theatres in Europe: A Critical Companion,* ed. Joe Kelleher and Nicholas Ridout (London: Routledge, 2006), 64–65.

3. 8 U.S.C. § 1225(a)(3) (2013).
4. Diana Taylor, *The Archive and the Repertoire: Performing Cultural Memory in the Americas* (Durham: Duke University Press, 2003), esp. 28–33.
5. Diana Taylor, "Double-Blind: The Torture Case," *Critical Inquiry* 33, no. 4 (Summer 2007): 717 (italics in original); Sophie Nield, "The Proteus Cabinet, or 'We Are Here but Not Here,'" *Research in Drama Education* 13, no. 2 (June 2008): 144; and Diana Taylor, "Afterword: War Play," *PMLA* 124, no. 5 (October 2009): 1890.
6. Janet A. Gilboy, "Deciding Who Gets In: Decisionmaking by Immigration Inspectors," *Law & Society Review* 25, no. 3 (1991): 571–600 and "Penetrability of Administrative Systems: Political 'Casework' and Immigration Inspections," *Law & Society Review* 26, no. 2 (1992): 273–314. Although her publications predate 9/11, Gilboy remains an authority and an often-cited voice in discussions about screening practices.
7. Gad Guterman, "Reviewing the Rosenbergs: Donald Freed's *Inquest* and Its Jurors," *Theatre Survey* 48, no. 2 (November 2007): 265–87. I refer to Eugenio Barba and Nicola Savarese's *A Dictionary of Theatre Anthropology: The Secret Art of the Performer*, 2nd ed. (New York: Routledge, 2006), esp. 6–20.
8. Konstantin Stanislavski, *An Actor's Work: A Student's Diary*, trans. Jean Benedetti (New York: Routledge, 2008), 306–21.
9. "Modes of Entry for the Unauthorized Migrant Population," Pew Research Center website, 22 May 2006, pewhispanic.org/factsheets/factsheet.php ?FactsheetID=19 (accessed 1 July 2013).
10. Taylor, "Double-Blind," 728.
11. Harold Fernandez, *Undocumented* (Mustang, OK: Tate Publishing, 2012), 61; Rubén Martínez, *Crossing Over: A Mexican Family on the Migrant Trail* (New York: Metropolitan Books, 2001), 202; Debbie Nathan, *Women and Other Aliens: Essays from the U.S.-Mexico Border* (El Paso: Cinco Puntos Press, 1991), 17–34; Shahram Khosravi, *"Illegal" Traveller: An Auto-Ethnography of Borders* (New York: Palgrave Macmillan, 2010), 63; and Susan Bibler Coutin, *Nations of Emigrants: Shifting Boundaries of Citizenship in El Salvador and the United States* (Ithaca: Cornell University Press, 2007), 103 (italics in original).
12. Cecilia Olivares, "Seeking Divine Intervention: Votive Iconography and Processes of U.S.-Mexican Migration," in *Mediating Chicana/o Culture: Multicultural American Vernacular*, ed. Scott L. Baugh (Newcastle, UK: Cambridge Scholars Press, 2006), 100, 102; Linda S. Bosniak, *The Citizen and the Alien: Dilemmas of Contemporary Membership* (Princeton: Princeton University Press, 2006), 4. I expand on the increased dangers of crossing the border in chapter 5.
13. Christine Koyama, "A Novice Playwright Finds Inspiration in Her Heritage," *New York Times*, 16 June 1985, 29. Lai, Lim, and Young's *Island* was first published in 1981 through the San Francisco Study Center (H. Mark Lai, Genny Lim, and Judy Young, *Island: Poetry and History of Chinese Immigrants on Angel Island 1910–1940* [Seattle: University of Washington Press, 1991]). Genny Lim, *Paper Angels*, in *Unbroken Thread: An Anthology of Plays by Asian American Women*, ed. Roberta Uno (Amherst: University

of Massachusetts Press, 1993), 11–52. References to this play will be noted parenthetically and abbreviated *PA* (all italics are in the original script).

14. See Joseph Nevins, *Operation Gatekeeper and Beyond: The War on "Illegals" and the Remaking of the U.S.-Mexico Boundary* (New York: Routledge, 2010); and Peter Yoxall, "The Minuteman Project, Gone in a Minute or Here to Stay? The Origin, History and Future of Citizen Activism on the United States-Mexico Border," *University of Miami Inter-American Law Review* 37, no. 3 (Spring–Summer 2006): 517–66.

15. I base my descriptions of audience reactions on L.A. Theatre Works' recording of *Bordertown*.

16. For more on paper sons, see Tung Pok Chin, with Winifred C. Chin, *Paper Son: One Man's Story* (Philadelphia: Temple University Press, 2000); Peter S. Li, "Fictive Kinship, Conjugal Tie and Kinship Chain among Chinese Immigrants in the United States," *Journal of Comparative Family Studies* 3, no. 1 (Spring 1977): 47–63; Mae M. Ngai, *Impossible Subjects: Illegal Aliens and the Making of Modern America* (Princeton: Princeton University Press, 2004), esp. ch. 6; Lucy Salyer, *Laws Harsh as Tigers: Chinese Immigrants and the Shaping of Modern Immigration Law* (Chapel Hill: University of North Carolina Press, 1995); and Betty Lee Sung, *The Story of Chinese in America* (New York: Collier Books, 1967).

17. Ngai, *Impossible Subjects*, 205.

18. Julian Samora, with the assistance of Jorge A. Bustamante F., and Gilbert Cardenas, *Los Mojados: The Wetback Story* (Notre Dame: University of Notre Dame Press, 1971), 11. Strategies to curb undocumented immigration spiked and ebbed throughout the twentieth century following economic and political tides. Especially during the Cold War, there were some isolated, intensified attempts to sweep "illegals" out from the country. Operation Wetback, for example, apprehended hundreds of thousands of undocumented workers in the Southwest in just one year. The Justice Department and the Immigration and Naturalization Service (INS) similarly conducted investigations in San Francisco's and New York City's Chinatowns to uncover and charge paper sons for fraud, perjury, and conspiracy (Ngai, *Impossible Subjects*, 155–56, 212–24).

19. Genny Lim, quoted by Richard Louv, "Of Poems Carved in Walls, and Angel Island's Ghosts," *San Diego Union-Tribune*, 6 July 1986, A3.

20. Hiroshi Motomura, *Americans in Waiting: The Lost Story of Immigration and Citizenship in the United States* (Oxford: Oxford University Press, 2006), 9.

21. For more on the entwining of consumption and the obligations of citizenship, see Lizabeth Cohen, *A Consumers' Republic: The Politics of Mass Consumption in Postwar America* (New York: Knopf, 2003).

22. Coutin, *Nations of Emigrants*, 101; Olivares, "Seeking Divine Intervention," 101.

23. Sung, *Story of Chinese in America*, 99, 104.

24. Dorinne Kondo, "(Re)Visions of Race: Contemporary Race Theory and the Cultural Politics of Racial Crossover in Documentary Theatre," *Theatre Journal* 52, no. 1 (2000): 82, 106. I problematize cross-document performance further in chapter 3.

25. Peter Brimelow, *Alien Nation: Common Sense about America's Immigration Disaster* (New York: HarperPerennial, 1995), 235.

26. Culture Clash Archive, Oviatt Library, California State University, Northridge (Box CCHS1, File 22).

27. The semiautobiographical *The Mission* calls attention to the three artists' struggles as "frustrated Latino actors," contending with a business that sees them as "either too Hispanic or not Hispanic enough" (Ricardo Salinas, introduction to *The Mission*, in *Culture Clash: Life, Death and Revolutionary Comedy* [New York: Theatre Communications Group, 1997], 5).

28. The performance, directed by Victoria Linchong, was produced by Direct Arts and the Performance Project @ University Settlement in April and May of 2009 in New York City.

29. Ellen MacKay, "Auditioning for the Role of a Lifetime: Performing Self-Translation at the American Immigration and Naturalization Service," *Canadian Theatre Review* 102 (Spring 2000): 23; subsequent quote also from p. 23. In their *American Night: The Ballad of Juan José* (Ashland: Oregon Shakespeare Festival Scripts, 2010), Culture Clash focuses on the title character's studies for a citizenship test, a framing device for a theatrical journey through US history.

30. This is my translated summary of two of the song's lines.

31. Josefina López, *Real Women Have Curves* (Woodstock, IL: Dramatic Publishing, 1996). References to this play will be noted parenthetically and abbreviated *RW* (all bold text, used for words in Spanish, and all italics are found in the original).

32. Jorge Huerta, "Looking for the Magic: Chicanos in the Mainstream," in *Negotiating Performance: Gender, Sexuality, and Theatricality in Latin/o America*, ed. Diana Taylor and Juan Villegas (Durham: Duke University Press, 1994), 42–43. Notable productions include the Teatro de la Esperanza premiere (1990), a long-running Spanish-language staging at Repertorio Español in New York City (1993–1996), one directed by López at her theatre in East Los Angeles (2006), and a version adapted and directed by Garbi Losada in Spain that transposed the action to the European country and depicted the characters as Cuban immigrants (2003). For more on the complications of this switch, see Tiffany Ana López, "Suturing Las Ramblas to East LA: Transnational Performances of Josefina López' *Real Women Have Curves*," in *Performing the US Latina and Latino Borderlands*, ed. Arturo J. Aldama, Chela Sandoval, and Peter J. García (Bloomington: Indiana University Press, 2012), 296–308.

33. Christie Launius, for example, attempts to move beyond strict questions about gender and ethnicity in order to further a conversation about class. But she acknowledges her "de-emphasiz[ing] the text's focus on immigration politics, something that deserves much more time to in the classroom" ("*Real Women Have Curves*: A Feminist Narrative of Upward Mobility," *American Drama* 16, no. 2 [Summer 2007], 26). Elizabeth C. Ramírez similarly posits issues of immigration law merely as secondary to or metaphoric of her exploration of "the female as subject on display" (*Chicanas/Latinas in American*

Theatre: A History of Performance [Bloomington: Indiana University Press, 2000], 118). In her celebratory reading of *Real Women*, Alicia Arrizón discusses differences between the film and the play, but does not at all engage with the shift away from depicting undocumentedness (*Queering Mestizaje: Transculturation and Performance* [Ann Arbor: University of Michigan Press, 2006], 38). And in examining López's introductory notes, Linda Saborío does not comment on the playwright's focus on immigration status (*Embodying Difference: Scripting Social Images of the Female Body in Latina Theatre* [Madison: Fairleigh Dickinson University Press, 2012], 70). I am interested in what happens when we approach López's work as one that places a so-called *illegal* female immigrant subject on display.

34. Jeff Kaliss, "Heavy Topic Handled with Humor," *San Francisco Chronicle*, 20 May 1990, Datebook 31. Immigration law is central in several of López's works: *Hungry Woman in Paris*, *Simply María or the American Dream*, and *Detained in the Desert*, for example.

35. IRCA set strict parameters for legalization. Only immigrants who could prove continuous residence in the United States since before 1 January 1982 could apply for a new status and had to do so within a limited time frame. The law was not entirely immigrant-friendly, as it also increased border enforcements and made the willful hiring of undocumented immigrants a punishable offense. The immigration bill currently under Congressional consideration (BSEOIM) is also set to adjust the status of many in undocumentedness, as well as to police and punish violations with increased severity.

36. María P. Figueroa, "Resisting 'Beauty' and *Real Women Have Curves*," in *Velvet Barrios: Popular Culture & Chicana/o Sexualities*, ed. Alicia Gaspar de Alba (New York: Palgrave Macmillan, 2003), 273 (my emphasis).

37. Ramón "Tianguis" Pérez, *Diary of an Undocumented Immigrant*, trans. Dick J. Reavis (Houston: Arte Público Press, 1991), 108.

38. Saborío, *Embodying Difference*, 77. For more on *Real Women*'s engagement with and critique of the American Dream, see Figueroa, "Resisting 'Beauty'"; Launius, "Feminist Narrative"; and López, "Suturing Las Ramblas."

39. Homi K. Bhabha, *The Location of Culture* (London: Routledge, 2004), 201, 213.

40. Pierre Bourdieu, "The Field of Cultural Production, or: The Economic World Reversed" and "The Production of Belief: Contribution to an Economy of Symbolic Goods," trans. Richard Nice, in *The Field of Cultural Production*, ed. Randal Johnson (New York: Columbia University Press, 1993), 29–73 and 74–111.

41. Culture Clash, interviewed by Philip Kan Gotanda, in *Life, Death and Revolutionary Comedy*, xviii.

42. See Center Theatre Group website, centertheatregroup.org/tickets /productiondetail.aspx?id=7710 (accessed 3 July 2013); Yale Repertory Theatre website, yalerep.org/on_stage/2012-13/american.html (accessed 1 July 2013); and La Jolla Playhouse website, lajollaplayhouse.org/the-season/2011-2012 -season/american-night (accessed 1 July 2013). See also Culture Clash's website, cultureclash.com/about (accessed 2 July 2013).

43. Josefina López, interview by Jorge Huerta, *Necessary Theatre*, UCtelevision, July 2003, youtube.com/watch?v=YL56dth0mj0 (accessed 3 July 2013); Josefina López, *Unconquered Spirits* (Woodstock, IL: Dramatic Publishing, 1997), 5; and Dramatic Publishing website, www.dramaticpublishing.com/AuthorBio .php?titlelink=9581 (accessed 3 July 2013).

44. "Genny Lim, Poet and Beyond," interview with Jaime Wright, www.jaimewright .ws/intergenny.html (accessed 2 September 2013); Miseong Woo, "Diaspora and Geographies of Identity: Genny Lim's *Paper Angels* and *Bitter Cane*," *Journal of Modern British and American Drama* 17, no. 1 (April 2004): 193.

45. Huerta, interviewing López, *Necessary Theatre*, UCtelevision; Alicia Arrizón, *Latina Performance: Traversing the Stage* (Bloomington: Indiana University Press, 1999), 11.

46. Stephen H. Sumida, "The More Things Change: Paradigm Shifts in Asian American Studies," *American Studies International* 38, no. 2 (June 2000): 103 (italics in original).

47. Questions of empire and economics aside, Puerto Rican natives and their US-born relatives can, with their US passports, travel freely between the island and the United States. For undocumented immigrants, however, travel between the United States and their countries of origin proves much more complicated and treacherous.

48. Woo, "Diaspora and Geographies of Identity," 179.

49. See, for example, Koyama, "Novice Playwright."

50. Louv, "Of Poems"; and Mel Gussow, "'Paper Angels,' about West Coast Ellis Island," *New York Times*, 26 March 1982, C3.

51. Program for *Paper Angels*, produced by Direct Arts and the Performance Project @ University Settlement, New York City, April–May 2009.

52. Culture Clash has toured extensively, performing in multiple venues not marked exclusively as Latina/o. Moreover, the group has performed at San Francisco's Asian American Theater and alongside Asian American companies such as 18 Mighty Mountain Warriors. The group has also attained a noteworthy presence on television: In 1992, PBS's *Great Performances* aired *A Bowl of Beings*; the following year, FOX hired the group to produce and star in 30 episodes of a sketch-comedy show, *Culture Clash*, which aired in several markets.

53. Richard Montoya, Ricardo Salinas, and Herbert Siguenza, *Bordertown*, sound recording (Venice, CA: L.A. Theatre Works, 2006), end track 3 into track 4.

54. Josefina López website, josefinalopez.co/?page_id=14 (accessed 12 September 2013). López is careful to explain that she did not write the screenplay alone and that many of the changes resulted from the work of co-screenwriter George LaVoo and director Patricia Cardoso. See also López, interview by Huerta, *Necessary Theatre*, UCtelevision.

55. Huerta, "Looking for the Magic," 43.

56. I quote one of many reviews of the film, which rely on phrases such as "well-told ethnic story" to describe the piece (Claudia Puig, "'*Real Women*' Reflects the *Real* World," *USA Today*, 25 October 2002, 15D).

57. Roberto Suro, featured in "Democracy in Age of New Media: A Report on the Media and the Immigration Debate" (panel presentation, Brookings Institution, Washington, DC, 25 September 2008), transcript available at www.brookings.edu/events/2008/0925_media_immigration.aspx (accessed 15 September 2013), 13–16.

3   Act § 274A—Unlawful Employment of Aliens

1. Portions of this chapter were published as "'The, Uh, Immigration Situation': *Living Out* and the Legal/Illegal Divide," *Journal of American Drama and Theatre* 23 (Spring 2011): 51–73.
2. Linda S. Bosniak, *The Citizen and the Alien: Dilemmas of Contemporary Membership* (Princeton: Princeton University Press, 2006), 116. To be sure, Bosniak believes this idea is too simplistic: "Citizenship is not a single currency that is transferred from some women to others in zero-sum fashion" (103).
3. Lisa Loomer, *Living Out* (New York: Dramatists Play Service, 2005); Milcha Sánchez-Scott, with Jeremy Blahnik, *Latina*, in *Necessary Theater: Six Plays about the Chicano Experience*, ed. Jorge Huerta (Houston: Arte Público Press, 1989), 75–141; and Octavio Solis, *Lydia* (New York: Samuel French, 2010). References to these plays will be noted parenthetically and abbreviated *LO*, *LA*, and *LY*, respectively (all italics appear in the original scripts).
4. Pierrette Hondagneu-Sotelo, *Doméstica: Immigrant Workers Cleaning and Caring in the Shadows of Affluence* (Berkeley: University of California Press, 2001). On changing demographics of immigrant labor, see Barbara Ehrenreich and Arlie Russell Hochschild, introduction to *Global Woman: Nannies, Maids, and Sex Workers in the New Economy*, ed. Ehrenreich and Hochschild (New York: Metropolitan Books, 2002), 1–13. To narrow the scope of the chapter, I do not delve deeply into questions of gender, focusing instead on questions of labor vis-à-vis immigration status. This said, a discussion of domestic work necessarily implicates gender. How that work "counts" ties into a long history of devaluing the labor of women. As immigrant women care for homes and children, they participate in perpetuating constructions of gender in the United States. At the same time, because they are breadwinners working outside their own homes and their own countries, domestic workers also challenge cultural stereotypes.
5. Lisa Loomer, interviewed by Karen Grigsby Bates, "Lisa Loomer's New Play," *Morning Edition*, NPR, 27 February 2003, www.npr.org/templates/story/story.php?storyId=1176691 (accessed 28 September 2013).
6. Hondagneu-Sotelo, *Doméstica*, 8, 14–18. On occupational ghettoization, see also, Mary Romero, *Maid in the U.S.A.*, 10th anniversary ed. (New York: Routledge, 2002), 57.
7. Shannon Gleeson, "Labor Rights for All? The Role of Undocumented Immigrant Status for Worker Claims Making," *Law & Social Inquiry* 35, no. 3 (Summer 2010): 561–602.
8. These are my translations from Spanish and emphases of cries urged at the 2007 protest that I attended.

9. For restrictions on the work that noncitizens can perform, see Foley v. Connelie, 435 U.S. 291 (1978); Cabell v. Chavez-Salido, 454 U.S. 432 (1982); Ambach v. Norwich, 441 U.S. 68 (1979); and the Aviation and Transportation Security Act of 2001, Pub. L. 107-71, 115 Stat. 230 (2001). Court decisions as to whether an unauthorized immigrant can be admitted to the bar have varied by state. Against the urging of the Obama administration, California has determined that immigration status alone should not preclude membership in the state bar (In re Sergio C. Garcia on Admission, No. S202512 [Cal. Sup. Filed 2 January 2014]). Florida has ruled that such applicants are ineligible for admission to the state bar (Florida Board of Bar Examiners Re: Undocumented Immigrants, No. SC11-2568 [Fla. Sup. 6 March 2014]). And in New York the question remains open (Kirk Semple, "Bar Exam Passed, Immigrant Still Can't Practice Law," *New York Times*, 4 December 2013, A30).

10. 8 U.S.C. § 1324a(f) (2013).

11. Jeffrey S. Passel and D'Vera Cohn, *Unauthorized Immigrant Population: National and State Trends, 2010*, Pew Research Center Report, 1 February 2011, pewhispanic.org/2011/02/01/unauthorized-immigrant-population-brnational-and-state-trends-2010/ (accessed 19 July 2013) and *A Portrait of Unauthorized Immigrants in the United States*, Pew Research Center Report, 14 April 2009, pewhispanic.org/files/reports/107.pdf (accessed 19 July 2013).

12. Ehrenreich and Hochschild, *Global Woman*, 8.

13. Jeffrey S. Passel and D'Vera Cohn, *U.S. Unauthorized Immigration Flows Are Down Sharply since Mid-Decade*, Pew Research Center Report, 1 September 2010, pewhispanic.org/files/reports/126.pdf (accessed 3 September 2010). The decline in unauthorized immigration that accompanied the Great Recession has leveled off and may be once again on the rise (Jeffrey S. Passel, D'Vera Cohn, and Ana Gonzalez-Barrera, *Population Decline of Unauthorized Immigrants Stalls, May Have Reversed*, Pew Research Center Report, 23 September 2013, www.pewhispanic.org/2013/09/23/population-decline-of-unauthorized-immigrants-stalls-may-have-reversed/ [accessed 23 September 2013], 6).

14. Karen Shimakawa, "Staging a Moving Map in Byron Au Yong's and Aaron Jafferis's *Stuck Elevator*," in *Neoliberalism and Global Theatres: Performance Permutations*, ed. Lara D. Nielsen and Patricia Ybarra (New York: Palgrave Macmillan, 2012), 103.

15. Neda Ulaby, "A Rising-Star Writer and a Miraculous Maid," *All Things Considered*, NPR, 18 April 2009, www.npr.org/templates/story/story.php?storyId=103174270 (accessed 28 September 2013).

16. David Bacon, *Illegal People: How Globalization Creates Migration and Criminalizes Immigrants* (Boston: Beacon Press, 2008), 23. On the economic forces compelling women to migrate, see also Grace Chang, *Disposable Domestics: Immigrant Women Workers in the Global Economy* (Cambridge, MA: South End Press, 2000); and Ehrenreich and Hochschild, *Global Woman*.

17. Grant McCracken, *Culture and Consumption: New Approaches to the Symbolic Character of Consumer Goods and Activities* (Bloomington: Indiana University Press, 1988), 117.

18. Charles Isherwood, review of *Living Out*, *Variety*, 5 October 2003, 94.
19. Hondagneu-Sotelo, *Doméstica*, 9, 12.
20. See Peggy R. Smith, "Organizing the Unorganizable: Private Paid Household Workers and Approaches to Employee Representation," *North Carolina Law Review* 79, no. 1 (2000): 45–110; Hondagneu-Sotelo, *Doméstica*, esp. 21; and Linda Burnham and Nik Theodore, *Home Economics: The Invisible and Unregulated World of Domestic Work* (New York: National Domestic Workers Alliance, 2012).
21. Hoffman Plastic Compounds v. NLRB, 535 U.S. 137, 148 (2002).
22. Kevin Parker, "The 'True' Nanny Experience," introduction to Nandi, *The True Nanny Diaries* (Brooklyn: Bread for Brick, 2009), unnumbered page. On the ineffectiveness of legal protection, see Russ Buettner, "For Nannies, Hope for Workplace Protection," *New York Times*, 3 June 2010, A1. On how fears of deportation sustain this ineffectiveness, see Gleeson, "Labor Rights for All?," esp. 586.
23. Bacon, *Illegal People*, 150.
24. Jill Smolowe, "How It Happened," *Time*, 1 February 1993, 35. The fine was about as high as IRCA allowed and came on top of $8,000 paid in back Social Security taxes (Clifford Krauss, "Nominee Pays Fine for Hiring of Illegal Aliens," *New York Times*, 17 January 1993, 22).
25. Paul Leavitt, "Ex-Baird Worker Feels 'Like a Hunted Animal,'" *USA Today*, 26 January 1993, 3A.
26. Linda Saborío, *Embodying Difference: Scripting Social Images of the Female Body in Latina Theatre* (Madison: Fairleigh Dickinson University Press, 2012), 35.
27. Judith Rollins, *Between Women: Domestics and Their Employers* (Philadelphia: Temple University Press, 1985), 186. I paraphrase John B. Thompson's introduction to Pierre Bourdieu's *Language & Symbolic Power*, trans. Gino Raymond and Matthew Adamson, ed. Thompson (Cambridge, MA: Harvard University Press, 1991), to describe a mask of control (24).
28. Rollins, *Between Women*, 155–56; subsequent quotation from p. 185.
29. Romero, *Maid in U.S.A.*, 101; Rollins, *Between Women*, 7–8.
30. I base this observation on the archival recording of *Living Out* available at the New York Public Library for the Performing Arts.
31. Hondagneu-Sotelo, *Doméstica*, 18, 13, 18–19 (my emphasis).
32. Edward Said, *Orientalism* (New York: Vintage Books, 1978), 21.
33. "A summary analysis of Voting in the 1994 General Election," p. 5, field.com /fieldpollonline/subscribers/COI-94-95-Jan-Election.pdf (accessed 22 July 2013).
34. Alberto Acereda, "Conservative Republican Values and the American Hispanic Mind," American Thinker website, 31 May 2008, americanthinker .com/2008/05/conservative_republican_values.html (accessed 22 July 2013).
35. Hondagneu-Sotelo, *Doméstica*, 188.
36. Rhacel Salazar-Parreñas, *The Force of Domesticity: Filipina Migrants and Globalization* (New York: New York University Press, 2008), 1.
37. Hondagneu-Sotelo, *Doméstica*, 109.
38. Hondagneu-Sotelo, *Doméstica*, 186.

39. Romero, *Maid in U.S.A.*, 130.
40. Rollins, *Between Women*, 147. Through the performances that Zoila undertakes during phone conversations with her boss, retaining a deferential, agreeable tone but simultaneously lying and avoiding commands, Loomer demonstrates some of the ways in which employees maintain some control (*LO* 29, 50).
41. Romero posits the general tendency between domestic workers and employers to use uneven terms of address as part of several practices through which status is reaffirmed daily (*Maid in U.S.A.*, 145).
42. Hondagneu-Sotelo, *Doméstica*, 12.
43. Romero, *Maid in U.S.A.*, 147–48; Rollins, *Between Women*, 209; Hondagneu-Sotelo, *Doméstica*, 197.
44. Isherwood, *Living Out* review, *Variety*.
45. Josefina López, quoted in Yvonne Villarreal, "Ode to the Women Who Give So Much," *Los Angeles Times*, 26 May 2010, D10.
46. Lorena Moran, interviewed by author at Cornerstone's offices in Los Angeles, 11 June 2010.
47. "Senator Savino on the Domestic Workers Bill of Rights," YouTube, 1 June 2010, youtube.com/watch?v=r4mknIO4aeg&feature=player_embedded (accessed 18 July 2013).
48. Savino was a featured speaker at the 22 April 2010 event at Riverside Church in New York City, which I attended. Lisa Ramirez conceived and directed *Invisible Women-Rise* in collaboration with members of the DWU as part of the Foundry Theatre's This Is My City/Esta Es Mi Ciudad series (Foundry Theatre website, thefoundrytheatre.org/forums.html [accessed 18 July 2013]). *Esclavitud moderna* is one of several plays created by Teatro Jornalero Sin Fronteras specifically for day laborers and seeks to empower domestic workers. *Super Doméstica* is likewise meant to galvanize members of the DWA at group meetings. For more on this superheroine and her play, see Anayansi Prado's documentary *Maid in America* (Los Angeles: Impacto Films, 2004) and Hondagneu-Sotelo, *Doméstica*, 224.
49. Jorge Huerta, "A Comic and Sensitive Look at Undocumented Nannies: *Living Out* by Lisa Loomer," *Gestos* 36 (November 2003): 185; Michael Quintanilla, "Domestic Drama," *Los Angeles Times*, 1 March 2003, E26; and Alys Marshall and Shalini Dore, "Theater Crowd Fetes 'Living' Stage Birth," *Daily Variety*, 5 February 2003, 11.
50. Lisa Loomer, interviewed by Carlo Botero, "Telling the Stories," *Revolutionary Worker* 1227, 1 February 2004, revcom.us/a/1227/lisainterview.htm (accessed 21 April 2014).
51. Sánchez-Scott, quoted in Huerta's introduction to *Latina*, 77. A glance at the Internet Movie Database offers a sampling of the various maids, nannies, housekeepers, and cleaning ladies played by actors who have been cast in *Living Out* (e.g., Zilah Mendoza, Maricela Ochoa, Maria Elena Ramirez), *Lydia* (e.g., Adriana Gaviria), and *Latina* (e.g., Christine Avila, Alma Beltran, Rita Conde, and Perla Walter).
52. Hondagneu-Sotelo, *Doméstica*, 110. That only one of the major productions on which I focus in this chapter was helmed by a Latina/o director

further complicates the power structures (Juliette Carrillo directed *Lydia*'s premiere).

53. Sau-ling C. Wong, "Diverted Mothering: Representations of Caregivers of Color in the Age of 'Multiculturalism,'" in *Mothering: Ideology, Experience, and Agency*, ed. Evelyn Nakano Glenn, Grace Chang, and Linda Rennie Forcey (New York: Routledge, 1994), 69.

54. Octavio Solis, interviewed by Elaine Romero, "Memories on the Border," *American Theatre* 25, no. 10 (December 2008): 64.

55. Ulaby, "Rising-Star."

56. Robert Machray, "Theatre Review (LA): Lydia by Octavio Solis at the Mark Taper Forum,' Blogcritics.org, 18 April 2009, blogcritics.org/culture/article /theatre-review-la-lydia-by-octavio/ (accessed 7 July 2013); John Moore, review of *Lydia*, *Denver Post*, 27 January 2008, www.denverpost.com/theater /ci_8086972 (accessed 7 July 2013); Anita Gates, "Amid Lives Gone Awry, a Struggle to Be Heard," *New York Times*, 15 February 2009, CT3; and Bob Bows, review of *Lydia*, *Variety*, 4 February 2008, 104.

57. William Harris, untitled, *Soho Weekly News*, 2 July 1980, n.p., in "Latina by Milcha Scott" clippings file, New York Public Library for the Performing Arts; Christopher Breyer, "Between the Lines," Center Theatre Group, www .centertheatregroup.org/uploadedFiles/Plays_and_Tickets/Productions/2009 /Lydia/files/Lydia_BTL(1).pdf (accessed 28 September 2013).

58. See Julie Salamon, "Playwright Maps Limits of the Best Intentions," *New York Times*, 14 October 2003, E1; and Huerta, "Comic and Sensitive Look," 185.

59. Milcha Sánchez-Scott, introduction to *Roosters*, in *On New Ground: Contemporary Hispanic-American Plays*, ed. M. Elizabeth Osborn (New York: Theatre Communications Group, 1987), 245.

60. Since the 1970s, multiple books, audiobooks, and flash cards have educated English-speaking employers with basic Spanish words and phrases to communicate with domestic workers. Representative titles include *Home Maid Spanish* (Los Angeles: Brooke House, 1976) by Margaret Storm and Elsie Ginnett; *Politely Tell a Maid* (Canoga Park, CA: Tell-a-Maid, 1981) by Linda Wolf; and *Spanish around the House: The Quick Guide to Communicating with Your Spanish-Speaking Employees* (Chicago: McGraw Hill, 2005) by José M. Díaz and María F. Nadel.

61. Gretchen Henkel, review of *Latina*, *Drama-Logue*, 12–18 June 1980, 5–6 (emphasis in original).

62. Bill Edwards, review of *Latina*, *Daily Variety*, 12 June 1980, 7.

63. A review of the original Los Angeles production, for instance, described the employers depicted in *Living Out* as "two caricatures and one character" (Steven Leigh Morris, "Familiarity and Contempt," *LA Weekly*, 20 February 2003, laweekly.com/2003-02-20/stage/familiarity-and-contempt [accessed 18 July 2013]). Subsequent productions have seemingly retained Wallace's and Linda's lack of multidimensionality. To offer just one example, Carolyn Clay describes these two characters as "more-vacuous rich bitches," as "spoiled, underemployed, and gossipy," in her review of the play's New England

premiere production ("Nanny Diaries," *Providence Phoenix*, 1–7 April 2005, www.providencephoenix.com/theater/tripping/documents/04570802.asp [accessed 28 September 2013]).

64. Bates, "Lisa Loomer's New Play."
65. Lisa Loomer, interviewed by Scott French, "Us and Them: A Conversation with Lisa Loomer," performance guide for schools, TheatreWorks, 2004, worksheet 4.
66. Baz Kershaw, *The Politics of Performance: Radical Theatre as Cultural Intervention* (London: Routledge, 1992), 1.
67. Lena Williams, "Relatively Few Taxpayers Are Jolted by the Nanny Scandal," *New York Times*, 4 November 1993, C8.
68. Warren Etheredge, interview with Loomer, "Living Out—Screenwriter, Lisa Loomer," The Warren Report, 18 January 2003, thewarrenreport.com /2003/01/18/living-out-screeenwriter-lisa-loomer/ (accessed 22 July 2013). For size of initial television audience of "Beef," see TV by the Numbers website, 22 April 2010 posting, tvbythenumbers.zap2it.com/2010/04/22/wednesday-broadcast -finals-idol-l-accidentally-on-purpose-down/49489/ (accessed 22 July 2013).
69. Bates, "Lisa Loomer's New Play."
70. I follow Sean Metzger's work on yellowface here, even if *Living Out* does not aim to animate stereotypes as do the performances of "Chinamen" that he analyzes (Sean Metzger, "Charles Parsloe's Chinese Fetish: An Example of Yellowface Performance in Nineteenth-Century American Melodrama," *Theatre Journal* 56, no. 4 [December 2004]: 627–51).
71. First, not all theatre productions are professional. The immigration status of amateur, student, and community theatre-makers is irrelevant, as they are not officially employed. Second, not all professional participants are subject to a theatre company's I-9 forms. "Independent contractors," a category that may include some self-employed artists, allows for a company to contract out a service (e.g., writing a play, teaching a workshop) without the responsibility of checking immigration status. This is not some easily exploitable loophole, as the Department of Labor regularly monitors "misclassification" (Department of Labor website, dol.gov/whd/workers/misclassification/ [accessed 21 July 2013]). Finally, some theatre artists do work in violation of immigration laws. On the specifics of *Latina*'s undocumented actor, see Sánchez-Scott, introduction to *Roosters*, 246; and Alicia Arrizón, *Latina Performance: Traversing the Stage* (Bloomington: Indiana University Press, 1999), 104.
72. Carlo Albán, interviewed by Rebecca Fuentes, Palabras Acentuadas home page, 22 May 2009, palabrasacentuadas.wordpress.com/2009/05/23/entrevista -con-carlo-alban-interview-with-carlo-alban/ (accessed 27 September 2013).
73. The collection of programs I studied reflects the bias of my theatre-going, and the vast majority of playbills are from professional New York City productions. With a handful of exceptions, I found no mention of housekeeping or the like in the myriad lists, which did detail each usher, refreshments vendor, and, in some cases, security staff member associated with the production and theatre in question. There may be viable explanations for such omissions. Some theatres may not have the names of the individual workers who clean because the labor has been contracted out to a company. However,

professional cleaning services are regularly absent from many of the rosters even though other contracted companies are expressly named. Cleaning duties may also fall on staff members whose official titles may disguise such tasks. A "building manager" may well be cleaning and/or administering an unnamed janitorial team. I was nonetheless struck by how challenging it is to match individual names to cleaning duties.

74. Hondagneu-Sotelo, *Doméstica*, 10; Second Stage Theatre website, 2st.com /about_2st/staff (accessed 20 July 2013). I would like to think that the single individual listed as "building staff" is not alone responsible for the herculean task of cleaning all 17 thousand square feet of Second Stage's space, a four-level building that includes "a 296-seat theatre with lobby on the second floor; dressing rooms, green room, and rehearsal and production spaces on the third floor; theatrical office space in the penthouse; and entrance foyer and box office at street level" (2st.com/about_2st/theatre).

75. Passel and Cohn, *Unauthorized Immigrant Population* and *Portrait of Unauthorized Immigrants*.

76. Huerta, "Comic and Sensitive Look," 186; Bates, "Lisa Loomer's New Play."

77. Denver Center Annual Reports, denvercenter.org/Libraries/Annual _Reports/Annual_Report_2008-2009.sflb.ashx (accessed 2 July 2010) and denvercenter.org/libraries/annual_reports/10-11_annual_report.sflb.ashx (accessed 21 July 2013). Target Stores is also a regular major donor for the Center Theatre Group in Los Angeles, where the Mark Taper Forum resides and where *Living Out* was commissioned (centertheatregroup.org/giving /corporate-support/corporate-circle-membership-listing/ [accessed 21 July 2013]). On Target's abuse of undocumented labor, see, for example, Jerry de Jaager, "Workplace Justice, Global Workers, Practical Lawyering: The Transnational Worker Rights Clinic," University of Texas at Austin website, utexas.edu/law/clinics/transnational/feature_2008_transnational_clinic .php (accessed 20 July 2013).

78. Bates, "Lisa Loomer's New Play."

79. Edwards, *Daily Variety*, 7.

4 Act § 212(a)(9)(B)(iii)(III)—Family Unity

1. Guillermo Reyes, *Deporting the Divas*, in *Gay Drama Now: An Anthology*, ed. John M. Clum (Amherst, NY: Cambria Press, 2013), 329. Subsequent references to the play will be noted parenthetically and abbreviated *DD* (all italics in the original script).

2. Teatro de la Esperanza, *La víctima*, in *Necessary Theater: Six Plays about the Chicano Experience*, ed. Jorge Huerta (Houston: Arte Público Press, 1989), 316–65. References to this play will be noted parenthetically and abbreviated *V*. All translations from the Spanish are mine (all italics in the original script).

3. Janet Noble, *Away Alone* (New York: Samuel French, 1990). References to this play will be noted parenthetically and abbreviated *AA* (all italics in the original script).

4. Bill Ong Hing, *Deporting Our Souls: Values, Morality, and Immigration Policy* (Cambridge: Cambridge University Press, 2006), 119.

5. Susan Bibler Coutin, *Legalizing Moves: Salvadoran Immigrants' Struggle for U.S. Residency* (Ann Arbor: University of Michigan Press, 2000), 32; and Susan Bibler Coutin, *Nations of Emigrants: Shifting Boundaries of Citizenship in El Salvador and the United States* (Ithaca: Cornell University Press, 2007), 18. The Illegal Immigration Reform and Immigrant Responsibility Act of 1996 (IIRIRA) severely limited the possibility of altering an unauthorized immigrant's status. Since 1996, an immigrant's unlawful status is "not subject to being reopened or reviewed [and] the alien is not eligible and may not apply for any relief" (8 U.S.C. § 1231[a][5] [2013]). In 2006, the Supreme Court upheld IIRIRA's retroactive power: individuals who entered the United States illegally before IIRIRA went into effect are also subject to the harsher mandate (Fernandez-Vargas v. Gonzalez, 548 U.S. 30 [2006]).

6. Ian F. Haney López, *White by Law: The Legal Construction of Race* (New York: New York University Press, 1996), 9–10, 3.

7. Bark v. INS, 511 F.2d 1200, 1201–2 (9th Cir. 1975).

8. See De Los Santos v. INS, 690 F.2d 56 (2nd Cir. 1982). The Court has continued to uphold the INA's differential treatment of mothers and fathers (Nguyen v. INS, 533 U.S. 53 [2001]).

9. Huerta, introduction to *La víctima*, 324.

10. See Jorge Huerta, "El Teatro de la Esperanza: Keeping in Touch with the People," *The Drama Review: TDR* 21, no. 1 (March 1977): 42–46; and Jorge Huerta, "Chicano Theatre in a Society in Crisis," in *Text & Presentation, 2007*, ed. Stratos E. Constantinidis (Jefferson, NC: McFarland, 2008), 11–12.

11. Mae M. Ngai, *Impossible Subjects: Illegal Aliens and the Making of Modern America* (Princeton: Princeton University Press, 2004), 72–73.

12. Eamonn Wall, *From the Sin-é Café to the Black Hills: Notes on the New Irish* (Madison: University of Wisconsin Press, 1999), 3; Coutin, *Legalizing Moves*, 33.

13. This line—"Our footprints are erased"—is spoken by the character Undocumented 1 in Hugo Alfredo Hinojosa's *Deserts* (unpublished script from translator, Caridad Svich, 40). Like other plays by Mexican writers (e.g., *Our Dad Is in Atlantis, Amarillo, La Casa Rosa*), *Deserts* deals with the disappearance of migrants in *el Norte* and those they leave behind.

14. Human Rights Watch, *Forced Apart: Families Separated and Immigrants Harmed by United States Deportation Policy*, 16 July 2007, available at www.hrw.org/en/publications (accessed 15 September 2013).

15. Sasha G. Lewis, *Slave Trade Today: American Exploitation of Illegal Aliens* (Boston: Beacon Press, 1979), 10; Huerta, introduction to *La víctima*, 324.

16. Hiroshi Motomura, "The Family and Immigration: A Roadmap for the Ruritanian Lawmaker," *American Journal of Comparative Law* 43, no. 4 (Autumn 1995): 540; Huerta, "Teatro de la Esperanza," 44.

17. For more on the Sanctuary Movement of the 1980s, see María Cristina García, *Seeking Refuge: Central American Migration to Mexico, the United States, and Canada* (Berkeley: University of California Press, 2006), esp. 98–108. For more on the New Sanctuary Movement of the 2000s, see Grace Yukich, *One*

Family under God: Immigration Politics and Progressive Religion in America (Oxford: Oxford University Press, 2013).

18. Michael Fix and Wendy Zimmerman, "All under One Roof: Mixed-Status Families in an Era of Reform," *International Migration Review* 35, no. 2 (Summer 2001): 397–419. Jeffrey Passel and Paul Taylor confirm that a substantial share of undocumented immigrants in the United States today live as part of a mixed-status family, with nearly 40 percent of undocumented adults being parents to US citizens (Jeffrey S. Passel and Paul Taylor, *Unauthorized Immigrants and Their U.S.-Born Children*, Pew Research Center Report, 11 August 2010, pewhispanic.org/files/reports/125.pdf [accessed 13 September 2010]).

19. Coutin, *Nations of Emigrants*, 13. On the difficulties of undocumentedness listed above, see Gabrielle Lessard and Leighton Ku, "Gaps in Coverage for Children in Immigrant Families," *The Future of Children* 13, no. 1 (Spring 2003): 100–115; and Ana Huerta-Macías, María Luisa González, and Linda Holman, "Children of Undocumented Immigrants: An Invisible Minority among Homeless Students," in *Children on the Streets of the Americas: Homelessness, Education and Globalization in the United States, Brazil and Cuba*, ed. Roslyn Arlin Mickelson (London: Routledge, 2000), 238–46. On medical repatriation, see *Discharge, Deportation, and Dangerous Journeys: A Study on the Practice of Medical Repatriation*, a joint project from the Center of Social Justice at Seton Hall Law School and the Health Justice Program at New York Lawyers for the Public Interest, available at www.nylpi.org/images/FE/chain234siteType8/site203/client/FINAL%20MED%20REPAT%20REPORT%20FOR%20WEBSITE.pdf (accessed 21 September 2013).

20. Fix and Zimmerman, "All Under One Roof," 400. On "collateral effects" of undocumentedness, see also Linda S. Bosniak, *The Citizen and the Alien: Dilemmas of Contemporary Membership* (Princeton: Princeton University Press, 2006), 65–70.

21. Coutin, *Nations of Emigrants*, 28; Helen Thorpe, *Just Like Us: The True Story of Four Mexican Girls Coming of Age in America* (New York: Scribner, 2009); Leisy Abrego and Roberto G. Gonzalez, "Blocked Paths, Uncertain Futures: The Postsecondary Education and Labor Market Prospects of Undocumented Latino Youth," *Journal of Education for Students Placed at Risk* 15, nos. 1–2 (January–June 2010): 145.

22. Huerta, introduction to *La víctima*, 317; Yvonne Yarbro-Bejarano, "The Female Subject in Chicano Theatre: Sexuality, 'Race,' and Class," *Theatre Journal* 38, no. 4 (December 1986): 399; and Sylvie Drake, "Political Ardor Revamped in 'La Victima,'" *Los Angeles Times*, 14 February 1987, Calendar 1.

23. See Jon D. Rossini's "Teatro Visión and the Limits of Chicano Politics in Neoliberal Space," in *Neoliberalism and Global Theatres: Performance Permutations*, ed. Lara D. Nielsen and Patricia Ybarra (New York: Palgrave Macmillan, 2012), for a reading of *La víctima* that highlights a growing "shift from the structural to the personal as a way of negotiating political thinking" (218).

24. The published script of *La víctima* follows the extensive use of Spanish in the play's original production. The 1987 English-language premiere at LATC

did away with most of the Spanish to appeal to a broader audience. So, some of my ideas here might not easily apply. This said, through sporadic use of Spanish phrases and a spoken English marked by accents, an English-language version of *La víctima* can still stress some of the differences between Sammy's and Amparo's manners of speech. For a twenty-fifth anniversary revival production at LATC in 2010, director José Luis Valenzuela decided to return to the original script, which more accurately presents a transition from Spanish to Spanglish to English as immigrants assimilate in the United States (Valenzuela, "*Víctima* Holds Relevancy Today," *LA Stage Times*, Blogs, 1 October 2010, lastagetimes.com/2010/10/the-story-of-la-victima -holds-relevancy-today/ [accessed 10 August 2013]).

25. Marvin Carlson, *Speaking in Tongues: Language at Play in the Theatre* (Ann Arbor: University of Michigan Press, 2006), 96.

26. Coutin, *Legalizing Moves*, 150; Josiah McC. Heyman, "U.S. Immigration Officers of Mexican Ancestry as Mexican Americans, Citizens, and Immigration Police," *Current Anthropology* 43, no. 3 (June 2002): 479.

27. Yarbro-Bejarano, "Female Subject in Chicano Theatre," 399.

28. Eithne Luibhéid, *Entry Denied: Controlling Sexuality at the Border* (Minneapolis: University of Minnesota Press, 2002), 3.

29. Yarbro-Bejarano, "Female Subject in Chicano Theatre," 398, 400.

30. Anthony G. Amsterdam and Jerome Bruner, *Minding the Law* (Cambridge, MA: Harvard University Press, 2000), 283 (emphasis in original).

31. Coutin, *Legalizing Moves*, 55.

32. Mulkerns, interviewed by Wall, *From the Sin-é Café*, 61; Brian Leahy Doyle, "'In the Pocket': Larry Kirwan's Restless Writings," *New Hibernia Review* 11, no. 3 (Autumn 2007): 132.

33. Stephen Holden, "Illegal Immigrants on the Irish Mile," *New York Times*, 16 December 1989, 18.

34. Gilberto Giménez, "Cultura, territorio y migraciones. Aproximaciones teóricas," *Alteridades* 11, no. 22 (July–December 2001): 5–14, my translation.

35. Jerry Tallmer, "Pretty Good Palaver from the Irish," *New York Post*, 9 February 1990, 37; Irene Backalenick, "A Grand Irish Night," *Westport News*, 2 February 1990, A36.

36. Don Nelsen, "A Dead End to Dreams," *New York Daily News*, 17 January 1990, 34.

37. Tallmer, "Pretty Good Palaver."

38. Ramón "Tianguis" Pérez, *Diary of an Undocumented Immigrant*, trans. Dick J. Reavis (Houston: Arte Público Press, 1991), 153.

39. Beginning in 1986, Congress approved various visa lottery programs for immigrants from a number of countries who failed to fit the family-reunification preferences established by INA. Irish immigrants were particularly poised to receive these lottery visas. Named after its sponsoring congressman, Brian Donnelly, the 1986 Donnelly Program distributed 40 percent of a total 40 thousand visas to Irish immigrants (Linda Dowling Almeida, *Irish Immigrants in New York City, 1945–1995* [Bloomington: Indiana University Press, 2001], 63).

40. Holden, "Illegal Immigrants on Irish Mile."
41. Bosniak, *Citizen and Alien*, 66; Erika Milvy, "A Shamrock Grows in the Bronx," *West Side Spirit*, 13 February 1990, 26.
42. Luibhéid, *Entry Denied*, 25, 78. Luibhéid's fascinating study addresses the history of these exclusions.
43. Luibhéid, *Entry Denied*, 99; Julia Preston, "For Gay Immigrants, Marriage Ruling Brings Relief and a Path to a Green Card," *New York Times*, 28 June 2013, A17.
44. Reyes's treatment of a self-identified gay and undocumented figure remains rare. Carlos Manuel's *La Vida Loca* (Sandy, UT: ECKO House Publishing, 2010) is a recent addition to the conversation. Cherríe L. Moraga's *The Hungry Woman: A Mexican Medea* (Albuquerque: West End Press, 2001) also deals with interrelated questions of gender, sexuality, law, nation, and the border, although her characters are less explicitly marked as undocumented. *Divas* premiered seven years before the Supreme Court finally disallowed antisodomy laws in 2003 (Lawrence v. Texas, 539 U.S. 558 [2003]). Although the ruling now protects private sexual conduct between consenting adults as a constitutional right, some states have refused to strike antisodomy laws from their books. As of this writing, a majority of states ban same-sex marriage, and many do not prohibit discrimination based on sexual orientation.
45. Beatriz Cortez, "Hybrid Identities and the Emergence of Dislocated Consciousness: *Deporting the Divas* by Guillermo Reyes," in *Chicano/Latino Homoerotic Identities*, ed. David William Foster (New York: Garland Publishing, 1999), 132.
46. Jorge Huerta, *Chicano Drama: Performance, Society and Myth* (Cambridge: Cambridge University Press, 2000), 173; Jon D. Rossini, *Contemporary Latina/o Theater: Wrighting Ethnicity* (Carbondale: Southern Illinois University Press, 2008), 132; Steven Winn, "Witty 'Divas' Crosses More than One Border," *San Francisco Chronicle*, 18 September 1996, B1. For more on Reyes's disruption of essentialist categories of identity, see also William Garcia, "Dragging the Borders: Transnational Queer Identities and Citizenship in Guillermo Reyes's *Deporting the Divas*," in *Trans/Acting: Latin American and Latino Performing Arts*, ed. Jacqueline Bixler and Laurietz Seda (Lewisburg, PA: Bucknell University Press, 2009); and Melissa A. Fitch, "Gender Bending in Latino Theater: *Johnny Diego, The His-panic Zone*, and *Deporting the Divas* by Guillermo Reyes," in *Latino/a Popular Culture*, ed. Michelle Habell-Pallán and Mary Romero (New York: New York University Press, 2002), 162–73.
47. Coutin, *Legalizing Moves*, 43.
48. See George Woodyard, "Rompiendo las fronteras: El teatro de Guillermo Reyes," in *Théâtre et territoires Espagne et Amérique Hispanique, 1950–1996/ Teatro y territorios España e Hispanoamérica*, ed. Sara Bonnardel and Geneviève Champeau (Bordeaux: Maison des Pays Ibériques, 1998), 333–43.
49. Jorge Huerta, "Some Thoughts on Casting *Deporting the Divas*," *Gestos* 27 (April 1999): 159.
50. Huerta, *Chicano Drama*, 181.

51. Cortez, "Hybrid Identities," 142–43; David William Foster, "Guillermo Reyes's *Deporting the Divas*," *Gestos* 27 (April 1999): 107.
52. Foster, "Guillermo Reyes's *Deporting the Divas*," 104.
53. William N. Eskridge Jr. and Darren R. Spedale, *Gay Marriage: For Better or for Worse?: What We've Learned from the Evidence* (Oxford: Oxford University Press, 2006), 17.
54. Cortez, "Hybrid Identities," 133.
55. Huerta, *Chicano Drama*, 177.
56. See, for example, Michelle J. Anderson, "A License to Abuse: The Impact of Conditional Status on Female Immigrants," *Yale Law Journal* 102 (1993): 1401–30; Luibhéid, *Entry Denied*, 24–25; and Joe A. Tucker, "Assimilation to the United States: A Study of the Adjustment of Status and the Immigration Marriage Fraud Statutes," *Yale Law & Policy Review* 7, no. 1 (1989): 94.
57. Luibhéid, *Entry Denied*, 71, xvii.
58. Michel Foucault, *Discipline & Punish: The Birth of the Prison*, trans. Alan Sheridan (New York: Vintage, 1977), 304.
59. Bosniak, *Citizen and Alien*, 69–70.
60. Foucault, *Discipline & Punish*, 173; Shahram Khosravi, *"Illegal" Traveller: An Auto-Ethnography of Borders* (New York: Palgrave Macmillan, 2010), 99.
61. Foucault, *Discipline & Punish*, 200, 304, 183 (italics in original).
62. Luibhéid, *Entry Denied*, 78–79, xv, 88–81. Luibhéid warrants that immigration processes do not affect individuals equally; questions of class, gender, race, and culture preclude the possibility of a uniform experience for all gay and lesbian border crossers. She adds that the ways in which immigrants can come under the scrutiny of border authorities are not limited to visible markers. We must also consider premigration screenings and medical checks; the location and timing of travel, particularly in association with well-known gay and lesbian destinations; information provided by third parties, especially fellow travelers; suitcase contents; and information contained in the various required forms needed for entering the United States (84–85).
63. 8 U.S.C. § 1186a(b)(1) (2013). The Board of Immigration Appeals has also contended with sham divorces, deciding whether a couple's separation was an act for obtaining preference status for unmarried adult children of permanent residents (Matter of Aldecoaotalora, 18 I & N Dec. 430 [BIA 1983]).
64. *Immigration Marriage Fraud, Hearing Before the Subcommittee on Immigration and Refugee Policy of the Committee of the Judiciary*, U.S. Senate, 99th Congress, 1st Sess., 26 July 1985 (Washington, DC: US Government Printing Office, 1986), 29, 30.
65. Luibhéid, *Entry Denied*, 25.
66. Rossini, *Contemporary Latina/o Theater*, 132, 136.
67. Huerta, *Chicano Drama*, 181; Robert Hitchcox, review of Diversionary Theatre's *Deporting the Divas*, April 2003, Total Theater website, totaltheater.com/?q=node/1643 (accessed 16 September 2013); Huerta, "Some Thoughts on Casting," 160.
68. Unsigned, undated review of Quinto Sol's production of *La víctima*, available at www.oocities.com/quintosolus/victima.html (accessed 16 September

2013); Anne Gelhaus, "Intimate Histories," review of Teatro Visión's production of *La víctima*, Metroactive website, 12–18 September 1996, www.metroactive .com/papers/metro/09.12.96/stage-9637.html (accessed 16 September 2013); Backalenick, "Grand Irish Night"; Roy Sander, review of *Away Alone*, *Backstage*, 9 February 1990, 48A; Holden, "Illegal Immigrants on Irish Mile"; Milvy, "Shamrock Grows in Bronx."
69. Thorpe, *Just Like Us*, 330.
70. Luibhéid, *Entry Denied*, 83.

5   Act § 331—Alien Enemies

1. Michael John Garcés, *Los Illegals*, Theatre 41, no. 2 (2011): 68–119. References to this play will be noted parenthetically and abbreviated *LI* (all italics in original script).
2. Ntare Guma Mbaho Mwine, *Biro* (Seattle: Amazon Digital Services, 2010). Citations to *Biro* are noted parenthetically and abbreviated *BI*. I refer to Kindle location numbers and maintain Mwine's line divisions and punctuation. I also base observations about *Biro* on the DVD recording of a performance at Uganda's National Theatre (Canoga Park, CA: Cinema Libre, 2007).
3. Yussef El Guindi, *Back of the Throat* (New York Dramatists Play Service, 2006). References to this play are noted parenthetically and abbreviated *BT* (all italics in original script).
4. El Guindi does not reveal where his protagonist is from; he offers the terms "Arab/Muslim" and "Arab/Muslim-American" ("Author's Introduction" to *Back of the Throat*, *TheatreForum* 29 [Summer/Fall 2006]: 26). I follow suit, aware that the terms are problematic as questions of national origin and religious practice do not neatly overlap.
5. Julian Samora, with the assistance of Jorge A. Bustamante F. and Gilbert Cardenas, *Los Mojados: The Wetback Story* (Notre Dame: University of Notre Dame Press, 1971), 11; Stephen H. Legomsky, "The New Path of Immigration Law: Asymmetric Incorporation of Criminal Justice Norms," *Washington and Lee Law Review* 64, nos. 2–3 (2007): 469.
6. Mathews v. Diaz, 426 U.S. 67, 77–80 (1976).
7. See 8 U.S.C. § 1357 (2013); INS v. Lopez-Mendoza, 468 U.S. 1032 (1984); Aguilera-Enriquez v. INS, 516 F.2d 565 (6th Cir. 1975), cert. denied, 423 U.S. 1050 (1976); and Demore v. Kim, 538 U.S. 510 (2003). I should note that individual states cannot discriminate as freely between aliens, legal or otherwise, and citizens (Graham v. Richardson, 403 U.S. 365 [1971]; and Plyler v. Doe, 457 U.S. 202 [1982]). Prior to *Graham* and *Plyler*, states had more discretion in making such distinctions so long as the discrimination related to special public interests. However, the Court's *Arizona v. U.S.* decision in 2012 (132 S. Ct. 2492 [2012]) has made it decidedly less clear how much discretion individual states now have in regulating noncitizens.
8. *Mathews*, 426 U.S. at 79–80; Judy Rabinovitz, Great Issues Forum, "Power & Law: Immigration Reform" (panel presentation, City University of New

York, 6 April 2009); and Perez v. Brownell, 356 U.S. 44, 64 (1958) (Warren, C. J., dissenting). See also Margaret R. Somers, *Genealogies of Citizenship: Markets, Statelessness, and the Right to Have Rights* (Cambridge: Cambridge University Press, 2008).

9. The literature on this subject is extensive. For excellent, up-to-date summaries, see Jonathan Xavier Inda and Julie A. Dowling, "Governing Migrant Illegality," introduction to *Governing Immigration through Crime: A Reader*, ed. Dowling and Inda (Stanford: Stanford Social Sciences, Stanford University Press, 2013), 1–36; and Ediberto Román, *Those Damned Immigrants: America's Hysteria over Undocumented Immigration* (New York: New York University Press, 2013).

10. Susan Bibler Coutin, *Nations of Emigrants: Shifting Boundaries of Citizenship in El Salvador and the United States* (Ithaca: Cornell University Press, 2007), 24; Joseph Nevins, *Operation Gatekeeper and Beyond: The War on "Illegals" and the Remaking of the U.S.-Mexico Boundary* (New York: Routledge, 2010), 150, 180, 176, 116. On the unreported crimes committed on immigrants, see Eithne Luibhéid, *Entry Denied: Controlling Sexuality at the Border* (Minneapolis: University of Minnesota Press, 2002), 104; see also various reports by Human Rights Watch, including *Cultivating Fear: The Vulnerability of Immigrant Farmworkers in the US to Sexual Violence and Sexual Harassment*, 16 May 2012; *Crossing the Line: Human Rights Abuses along the U.S. Border with Mexico Persist amid Climate of Impunity*, 1 April 1995; and *Brutality Unchecked: Human Rights Abuses along the U.S. Border with Mexico*, 1 June 1992, all available at www.hrw.org/en/publications (accessed 15 September 2013).

11. David M. Engel and Frank W. Munger, *Rights of Inclusion: Law and Identity in the Life Stories of Americans with Disabilities* (Chicago: University of Chicago Press, 2003), 11.

12. Nevins, *Operation Gatekeeper*, 177.

13. Biro's narrative contrasts reports of serious lapses in treatment for immigrant detainees with HIV/AIDS (see Human Rights Watch's *Chronic Indifference: HIV/AIDS Services for Immigrants Detained by the United States*, 5 December 2007, available at www.hrw.org/en/publications [accessed 15 September 2013]).

14. Coutin, *Nations of Emigrants*, 30, 111. For notable current examples of dehumanizing anti-immigrant rhetoric, see Lucas L. Johnson II, "State Rep. Curry Todd Likens Illegal Immigrant Births to Multiplying Rats," *Commercial Appeal* (Memphis), 11 November 2010, commercialappeal.com/news/2010/nov/11/lawmaker-makes-rat-comparison/ (accessed 17 August 2013); and Dana Milbank, "A Fruitless Attempt," *Washington Post*, 25 July 2013, A2.

15. Linda S. Bosniak, *The Citizen and the Alien: Dilemmas of Contemporary Membership* (Princeton: Princeton University Press, 2006), 71; Valerie Neal, "Slings and Arrows of Outrageous Fortune: The Deportation of 'Aggravated Felons,'" *Vanderbilt Journal of Transnational Law* 36 (November 2003): 1621–22.

16. Shahram Khosravi, *"Illegal" Traveller: An Auto-Ethnography of Borders* (New York: Palgrave Macmillan, 2010), 67.

17. "Alabama's Immigration Law Permanently Blocked in Justice Department Lawsuit," US Department of Justice website, 25 November 2013, www .justice.gov/usao/aln/News/November%202013/Nov%2025,%202013%20 Alabama%20Immigration.htm (accessed 26 December 2013).

18. Tram Nguyen, *We Are All Suspects Now: Untold Stories from Immigrant Communities after 9/11* (Boston: Beacon Press, 2005), xv.

19. Michael Garcés, interviewed by author at Cornerstone's offices in Los Angeles, 7 June 2010. For more on the Justice Cycle, see Anne García-Romero, "Cornerstone Theater Company's *Justice Cycle*," *TheatreForum* 38 (Winter/Spring 2011): 47–59; and Cornerstone's website, cornerstonetheater.org/work/2007-2010 -justice-cycle/ (accessed 21 August 2013).

20. I base my observations on a videotape of one of Cornerstone's performances, archived in its Los Angeles office.

21. Sally Engle Merry, *Getting Justice and Getting Even: Legal Consciousness among Working-Class Americans* (Chicago: University of Chicago Press, 1990), 5; Nevins, *Operation Gatekeeper*, 114, 8.

22. See Shonna L. Trinch, *Latinas' Narratives of Domestic Abuse: Discrepant Versions of Violence* (Amsterdam: John Benjamins, 2003), 2.

23. Michel Foucault, *Discipline & Punish: The Birth of the Prison*, trans. Alan Sheridan (New York: Vintage, 1977), 9.

24. Robert Hariman, "Performing the Laws: Popular Trials and Social Knowledge," in *Popular Trials: Rhetoric, Mass Media, and the Law*, ed. Hariman (Tuscaloosa: University of Alabama Press, 1990), 17 (italics in original).

25. Engel and Manger, *Rights of Inclusion*, 92.

26. I am indebted here to Diana Taylor's work on Argentina's *desaparecidos*. I do not wish to compare and contrast one system of violence to another but merely draw on the theoretical possibility that the "disappeared" are, "by definition, always already the object of representation" (Diana Taylor, *Disappearing Acts: Spectacles of Gender and Nationalism in Argentina's "Dirty War"* [Durham: Duke University Press, 1997], 140).

27. Foucault, *Discipline & Punish*, 95; Coutin, *Nations of Emigrants*, 22.

28. Peter H. Schuck, *Citizens, Strangers, and In-Betweens: Essays on Immigration and Citizenship* (Boulder: Westview Press, 1998), 35.

29. Dora Schriro, *Immigration Detention Overview and Recommendations*, report to DHS, 6 October 2009, available at www.iaumc.org/console/files /oFiles_Library_XZXLCZ/2010HomelandSecurityImmigrationDetention Overview_MJERXUXV.pdf (accessed 21 September 2013), 4, 6. On changing nature of immigration detention in the late twentieth and early twenty-first centuries, see also Mark Dow, *American Gulag: Inside U.S. Immigration Prisons* (Berkeley: University of California Press, 2004).

30. Inda and Dowling, "Governing Migrant Illegality," 17.

31. Inda and Dowling, "Governing Migrant Illegality," 16; Charlie Savage, "Dept. of Justice Seeks to Curtail Stiff Drug Terms," *New York Times*, 12 August 2013, A1. On immigration industrial complex, see also Deepa Fernandes, *Targeted: Homeland Security and the Business of Immigration*

(New York: Seven Stories Press, 2007); and Alissa R. Ackerman and Rich Furman, "The Criminalization of Immigration and the Privatization of the Immigration Detention: Implications for Justice," *Contemporary Justice Review* 16, no. 2 (2013): 251–63.

32. Moustafa Bayoumi, *How Does It Feel to Be a Problem?: Being Young and Arab in America* (New York: Penguin Press, 2008), 23–24, 28. On the length and condition of detention for immigrants, see Amnesty International, *Jailed without Justice: Immigration Detention in the USA*, 25 March 2009, available at www.amnestyusa.org/document.php?id=ENGUSA20090325002&lang=e (accessed 15 September 2013); David Cole, *Enemy Aliens: Double Standards and Constitutional Freedoms in the War on Terrorism* (New York: New Press, 2003); and various Human Rights Watch reports, including *Detained and at Risk: Sexual Abuse and Harassment in United States Immigration Detention*, 25 August 2010; *Costly and Unfair: Flaws in US Immigration Detention Policy*, 6 May 2010; *Locked Up Far Away: The Transfer of Immigrants to Remote Detention Centers in the United States*, 2 December 2009; *Detained and Dismissed: Women's Struggles to Obtain Health Care in United States Immigration Detention*, 17 March 2009; and *Detained and Deprived of Rights: Children in the Custody of the U.S. Immigration and Naturalization Service*, 1 December 1998, all available at www.hrw.org/en/publications (accessed 15 September 2013).

33. Jean Comaroff and John L. Comaroff, "Criminal Obsessions, after Foucault: Postcoloniality, Policing, and the Metaphysics of Disorder," in *Law and Disorder in the Postcolony*, ed. Comaroff and Comaroff (Chicago: University of Chicago Press, 2006), 276; Diana Taylor, "Afterword: War Play," *PMLA* 124, no. 5 (October 2009): 1892.

34. Nevins, *Operation Gatekeeper*, 177–78.

35. Pierre Bourdieu, *Language & Symbolic Power*, trans. Gino Raymond and Matthew Adamson, ed. John B. Thompson (Cambridge, MA: Harvard University Press, 1991), 140.

36. David Bacon, *Illegal People: How Globalization Creates Migration and Criminalizes Immigrants* (Boston: Beacon Press, 2008), 184.

37. Nevins, *Operation Gatekeeper*, 183 (my emphasis); Lisa Marie Cacho, *Social Death: Racialized Rightlessness and the Criminalization of the Unprotected* (New York: New York University Press, 2012), esp. her chapter, "Immigrant Rights versus Civil Rights," 115–45.

38. Sonja Kuftinec, *Staging America: Cornerstone and Community-Based Theater* (Carbondale: Southern Illinois University Press, 2003), 9–10.

39. For a most recent analysis on this much-studied phenomenon, see Natalie Masuoka and Jane Junn, *The Politics of Belonging: Race, Public Opinion, and Immigration* (Chicago: University of Chicago Press, 2013).

40. Nevins, *Operation Gatekeeper*, 168.

41. Kim Fellner, *Wrestling with Starbucks: Conscience, Capital, Cappuccino* (New Brunswick: Rutgers University Press, 2008), 2.

42. Michel Foucault, "Space, Knowledge, and Power" (1982), interview by Paul Rabinow, trans. Christian Hubert, in *The Foucault Reader*, ed. Rabinow (New York: Pantheon Books, 1984), 245.

43. Juan José Mangandi, quoted in David Montgomery, "Work, Then Play; Day Laborers at Night, Blurring the Border between Life and Art," *Washington Post*, 6 August 2007, C1.
44. Leisy Abrego, "Legitimacy, Social Identity, and the Mobilization of Law: The Effects of Assembly Bill 540 on Undocumented Students in California," *Law & Social Inquiry* 33, no. 3 (Summer 2008): 709–34.
45. Judith Butler and Gayatri Chakravorty Spivak, *Who Sings the Nation-State?: Language, Politics, Belonging* (London: Seagull Books, 2007), 58–69; Noa Ben-Asher, "Who Says 'I Do'?: Reviewing Judith Butler & Gayatri Chakravorty Spivak, *Who Sings the Nation-State? Language, Politics, Belonging*," *Yale Journal of Law and Feminism* 21 (2009): 250.
46. Butler and Spivak, *Who Sings the Nation-State?*, 68–69.
47. Peter Brooks, "The Law as Narrative and Rhetoric," in *Law's Stories: Narrative and Rhetoric in the Law*, ed. Brooks and Paul Gewirtz (New Haven: Yale University Press, 1996), 16; Engel and Munger, *Rights of Inclusion*, 40.
48. Michel Foucault, "Intellectuals and Power: A Conversation between Michel Foucault and Gilles Deleuze" (1972), in *Language, Counter-Memory, and Practice: Selected Essays and Interviews by Michel Foucault*, ed. Donald F. Bouchard (Ithaca: Cornell University Press, 1977), 209; and Foucault, *Discipline & Punish*, 200.
49. Coutin, *Nations of Emigrants*, 178, 112, 16. For stories referenced below, see, for example, Jose Antonio Vargas, "Outlaw," *New York Times*, 26 June 2011, MM22; Julia Preston, "Out of the Shadows: A Speech Makes History," *New York Times*, 7 September 2012, A14; Eva Longoria, "Dulce Matuz: Citizen-in-Waiting," *Time*, 30 April 2012, 68; and Manny Fernandez, "Vying for Campus President, Illegal Immigrant Gets a Gamut of Responses," *New York Times*, 10 March 2012, A11. On the success of the DREAMers as a viable political bloc, see Walter Nicholls, *The DREAMers: How the Undocumented Youth Movement Transformed the Immigrant Rights Debate* (Stanford: Stanford University Press, 2013).
50. Sally Engle Merry, *Colonizing Hawai'i: The Cultural Power of Law* (Princeton: Princeton University Press, 2000), 220.
51. Coutin, *Nations of Emigrants*, 47.
52. Giorgio Agamben, *State of Exception*, trans. Kevin Attell (Chicago: University of Chicago Press, 2005), 3, 39, 2. I do not engage here in philosophical arguments over "bare life," Agamben's conception for the kind of exposure to state violence that results from the state of exception. Rather, I am interested in the ways in which "exceptionality" seeps into discussions and analyses of cultural products.
53. Amnesty International, *U.S. of America—Amnesty International's Concerns Regarding Post September 11 Detentions in the USA* (London: International Secretariat, 2002), 1; Philip Shenon, "Report on U.S. Antiterrorism Law Alleges Violations of Civil Rights," *New York Times*, 21 July 2003, A1.
54. Bayoumi, *How Does It Feel*, 118, 133, 3; Dalia Basiouny, "The Powerful Voice of Women Dramatists in the Arab American Theatre Movement," PhD diss., The Graduate Center, City University of New York, 2009, 17, 3.

55. Nguyen, *We Are All Suspects Now*, 81; Allan Havis, introduction to *American Political Plays after 9/11*, ed. Havis (Carbondale: Southern Illinois University Press, 2010), 9.

56. On immigration and terrorism, see Bill Ong Hing, *Deporting Our Souls: Values, Morality, and Immigration Policy* (Cambridge: Cambridge University Press, 2006), 140–63. On immigration and violent crime, see, for example, Scott Akins, Rubén G. Rumbaut, and Richard Stansfield, "Immigration, Economic Disadvantage, and Homicide: A Community-Level Analysis of Austin, Texas," *Homicide Studies* 13, no. 3 (August 2009): 307–14.

57. Nguyen, *We Are All Suspects Now*, 14; Coutin, *Nations of Emigrants*, 28.

58. Nguyen, *We Are All Suspects Now*, 149; Nevins, *Operation Gatekeeper*, 179.

59. El Guindi, "Author's Introduction," 26.

60. Agamben, *State of Exception*, 28.

61. Yussef El Guindi, quoted in Jenn Q. Goddu, "A Play that Asks Tough Questions," *Chicago Tribune*, 7 April 2006, section 7, p. 7.

62. Nguyen, *We Are All Suspects Now*, 14; Bayoumi, *How Does It Feel*; and Sharon Perlmutter, review of *Back of the Throat*, Talkin' Broadway website, July 2006, www.talkinbroadway.com/regional/la/la215.html (accessed 18 September 2013) (emphasis in original).

63. Lisa Magaña and Erik Lee, eds., preface to *Latino Politics and Arizona's Immigration Law SB 1070* (New York: Springer, 2013), v.

64. Bayoumi, *How Does It Feel*, 134; Yussef El Guindi, interviewed by Ina Rometsch, Furious Theatre Company website, 22 June 2006, firioustheatre .blogspot.com/2006/06/interview-with-playwright-yussef-el.html (accessed 1 September 2013).

65. Yussef El Guindi, quoted by Tirdad Derakhshani, "A Funny, Ferocious Drama Post-9/11: An Egyptian-born Writer Mingles the Immigrant Experience, the War on Terror, and Office Politics," *Philadelphia Inquirer*, 9 March 2010, Daily Magazine D1. On English-Only legislation, see Carlos R. Soltero, *Latinos and American Law: Landmark Supreme Court Cases* (Austin: University of Texas Press, 2006), esp. chap. 14. For an example of language policing, see Miriam Jordan, "Arizona Grades Teachers on Fluency," *Wall Street Journal*, 30 April 2010, A3.

66. Bayoumi, *How Does It Feel*, 11.

67. Neil Genzlinger, "Homeland Spies Poking Around a Cluttered Apartment," *New York Times*, 14 February 2006, E5.

68. El Guindi, "Author's Introduction," 26.

69. Agamben, *State of Exception*, 8.

70. Juan José Mangandi, interviewed by author at Cornerstone's offices in Los Angeles, 11 June 2010; Ntare Mwine, interviewed in "Ugandan-American Filmmaker Discusses AIDS, Other Issues in Africa," America.gov, 19 February 2009, iipdigital.usembassy.gov/st/english/texttrans/2009/02/20090219145655xj snommis0.9413874.html#axzz2dgAmwcwU (accessed 18 August 2013).

71. Ntare Mwine, quoted in Misha Berson, "AIDS Theater Now," *Seattle Times*, 3 April 2005, J4.

72. García-Romero, "*Justice Cycle*," 48.

73. Nicole Kristal, "Coming Home," *Back Stage West*, 27 October 2005, 10.
74. Kuftinec, *Staging America*, 50; María Refugio Jacinto, quoted in Paula Díaz, "La vida de los jornaleros es dura," *Diario HOY* (Los Angeles), 14 May 2007, available through Cornerstone Theater's website, cornerstone.pbworks .com/w/page/16506966/LOS%20ILLEGALS (accessed 3 October 2010), my translation; Lorena Moreno, interviewed by author at Cornerstone's offices in Los Angeles, 11 June 2010. For more on the transformative nature of *Los Illegals*, see García-Romero, "Justice Cycle."
75. Bacon, *Illegal People*, 126; Montgomery, "Work, Then Play."
76. Nevins, *Operation Gatekeeper*, 216; Butler and Spivak, *Who Sings the Nation-State?*, 56.
77. "Biro: Uganda's Story," *Monitor* (Kampala), 30 January 2003; Damaso Reyes, "'Biro' Is Captivating," *New York Amsterdam News*, 22–28 April 2004, 19; Lyn Gardner, review of *Biro*, *The Guardian* (London), 11 November 2003, 28; and Steve Wiecking, review of *Biro*, *Seattle Weekly*, 13 April 2005, www .seattleweekly.com/2005-04-13/arts/biro/ (accessed 17 August 2013).
78. Catherine E. Wall, review of *Los Illegals*, *Latin American Theatre Review* 41, no. 1 (Fall 2007): 189.
79. Nevins, *Operation Gatekeeper*, 202.
80. See Karen W. Arenson, with Sean McManus, "Immigrant Game at N.Y.U. Draws Protesters," *New York Times*, 23 February 2007, B3; Margot Adler, "NYU Immigration Game Draws Protests," NPR, 23 February 2007, www .npr.org/templates/story/story.php?storyId=7565623; and "Hundreds Protest NYU Republicans' 'Find the Illegal Immigrant' Game," Democracy Now! website, www.democracynow.org/2007/2/23/hundreds_protest_nyu_republicans _find_the (both accessed 1 September 2013).

6   Act § 505—Appeals

1. Times Square Alliance, timessquarenyc.org/index.aspx and timessquarenyc .org/about-the-alliance/welcome/index.aspx#.Ujy3K9JJOuI (accessed 20 September 2013). On number of visitors, see Kate Appleton et al., "World's Most-Visited Tourist Attractions," *Travel + Leisure*, October 2011, travelandleisure.com/articles/worlds-most-visited-tourist-attractions/2 (accessed 28 September 2013).
2. David W. Dunlap, "Atop the New TKTS Booth, Ruby-Red Stairs with a View of the Great White Way," *New York Times*, 17 October 2008, A29. On explosion of costumed performers, see Michael Wilson, "Enforcement a Little Fuzzy on Elmos," *New York Times*, 30 June 2012, A17; and Matt Flegenheimer, "In the New Times Square, Still a Mix of Characters," *New York Times*, 14 August 2012, A13.
3. Eugenio Barba and Nicola Savarese, *A Dictionary of Theatre Anthropology: The Secret Art of the Performer*, 2nd ed. (New York: Routledge, 2006), 16–17.
4. Novack, quoted in Wilson, "Enforcement a Little Fuzzy." For regulating performers, see Edgar Sandoval, John Doyle, and Larry McShane, "Smiles in

Times Square," *NY Daily News*, 11 December 2011, News 5; Vivian Yee and Kirk Semple, "Nasty Elmo Is Gone, and the Others Are Tickled," *New York Times*, 26 June 2012, A19; Sumathi Reddy and Amber Benham, "Behind the Mickey Masks," *Wall Street Journal*, 27 September 2011, A17; and Christopher Robbins, "Are the Costumed Grifters of Times Square Diluting Disney's Brand?" *Gothamist*, 19 June 2011, gothamist.com/2011/06/19/are_the_costumed _grifters_of_times.php (accessed 19 September 2013).

5. Caramelito asked me to use his stage name rather than his given name. We conducted the interview by phone in Spanish, and all translations of his ideas are mine. The interview took place on 12 September 2012.

6. Reddy and Benham, "Behind the Mickey Masks"; and Bruce Wallace, "Mickey and Minnie May Be Undocumented," *The World*, PRI, 24 November 2011, www.pri.org/stories/2011-11-24/mickey-and-minnie-may-be-undocumented (accessed 16 April 2014). For the record, Caramelito and I did not discuss his immigration status.

7. Reddy and Benham, "Behind the Mickey Masks."

8. Reddy and Benham, "Behind the Mickey Masks."

9. Yee and Semple, "Nasty Elmo Is Gone"; Christina Boyle and Stephen Rex Brown, "Fast & Furriest," *New York Daily News*, 10 April 2013, 4.

10. Sandoval, Doyle, and McShane, "Smiles in Times Square"; Alissa Fleck, "Who's Really Behind that Furry Costume? A Look at NYC's Elmo Impersonators," *NY Press*, 29 June 2012, nypress.com/whos-really-behind-that-furry-costumes -after-central-park-arrest-a-look-at-nycs-elmo-impersonators/ (accessed 19 September 2013).

11. Novack, quoted in Wilson, "Enforcement a Little Fuzzy"; "Elmo Is Getting Arrested in Times Square," YouTube, 12 July 2009, www.youtube.com /watch?v=OvlyeECpB_Y (accessed 19 September 2013).

12. Wallace, "Mickey and Minnie May Be Undocumented"; Fleck, "Who's Really Behind that Furry Costume?"

13. Judith Butler and Gayatri Chakravorty Spivak, *Who Sings the Nation-State?: Language, Politics, Belonging* (London: Seagull Books, 2007), 69.

14. Jose Antonio Vargas, "Not Legal, Not Leaving," *Time*, 25 June 2012, 36.

15. *30 Rock*, season 6, episode 21, "The Return of Avery Jessup," first aired 10 May 2012. To be sure, the "creepy, off-brand Sesame Street characters," as they are described by protagonist Liz Lemon, are not portrayed positively. Marking the characters as immigrants also could be problematic.

16. Susan Bibler Coutin, *Nations of Emigrants: Shifting Boundaries of Citizenship in El Salvador and the United States* (Ithaca: Cornell University Press, 2007), 122–48.

17. See Reddy and Benham, "Behind the Mickey Masks"; and Wallace, "Mickey and Minnie May Be Undocumented."

18. "Remittances to Peru Reached $2.53 Billion in 2010," *Andean Air Mail & Peruvian Times*, 14 March 2011, www.peruviantimes.com/14/remittances -to-peru-reached-2-53-billion-in-2010/11230/ (accessed 19 September 2013); Ministerio de Relaciones Exteriores, Secretaría de Comunidades Peruanas en

el Exterior, "Guía para El Inmigrante Peruano Reciente," esp. 126–27, available at www.consuladoperubaires.org/Guia-Inmigrante-Peruano-Reciente .pdf (accessed 20 September 2013).

19. Kit Johnson, "The Wonderful World of Disney Visas," *Florida Law Review* 63 (2011): 915–58.

20. Coutin, *Nations of Emigrants*, 103, 110 (emphasis in original), 203, 110.

Bibliography

Selected List of Theatrical Works Engaging Undocumentedness and Immigration Law

* **Unpublished Text**

Adams, John (music), and June Jordan (libretto and lyrics). *I Was Looking at the Ceiling and Then I Saw the Sky: Earthquake/Romance.* New York: Scribner, 1995.

Akalaitis, JoAnne. *Green Card.* New York: Broadway Play Publishing, 1991.

Akhtar, Ayad. *Disgraced.* New York: Bloomsbury Methuen Drama, 2013.

*Albán, Carlo. *Intríngulis.* Unpublished script, NYC draft for INTAR production, 2011.

Albany Park Theater Project. *Home/Land: A Theatrical Journey.* In *The Goodman Theatre's Festival Latino: Six Plays,* edited by Henry D. Godinez and Ramón Rivera-Servera, 233–92. Evanston, IL: Northwestern University Press, 2013.

Andino, Peky. *Medea llama por cobrar.* Quito: Tribal Editores, 2005.

*Au Yong, Byron (music), and Aaron Jafferis (libretto). *Stuck Elevator,* 2013.

Bonilla, Alberto. *Walking to America.* In *Plays and Playwrights 2005,* edited by Martin Denton, 269–94. New York: The New York Theatre Experience, 2005.

*Cara Mía Theatre Co., *The Dreamers,* 2013.

Cardona, Ed., Jr. *American Jornalero.* South Gate, CA: NoPassport Press, 2012.

*———. *La Ruta,* 2013.

Carlos Manuel. *La Vida Loca.* Sandy, UT: ECKO House Publishing, 2010.

*Carrillo, Eduardo. *El proceso de Aurelio Pompa,* n.d.

Casas, José. *14.* In Sandoval, *Borders on Stage,* 69–128.

Chin, Frank. *The Year of the Dragon.* Seattle: University of Washington Press, 1981.

*Chua, Kat. *Undocumented,* 2011.

*Chung, Mia, Jessica Litwak, Chiori Miyagawa, Saviana Stanescu, and Andrea Thome. *Dream Acts,* 2012.

Cosson, Steve (The Civilians). *(I Am) Nobody's Lunch.* London: Oberon Books, 2006.

Culture Clash. *Bordertown.* In Culture Clash, *Culture Clash in Americca,* 9–64.

*Domestic Workers' Association (DWA). *Super Doméstica,* n.d.

Duarte-Clark, Rodrigo. *Brujerías.* In Kanellos and Huerta, *Nuevos Pasos,* 8–17.

El Guindi, Yussef. *Back of the Throat.* New York: Dramatists Play Service, 2006.

Gallagher, Mary. *¿De dónde?* New York: Dramatists Play Service, 1991.

Garcés, Michael John. *Los Illegals. Theatre* 41, no. 2 (2011): 68–119.

García, Saulo. *El Insomnio Americano,* DVD. Miami: Saulo García, 2007.

Gómez-Peña, Guillermo. *Dangerous Border Crossers: The Artist Talks Back.* London: Routledge, 2000.

———. *Mexterminator vs. The Global Predator.* In Bixler and Seda, *Trans/Acting,* 238–59.

———. *The New World Border: Prophecies, Poems, and Loqueras for the End of the Century.* San Francisco: City Lights Books, 2001.

———. *Warrior for Gringostroika: Essays, Performance Texts, and Poetry.* St. Paul, MN: Graywolf Press, 1993.

González S., Silvia. *Boxcar.* In Sandoval, *Borders on Stage,* 37–68.

González-Pando, Miguel. *The Great American Justice Game.* In *Cuban Theater in the United States: A Critical Anthology,* edited by Luis F. González-Cruz and Francesca M. Colecchia, 78–108. Tempe: Bilingual Press, 1992.

Hartzler, Kara. *No Roosters in the Desert,* based on the fieldwork by Anna Ochoa O'Leary. South Gate, CA: NoPassport Press, 2010.

*———. *Trash,* 2014.

Havis, Allan. *Hospitality.* New York: Broadway Play Publishing, 1989.

*Helú, Antonio. *Los mexicanos se van,* 1932.

*Hinojosa Díaz, Hugo Alfredo. *Deserts.* Translated by Caridad Svich. Unpublished script from translator, 2007.

———. *Desiertos.* Col. Cuauhtémoc, México, DF: Consejo Nacional para la Cultura y las Artes, 2007.

Houston, Velina Hasu. *Tea.* In Uno, *Unbroken Thread,* 161–200.

Hwang, David Henry. *FOB.* In *FOB and Other Plays,* 1–50. New York: Plume, 1990.

*Jones, Sarah. *Bridge and Tunnel.* Typescript dated 8 February 2006 available at New York Public Library for the Performing Arts.

Lacámara, Carlos. *Nowhere on the Border.* In *Nuestras Voces: Latino Plays from Repertorio Español's MetLife Playwriting Competition,* vol. 1, 257–335. South Gate, CA: NoPassport Press, 2012.

*LaChiusa, Michael, and Ellen Fitzhugh. *Tres Niñas* (part of *Inner Voices: Three Solo Musicals*). Typescript dated 16 May 2008 available at New York Public Library for the Performing Arts.

*LeFranc, Dan. *In the Labyrinth,* 2008.

Leguizamo, John. *Mambo Mouth.* In *The Works of John Leguizamo,* 161–248. New York: Harper, 2008.

Lim, Genny. *Paper Angels.* In Uno, *Unbroken Thread,* 11–52.

———. *Paper Angels* on PBS. Directed by John Lone, aired on 17 June 1985. Recording available at Paley Center for Media in New York City.

Loomer, Lisa. *¡Bocón!* Woodstock, IL: Dramatic Publishing, 1998.

———. *Living Out.* New York: Dramatists Play Service, 2005.

López, Josefina. *Detained in the Desert.* In *Detained in the Desert & Other Plays,* 16–65. Carlsbad, CA: WPR Books, 2011.

———. *Real Women Have Curves.* Woodstock, IL: Dramatic Publishing, 1996.

———. *Simply María or the American Dream*. In Feyder, *Shattering the Myth*, 113–41.

———. *Unconquered Spirits*. Woodstock, IL: Dramatic Publishing, 1997.

López, Josefina, and George LaVoo. *Real Women Have Curves*, DVD. Directed by Patricia Cardoso. New York: HBO Video, 2003.

Malpica, Javier. *Our Dad Is in Atlantis*. Translated by Jorge Ignacio Cortiñas. *American Theatre* 25, no. 6 (July–August 2008): 69–82.

*Marting, Kristin, Mahayana Landowne, and Tal Yarden. *Lush Valley*, 2011.

Mayer, Oliver. *Conjunto*. In *Oliver Mayer: Collected Plays*, 159–225. South Gate, CA: No Passport Press, 2007.

Miller, Arthur. *A View from the Bridge* (two-act version, 1956). In *Arthur Miller: Collected Plays 1944–1961*, 569–636. New York: Library of America, 2006.

*Miyagawa, Chiori. *A Winter's Captive*, in development.

Montoya, Richard, and Culture Clash. *American Night: The Ballad of Juan José*. Ashland: Oregon Shakespeare Festival Scripts, 2010.

Montoya, Richard, Ricardo Salinas, and Herbert Siguenza. *Bordertown*, sound recording. Venice, CA: L.A. Theatre Works, 2006.

Moraga, Cherríe L. *The Hungry Woman: A Mexican Medea*. Albuquerque: West End Press, 2001.

———. *Watsonville: Some Place Not Here* and *Circle in the Dirt: El Pueblo de East Palo Alto*. Albuquerque: West End Press, 2002.

Mwine, Ntare Guma Mbaho. *Biro*. Seattle: Amazon Digital Services, 2010.

———. *Biro*, DVD. Canoga Park, CA: Cinema Libre, 2007.

Najera, Rick. *Latinologues*, DVD, vols. 1 and 2. Chatsworth, CA: Image Entertainment, 2005.

———. *The Pain of the Macho and Other Plays*. Houston: Arte Público Press, 1997.

*Navarro, Gabriel. *Los emigrados*, n.d.

Noble, Janet. *Away Alone*. New York: Samuel French, 1990.

Noble, Janet, and Noel Pearson. *Gold in the Streets*, DVD. Directed by Elizabeth Gill. London: ITV Studios Home Entertainment, 1996.

*Okai-Davies, Kabu. *In Another Man's Name*, 1992. Unpublished manuscript available at New York Public Library Schomburg Center.

*Ordaz, Evangeline. *Visitor's Guide to Arivaca (Map Not to Scale)*, 2006.

Portillo Trambley, Estela. *Puente Negro*. In *Sor Juana and Other Plays*, 1–35. Tempe: Bilingual Press, 1983.

———. *Sun Images*. In Kanellos and Huerta, *Nuevos Pasos*, 18–42.

Powers, Frank. *The First Born*. In Williams, *Chinese Other*, 149–73.

Prida, Dolores. *Beautiful Señoritas & Other Plays*, edited by Judith Weiss. Houston: Arte Público Press, 1991.

*Ramirez, Lisa, and Domestic Workers United (DWU). *Invisible Women-Rise/ mujeres invisibles-superan*, 2010.

Rascón Banda, Victor Hugo. *La mujer que cayó del cielo*. México, DF: Escenología, 2000.

Reyes, Guillermo. *Deporting the Divas*. In *Gay Drama Now: An Anthology*, edited by John M. Clum, 323–411. Amherst, NY: Cambria Press, 2013.

Reyes, Guillermo. *Men on the Verge of a His-panic Breakdown*. Woodstock, IL: Dramatic Publishing, 1999.

——. *Places to Touch Him*. In Sandoval, *Borders on Stage*, 177–221.

Rodgers, Richard (music), Oscar Hammerstein II (lyrics), and Joseph Fields (book). *Flower Drum Song*. New York: Farrar, Straus and Cudahy, 1959.

——. *Flower Drum Song*, DVD. Directed by Henry Coster. 1961. Universal City, CA: Universal Studios Home Entertainment, 2006.

Rodgers, Richard (music), Oscar Hammerstein II (lyrics), and David Henry Hwang (book). *Flower Drum Song*. New York: Theatre Communications Group, 2003.

*Romero, Elaine. *Wetback*, 2010.

Sánchez-Scott, Milcha, with Jeremy Blahnik. *Latina*. In Huerta, *Necessary Theater*, 76–141.

*Saracho, Tanya. *Kita y Fernanda*, 2002.

*——. *Our Lady of the Underpass*, 2009.

Schimmelpfennig, Roland. *The Golden Dragon*. Translated by David Tushingham. London: Oberon Books, 2011.

*Soame Citlalime, and Daniel Carlton. *La Casa Rosa*, 2010.

Solis, Octavio. *Lydia*. New York: Samuel French, 2010.

——. *River Plays (El Otro, Dreamlandia, Bethlehem)*. South Gate, CA: NoPassport Press, 2010.

*Solomon, Jeffrey. *De Novo*, 2010.

*Spangler, Matthew. *Tortilla Curtain* (based on the novel by T.C. Boyle), 2012.

Stanescu, Saviana. *Aliens with Extraordinary Skills*. New York: Samuel French, 2009.

Teatro de la Esperanza. *Guadalupe*. In Huerta, *Necessary Theater*, 208–57.

——. *La víctima*. In Huerta, *Necessary Theater*, 316–65.

*Teatro Jornalero Sin Fronteras. *Esclavitud Moderna*, 2009.

*Teatro Línea de Sombra. *Amarillo*, 2009. Video of 9 November 2012 performance available for viewing through On the Boards (www.ontheboards.tv).

Teatro Raíces. *E. T.—The Alien*. In *Teatro Chicana: A Collective Memoir and Selected Plays*, edited by Laura E. Garcia, Sandra M. Gutierrez, and Felicitas Nuñez, 229–40. Austin: University of Texas Press, 2008.

*Torres-Tama, José. *Aliens, Immigrants & Other Evildoers*, 2010.

Valdez, Luis. *Quinta Temporada* and *Los Vendidos*. In *Luis Valdez—Early Works: Actos, Bernabé, and Pensamiento Serpentino*, 28–39 and 40–52. Second printing. Houston: Arte Público Press, 1994.

Villarreal, Edit. *My Visits with MGM (My Grandmother Marta)*. In Feyder, *Shattering the Myth*, 143–207.

Wallace, Naomi. *The War Boys*. In *In the Heart of America and Other Plays*, 144–96. New York: Theatre Communications Group, 2001.

Wong, Elizabeth. *Letters to a Student Revolutionary*. In Uno, *Unbroken Thread*, 261–308.

Yew, Chay. *A Beautiful Country*. In *The Hyphenated American: Four Plays by Chay Yew*, 167–275. New York: Grove Press, 2002.

Legal Cases and Statutes

*Adams v. Howerto*n, 673 F.2d 1036 (9th Cir.), cert. denied, 458 U.S. 1111 (1982).

AEDPA: *Antiterrorism and Effective Death Penalty Act of 1996.* Public Law 104-132, *U.S. Statutes at Large* 110 (1996): 1214.

Aguilera-Enriquez v. INS, 516 F.2d 565 (6th Cir. 1975), cert. denied, 423 U.S. 1050 (1976).

Alabama HB 56: *Beason-Hammon Alabama Taxpayer and Citizen Protection Act*, 2011 Ala. Acts 535.

Ambach v. Norwich, 441 U.S. 68 (1979).

Arizona SB 1070: *Support Our Law Enforcement and Safe Neighborhoods Act*, 2010 *Ariz. Sess. Laws* 113, as amended by 2010 *Ariz. Sess. Laws* 211, invalidated in part by *Arizona v. U.S.*

Arizona v. U.S., 132 S. Ct. 2492 (2012).

Aviation and Transportation Security Act of 2001. Public Law 107-71, *U.S. Statutes at Large* 115 (2001): 230.

Bark v. INS, 511 F 2d 1200 (9th Cir. 1975).

BSEOIM: *Border Security, Economic Opportunity, and Immigration Modernization Act*, S. 744, 113th Cong. (2013).

Cabell v. Chavez-Salido, 454 U.S. 432 (1982).

Carachuri-Rosendo v. Holder, 560 U.S. 563 (2010).

Chinese Exclusion Act of 1882. Ch. 126, *U.S. Statutes at Large* 22 (1882): 58 (repealed 1943).

Comite de Jornaleros de Redondo Beach v. Redondo Beach, 607 F.3d 1178 (9th Cir. 2010).

Dabaghian v. Civiletti, 607 F.2d 868 (9th Cir. 1979).

De Los Santos v. INS, 690 F.2d 56 (2nd Cir. 1982).

Demore v. Kim, 538 U.S. 510 (2003).

DOMA: *Defense of Marriage Act.* Public Law 104-99, *U.S. Statutes at Large* 110 (1997): 2419, invalidated in part by *U.S. v. Windsor*.

Domestic Worker Bill of Rights, 2013 Cal. Stat. 374.

Domestic Workers Bill of Rights, Hawaii Act 248 (1 July 2013).

Domestic Workers' Bill of Rights, 2010 N.Y. Sess. Laws 1315 (McKinney).

EBSVERA: *Enhanced Border Security and Visa Entry Reform Act.* Public Law 107-173, *U.S. Statutes at Large* 116 (2002): 543.

Fernandez-Vargas v. Gonzalez, 548 U.S. 30 (2006).

Fiallo v. Bell, 430 U.S. 787 (1977).

Florida Board of Bar Examiners Re: Undocumented Immigrants, No. SC11-2568 (Fla. Sup. 6 March 2014).

FLSA: *Fair Labor Standards Act of 1938.* Public Law 75-718, *U.S. Statutes at Large* 52 (1938): 1060.

Foley v. Connelie, 435 U.S. 291 (1978).

Graham v. Richardson, 403 U.S. 365 (1971).

Hoffman Plastic Compounds v. NLRB, 535 U.S. 137 (2002).

Homeland Security Act of 2002. Public Law 107-296, *U.S. Statutes at Large* 116 (2002): 2135.

IIRIRA: *Illegal Immigration Reform and Immigrant Responsibility Act of 1996*. Public Law 104-208, *U.S. Statutes at Large* 110 (1996): 3009.

Immigration Act of 1924 (Johnson-Reed Immigration Act). Public Law 68-139, *U.S. Statutes at Large* 43 (1924): 153 (repealed 1965).

Immigration Act of 1990. Public Law 101-649, *U.S. Statutes at Large* 104 (1990): 4978.

Immigration Marriage Fraud Amendments of 1986. Public Law 99-639, *U.S. Statutes at Large* 100 (1986): 3537.

1952 INA: *Immigration and Nationality Act of 1952* (McCarran-Walter Act). Public Law 82-414, *U.S. Statutes at Large* 66 (1952): 163.

INA: *Immigration and Nationality Act of 1965*. Public Law 89-236, *U.S. Statutes at Large* 79 (1965): 911.

In re Sergio C. Garcia on Admission, No. S202512 (Cal. Sup. Filed 2 January 2014).

INS v. Lopez-Mendoza, 468 U.S. 1032 (1984).

IRCA: *Immigration Reform and Control Act*. Public Law 99-603, *U.S. Statutes at Large* 100 (1986): 3359.

Lawrence v. Texas, 539 U.S. 558 (2003).

Mathews v. Diaz, 426 U.S. 67 (1976).

Matter of Aldecoaotalora, 18 I & N Dec. 430 (BIA 1983).

Nguyen v. INS, 533 U.S. 53 (2001).

Nikrodhanondha v. Reno, 202 F.3d 922 (7th Cir. 2000).

Patel v. Quality Inn South, 846 F.2d 700 (11th Cir. 1988).

Patriot Act: *Uniting and Strengthening America by Providing Appropriate Tools Required to Intercept and Obstruct Terrorism Act of 2001*. Public Law 107-56, *U.S. Statutes at Large* 115 (2001): 272.

Perez v. Brownell, 356 U.S. 44 (1958).

Plyler v. Doe, 457 U.S. 202 (1982).

Proposition 187: 1994 Cal. Legis. Serv. Prop 187 (West), invalidated largely by *League of United Latin Am. Citizens v. Wilson*, 997 F. Supp. 1253 (C.D. Cal. 1997).

Refugee Act of 1980. Public Law 96-212, *U.S. Statutes at Large* 94 (1980): 102.

U.S. v. Windsor, 133 S. Ct. 2675 (2013).

Young v. Reno, 114 F.3d 879 (9th Cir. 1997).

Secondary Sources

Abrego, Leisy. "Legitimacy, Social Identity, and the Mobilization of Law: The Effects of Assembly Bill 540 on Undocumented Students in California." *Law & Social Inquiry* 33, no. 3 (Summer 2008): 709–34.

Abrego, Leisy, and Roberto G. Gonzalez. "Blocked Paths, Uncertain Futures: The Postsecondary Education and Labor Market Prospects of Undocumented Latino Youth." *Journal of Education for Students Placed at Risk* 15, nos. 1–2 (January–June 2010): 144–57.

Ackerman, Alissa R., and Rich Furman. "The Criminalization of Immigration and the Privatization of the Immigration Detention: Implications for Justice." *Contemporary Justice Review* 16, no. 2 (2013): 251–63.

Agamben, Giorgio. *State of Exception.* Translated by Kevin Attell. Chicago: University of Chicago Press, 2005.

Akins, Scott, Rubén G. Rumbaut, and Richard Stansfield. "Immigration, Economic Disadvantage, and Homicide: A Community-Level Analysis of Austin, Texas." *Homicide Studies* 13, no. 3 (August 2009): 307–14.

Almeida, Linda Dowling. *Irish Immigrants in New York City, 1945–1995.* Bloomington: Indiana University Press, 2001.

Amnesty International. *Jailed without Justice: Immigration Detention in the USA,* 25 March 2009. Available at www.amnestyusa.org/document .php?id=ENGUSA20090325002&lang=e (accessed 15 September 2013).

———. *U.S. of America—Amnesty International's Concerns Regarding Post September 11 Detentions in the USA.* London: International Secretariat, 2002.

Amsterdam, Anthony G., and Jerome Bruner. *Minding the Law.* Cambridge, MA: Harvard University Press, 2000.

Anderson, Michelle J. "A License to Abuse: The Impact of Conditional Status on Female Immigrants." *Yale Law Journal* 102 (1993): 1401–30.

Arrizón, Alicia. *Latina Performance: Traversing the Stage.* Bloomington: Indiana University Press, 1999.

———. *Queering Mestizaje: Transculturation and Performance.* Ann Arbor: University of Michigan Press, 2006.

Associated Press. *The Associated Press Stylebook and Briefing on Media Law, 2013.* New York: Basic Books, 2013.

Bacon, David. *Illegal People: How Globalization Creates Migration and Criminalizes Immigrants.* Boston: Beacon Press, 2008.

Barba, Eugenio, and Nicola Savarese. *A Dictionary of Theatre Anthropology: The Secret Art of the Performer.* 2nd ed. New York: Routledge, 2006.

Basiouny, Dalia. "The Powerful Voice of Women Dramatists in the Arab American Theatre Movement." PhD diss., The Graduate Center, City University of New York, 2009.

Bayoumi, Moustafa. *How Does It Feel to Be a Problem?: Being Young and Arab in America.* New York: Penguin Press, 2008.

Ben-Asher, Noa. "Who Says 'I Do'?: Reviewing Judith Butler & Gayatri Chakravorty Spivak, *Who Sings the Nation-State? Language, Politics, Belonging.*" *Yale Journal of Law and Feminism* 21 (2009): 245–60.

Bhabha, Homi K. *The Location of Culture.* London: Routledge, 2004.

Bigsby, Christopher. *Arthur Miller: A Critical Study.* Cambridge: Cambridge University Press, 2005.

Bixler, Jacqueline, and Laurietz Seda, eds. *Trans/Acting: Latin American and Latino Performing Arts.* Lewisburg, PA: Bucknell University Press, 2009.

Bosniak, Linda S. *The Citizen and the Alien: Dilemmas of Contemporary Membership.* Princeton: Princeton University Press, 2006.

Bourdieu, Pierre. "The Field of Cultural Production, or: The Economic World Reversed" and "The Production of Belief: Contribution to an Economy of Symbolic Goods." Translated by Richard Nice. In *The Field of Cultural Production,* edited by Randal Johnson, 29–73 and 74–111. New York: Columbia University Press, 1993.

Bourdieu, Pierre. *Language & Symbolic Power.* Translated by Gino Raymond and Matthew Adamson. Edited by John B. Thompson. Cambridge, MA: Harvard University Press, 1991.

Brater, Enoch. "A Dominican *View*: An Interview with Darryl V. Jones." In *Arthur Miller's Global Theater,* edited by Brater, 87–95. Ann Arbor: University of Michigan Press, 2007.

Brimelow, Peter. *Alien Nation: Common Sense about America's Immigration Disaster.* New York: HarperPerennial, 1995.

Brooks, Peter. "The Law as Narrative and Rhetoric." In *Law's Stories: Narrative and Rhetoric in the Law,* edited by Brooks and Paul Gewirtz, 14–22. New Haven: Yale University Press, 1996.

Burnham, Linda, and Nik Theodore. *Home Economics: The Invisible and Unregulated World of Domestic Work.* New York: National Domestic Workers Alliance, 2012.

Butler, Judith, and Gayatri Chakravorty Spivak. *Who Sings the Nation-State?: Language, Politics, Belonging.* London: Seagull Books, 2007.

Cacho, Lisa Marie. *Social Death: Racialized Rightlessness and the Criminalization of the Unprotected.* New York: New York University Press, 2012.

Carlson, Marvin. *Speaking in Tongues: Language at Play in the Theatre.* Ann Arbor: University of Michigan Press, 2006.

Chambers-Letson, Joshua Takano. *A Race So Different: Performance and Law in Asian America.* New York: New York University Press, 2013.

Chang, Grace. *Disposable Domestics: Immigrant Women Workers in the Global Economy.* Cambridge, MA: South End Press, 2000.

Chin, Tung Pok, with Winifred C. Chin. *Paper Son: One Man's Story.* Philadelphia: Temple University Press, 2000.

Christie, John S., and José B. Gonzalez, eds. *Latino Boom: An Anthology of U.S. Latino Literature.* New York: Pearson/Longman, 2006.

Cohen, Lizabeth. *A Consumers' Republic: The Politics of Mass Consumption in Postwar America.* New York: Knopf, 2003.

Cole, David. *Enemy Aliens: Double Standards and Constitutional Freedoms in the War on Terrorism.* New York: New Press, 2003.

Comaroff, Jean, and John L. Comaroff. "Criminal Obsessions, after Foucault: Postcoloniality, Policing, and the Metaphysics of Disorder." In *Law and Disorder in the Postcolony,* edited by Comaroff and Comaroff, 273–98. Chicago: University of Chicago Press, 2006.

Cortez, Beatriz. "Hybrid Identities and the Emergence of Dislocated Consciousness: *Deporting the Divas* by Guillermo Reyes." In *Chicano/Latino Homoerotic Identities,* edited by David William Foster, 131–45. New York: Garland Publishing, 1999.

Coutin, Susan Bibler. *Legalizing Moves: Salvadoran Immigrants' Struggle for U.S. Residency.* Ann Arbor: University of Michigan Press, 2000.

———. *Nations of Emigrants: Shifting Boundaries of Citizenship in El Salvador and the United States.* Ithaca: Cornell University Press, 2007.

Culture Clash. *Culture Clash in Americca.* New York: Theatre Communications Group, 2003.

―――. *Culture Clash: Life, Death and Revolutionary Comedy*. New York: Theatre Communications Group, 1997.

Díaz, José M., and María F. Nadel. *Spanish around the House: The Quick Guide to Communicating with Your Spanish-Speaking Employees*. Chicago: McGraw Hill, 2005.

Discharge, Deportation, and Dangerous Journeys: A Study on the Practice of Medical Repatriation. A joint project from the Center of Social Justice at Seton Hall Law School and the Health Justice Program at New York Lawyers for the Public Interest, available at www.nylpi.org/images/FE/chain234siteType8/site203 /client/FINAL%20MED%20REPAT%20REPORT%20FOR%20WEBSITE.pdf (accessed 21 September 2013).

Dow, Mark. *American Gulag: Inside U.S. Immigration Prisons*. Berkeley: University of California Press, 2004.

Doyle, Brian Leahy. "'In the Pocket': Larry Kirwan's Restless Writings." *New Hibernia Review* 11, no. 3 (Autumn 2007): 131–44.

Ehrenreich, Barbara, and Arlie Russell Hochschild. Introduction to *Global Woman: Nannies, Maids, and Sex Workers in the New Economy*, edited by Ehrenreich and Hochschild, 1–13. New York: Metropolitan Books, 2002.

El Guindi, Yussef. "Author's Introduction" to *Back of the Throat*. *TheatreForum* 29 (Summer/Fall 2006): 26.

Engel, David M., and Frank W. Munger. *Rights of Inclusion: Law and Identity in the Life Stories of Americans with Disabilities*. Chicago: University of Chicago Press, 2003.

Eskridge, William N., Jr., and Darren R. Spedale. *Gay Marriage: For Better or for Worse?: What We've Learned from the Evidence*. Oxford: Oxford University Press, 2006.

Ewick, Patricia, and Susan S. Silbey. *The Common Place of Law: Stories from Everyday Life*. Chicago: University of Chicago Press, 1998.

―――. "Narrating Social Structure: Stories of Resistance to Legal Authority." *American Journal of Sociology* 108, no. 6 (May 2003): 1328–72.

Fellner, Kim. *Wrestling with Starbucks: Conscience, Capital, Cappuccino*. New Brunswick: Rutgers University Press, 2008.

Fernandes, Deepa. *Targeted: Homeland Security and the Business of Immigration*. New York: Seven Stories Press, 2007.

Fernandez, Harold. *Undocumented*. Mustang, OK: Tate Publishing, 2012.

Feyder, Linda, ed. *Shattering the Myth: Plays by Hispanic Women*. Houston: Arte Público Press, 1992.

Figueroa, María P. "Resisting 'Beauty' and *Real Women Have Curves*." In *Velvet Barrios: Popular Culture & Chicana/o Sexualities*, edited by Alicia Gaspar de Alba, 265–82. New York: Palgrave Macmillan, 2003.

Fitch, Melissa A. "Gender Bending in Latino Theater: *Johnny Diego, The Hispanic Zone*, and *Deporting the Divas* by Guillermo Reyes." In *Latino/a Popular Culture*, edited by Michelle Habell-Pallán and Mary Romero, 162–73. New York: New York University Press, 2002.

Fix, Michael, and Wendy Zimmerman. "All under One Roof: Mixed-Status Families in an Era of Reform." *International Migration Review* 35, no. 2 (Summer 2001): 397–419.

Foster, David William. "Guillermo Reyes's *Deporting the Divas*." *Gestos* 27 (April 1999): 103–8.

Foucault, Michel. *Discipline & Punish: The Birth of the Prison.* Translated by Alan Sheridan. New York: Vintage, 1977.

———. "Intellectuals and Power: A Conversation between Michel Foucault and Gilles Deleuze" (1972). In *Language, Counter-Memory, and Practice: Selected Essays and Interviews by Michel Foucault*, edited by Donald F. Bouchard, 205–17. Ithaca: Cornell University Press, 1977.

———. "Space, Knowledge, and Power" (1982). Interview by Paul Rabinow. Translated by Christian Hubert. In *The Foucault Reader*, edited by Rabinow, 239–56. New York: Pantheon Books, 1984.

García, María Cristina. *Seeking Refuge: Central American Migration to Mexico, the United States, and Canada.* Berkeley: University of California Press, 2006.

García, William. "Dragging the Borders: Transnational Queer Identities and Citizenship in Guillermo Reyes's *Deporting the Divas*." In Bixler and Seda, *Trans/Acting*, 211–26.

García-Romero, Anne. "Cornerstone Theater Company's *Justice Cycle*." *TheatreForum* 38 (Winter/Spring 2011): 47–59.

Gilboy, Janet A. "Deciding Who Gets In: Decisionmaking by Immigration Inspectors." *Law & Society Review* 25, no. 3 (1991): 571–600.

———. "Penetrability of Administrative Systems: Political 'Casework' and Immigration Inspections." *Law & Society Review* 26, no. 2 (1992): 273–314.

Giménez, Gilberto. "Cultura, territorio y migraciones. Aproximaciones teóricas." *Alteridades* 11, no. 22 (July–December 2001): 5–14.

Gleeson, Shannon. "Labor Rights for All? The Role of Undocumented Immigrant Status for Worker Claims Making." *Law & Social Inquiry* 35, no. 3 (Summer 2010): 561–602.

Gotanda, Philip Kan. "Chicano Is a State of Mind: An Interview with Culture Clash." In Culture Clash, *Culture Clash: Life, Death and Revolutionary Comedy*, ix–xviii.

Guterman, Gad. "Field Tripping: The Power of *Inherit the Wind*." *Theatre Journal* 60, no. 4 (December 2008): 563–83.

———. "Reviewing the Rosenbergs: Donald Freed's *Inquest* and Its Jurors." *Theatre Survey* 48, no. 2 (November 2007): 265–87.

Harding, Rosie. *Regulating Sexuality: Legal Consciousness in Lesbian and Gay Lives.* New York: Routledge, 2011.

Hariman, Robert. "Performing the Laws: Popular Trials and Social Knowledge." In *Popular Trials: Rhetoric, Mass Media, and the Law*, edited by Hariman, 17–30. Tuscaloosa: University of Alabama Press, 1990.

Havis, Allan. Introduction. In *American Political Plays after 9/11*, edited by Havis. Carbondale: Southern Illinois University Press, 2010.

Heyman, Josiah McC. "U.S. Immigration Officers of Mexican Ancestry as Mexican Americans, Citizens, and Immigration Police." *Current Anthropology* 43, no. 3 (June 2002): 479–507.

Hing, Bill Ong. *Deporting Our Souls: Values, Morality, and Immigration Policy.* Cambridge: Cambridge University Press, 2006.

Hondagneu-Sotelo, Pierrette. *Doméstica: Immigrant Workers Cleaning and Caring in the Snadows of Affluence*. Berkeley: University of California Press, 2001.

Huerta, Jorge. *Chicano Drama: Performance, Society and Myth*. Cambridge: Cambridge University Press, 2000.

———. "Chicano Theatre in a Society in Crisis." In *Text & Presentation, 2007*, edited by Stratos E. Constantinidis, 5–23. Jefferson, NC: McFarland, 2008.

———. "El Teatro de la Esperanza: Keeping in Touch with the People." *The Drama Review: TDR* 21, no. 1 (March 1977): 37–46.

———. Introduction to *La víctima*. In Huerta, *Necessary Theater*, 316–24.

———. Introduction to *Latina*. In Huerta, *Necessary Theater*, 76–84.

———. "Looking for the Magic: Chicanos in the Mainstream." In *Negotiating Performance: Gender, Sexuality, and Theatricality in Latin/o America*, edited by Diana Taylor and Juan Villegas, 37–48. Durham: Duke University Press, 1994.

———, ed. *Necessary Theater: Six Plays about the Chicano Experience*. Houston: Arte Público Press, 1989.

———. "Some Thoughts on Casting *Deporting the Divas*." *Gestos* 27 (April 1999): 159–61.

Huerta-Macías, Ana, María Luisa González, and Linda Holman. "Children of Undocumented Immigrants: An Invisible Minority among Homeless Students." In *Children on the Streets of the Americas: Homelessness, Education and Globalization in the United States, Brazil and Cuba*, edited by Roslyn Arlin Mickelson, 238–46. London: Routledge, 2000.

Human Rights Watch. *Brutality Unchecked: Human Rights Abuses along the U.S. Border with Mexico*, 1 June 1992. Available at www.hrw.org/en/publications (accessed 15 September 2013).

———. *Chronic Indifference: HIV/AIDS Services for Immigrants Detained by the United States*, 5 December 2007. Available at www.hrw.org/en/publications (accessed 15 September 2013).

———. *Costly and Unfair: Flaws in US Immigration Detention Policy*. 6 May 2010. Available at www.hrw.org/en/publications (accessed 15 September 2013).

———. *Crossing the Line: Human Rights Abuses along the U.S. Border with Mexico Persist amid Climate of Impunity*, 1 April 1995. Available at www.hrw.org/en/publications (accessed 15 September 2013).

———. *Cultivating Fear: The Vulnerability of Immigrant Farmworkers in the US to Sexual Violence and Sexual Harassment*, 16 May 2012. Available at www.hrw.org/en/publications (accessed 15 September 2013).

———. *Detained and at Risk: Sexual Abuse and Harassment in United States Immigration Detention*, 25 August 2010. Available at www.hrw.org/en/publications (accessed 15 September 2013).

———. *Detained and Deprived of Rights: Children in the Custody of the U.S. Immigration and Naturalization Service*, 1 December 1998. Available at www.hrw.org/en/publications (accessed 15 September 2013).

———. *Detained and Dismissed: Women's Struggles to Obtain Health Care in United States Immigration Detention*, 17 March 2009. Available at www.hrw.org/en/publications (accessed 15 September 2013).

Human Rights Watch. *Forced Apart: Families Separated and Immigrants Harmed by United States Deportation Policy*, 16 July 2007. Available at www.hrw.org /en/publications (accessed 15 September 2013).

———. *Locked Up Far Away: The Transfer of Immigrants to Remote Detention Centers in the United States*, 2 December 2009. Available at www.hrw.org /en/publications (accessed 15 September 2013).

Hwang, David Henry, and Laurence Maslon. Interviewed in "A Classic Evolves: From Print to Stage to Screen." In Rodgers, Hammerstein, and Fields, *Flower Drum Song*, DVD.

Immigration Marriage Fraud, Hearing Before the Subcommittee on Immigration and Refugee Policy of the Committee of the Judiciary. U.S. Senate, 99th Congress, 1st Sess., 26 July 1985. Washington, DC: US Government Printing Office, 1986.

Inda, Jonathan Xavier, and Julie A. Dowling, "Governing Migrant Illegality." Introduction to *Governing Immigration through Crime: A Reader*, edited by Dowling and Inda, 1–36, Stanford: Stanford Social Sciences, Stanford University Press, 2013.

Johnson, Kit. "The Wonderful World of Disney Visas." *Florida Law Review* 63 (2011): 915–58.

Kanellos, Nicolás. *A History of Hispanic Theatre in the United States: Origins to 1940*. Austin: University of Texas Press, 1990.

Kanellos, Nicolás, and Jorge A. Huerta, eds. *Nuevos Pasos: Chicano and Puerto Rican Drama*. Houston: Arte Público Press, 1989.

Kershaw, Baz. *The Politics of Performance: Radical Theatre as Cultural Intervention*. London: Routledge, 1992.

Khosravi, Shahram. *"Illegal" Traveller: An Auto-Ethnography of Borders*. New York: Palgrave Macmillan, 2010.

Kondo, Dorinne. "(Re)Visions of Race: Contemporary Race Theory and the Cultural Politics of Racial Crossover in Documentary Theatre." *Theatre Journal* 52, no. 1 (2000): 81–107.

Kuftinec, Sonja. *Staging America: Cornerstone and Community-Based Theater*. Carbondale: Southern Illinois University Press, 2003.

Lai, H. Mark, Genny Lim, and Judy Young. *Island: Poetry and History of Chinese Immigrants on Angel Island 1910–1940*. Seattle: University of Washington Press, 1991.

Launius, Christie. "*Real Women Have Curves*: A Feminist Narrative of Upward Mobility." *American Drama* 16, no. 2 (Summer 2007): 15–27.

Lee, Esther Kim. *A History of Asian American Theatre*. Cambridge: Cambridge University Press, 2006.

Lee, Robert G. *Orientals: Asian Americans in Popular Culture*. Philadelphia: Temple University Press, 1999.

Legomsky, Stephen H. "The New Path of Immigration Law: Asymmetric Incorporation of Criminal Justice Norms." *Washington and Lee Law Review* 64, nos. 2–3 (2007): 469–528.

Lessard, Gabrielle, and Leighton Ku. "Gaps in Coverage for Children in Immigrant Families." *The Future of Children* 13, no. 1 (Spring 2003): 100–115.

Levit, Nancy. *The Gender Line: Men, Women, and the Law.* New York: New York University Press, 1998.

Lewis, Sasha G. *Slave Trade Today: American Exploitation of Illegal Aliens.* Boston: Beacon Press, 1979.

Li, Peter S. "Fictive Kinship, Conjugal Tie and Kinship Chain among Chinese Immigrants in the United States." *Journal of Comparative Family Studies* 3, no. 1 (Spring 1977): 47–63.

Lope de Vega. *Fuerte Ovejuna.* Translated by Roy Campbell. In *Life Is a Dream and Other Spanish Classics*, edited by Eric Bentley, 67–135. New York: Applause, 1985.

López, Ian F. Haney. *White by Law: The Legal Construction of Race.* New York: New York University Press, 1996.

López, Josefina. *Hungry Woman in Paris.* New York: Hachette Book Group, 2009.

López, Tiffany Ana. "Suturing Las Ramblas to East LA: Transnational Performances of Josefina López' *Real Women Have Curves*." In *Performing the US Latina and Latino Borderlands*, edited by Arturo J. Aldama, Chela Sandoval, and Peter J. García, 296–308. Bloomington: Indiana University Press, 2012.

Luibhéid, Eithne. *Entry Denied: Controlling Sexuality at the Border.* Minneapolis: University of Minnesota Press, 2002.

MacKay, Ellen. "Auditioning for the Role of a Lifetime: Performing Self-Translation at the American Immigration and Naturalization Service." *Canadian Theatre Review* 102 (Spring 2000): 20–24.

Magaña, Lisa, and Erik Lee, eds. *Latino Politics and Arizona's Immigration Law SB 1070.* New York: Springer, 2013.

Martínez, Rubén. *Crossing Over: A Mexican Family on the Migrant Trail.* New York: Metropolitan Books, 2001.

Masuoka, Natalie, and Jane Junn. *The Politics of Belonging: Race, Public Opinion, and Immigration.* Chicago: University of Chicago Press, 2013.

McCracken, Grant. *Culture and Consumption: New Approaches to the Symbolic Character of Consumer Goods and Activities.* Bloomington: Indiana University Press, 1988.

Merry, Sally Engle. *Colonizing Hawai'i: The Cultural Power of Law.* Princeton: Princeton University Press, 2000.

———. *Getting Justice and Getting Even: Legal Consciousness among Working-Class Americans.* Chicago: University of Chicago Press, 1990.

Metzger, Sean. "Charles Parsloe's Chinese Fetish: An Example of Yellowface Performance in Nineteenth-Century American Melodrama." *Theatre Journal* 56, no. 4 (December 2004): 627–51.

Motomura, Hiroshi. *Americans in Waiting: The Lost Story of Immigration and Citizenship in the United States.* Oxford: Oxford University Press, 2006.

———. "The Family and Immigration: A Roadmap for the Ruritanian Lawmaker." *American Journal of Comparative Law* 43, no. 4 (Autumn 1995): 511–44.

Nathan, Debbie. *Women and Other Aliens: Essays from the U.S.-Mexico Border.* El Paso: Cinco Puntos Press, 1991.

Neal, Valerie. "Slings and Arrows of Outrageous Fortune: The Deportation of 'Aggravated Felons.'" *Vanderbilt Journal of Transnational Law* 36 (November 2003): 1619–55.

Nevins, Joseph. *Operation Gatekeeper and Beyond: The War on "Illegals" and the Remaking of the U.S.-Mexico Boundary.* New York: Routledge, 2010.

Ngai, Mae M. *Impossible Subjects: Illegal Aliens and the Making of Modern America.* Princeton: Princeton University Press, 2004.

Nguyen, Tram. *We Are All Suspects Now: Untold Stories from Immigrant Communities after 9/11.* Boston: Beacon Press, 2005.

Nicholls, Walter. *The DREAMers: How the Undocumented Youth Movement Transformed the Immigrant Rights Debate.* Stanford: Stanford University Press, 2013.

Nield, Sophie. "On the Border as Theatrical Space: Appearance, Dis-Location and the Production of the Refugee." In *Contemporary Theatres in Europe: A Critical Companion,* edited by Joe Kelleher and Nicholas Ridout, 61–72. London: Routledge, 2006.

———. "The Proteus Cabinet, or 'We Are Here but Not Here.'" *Research in Drama Education* 13, no. 2 (June 2008): 137–45.

Nielsen, Lara D., and Patricia Ybarra, eds. *Neoliberalism and Global Theatres: Performance Permutations.* New York: Palgrave Macmillan, 2012.

Oboler, Suzanne. *Ethnic Labels, Latino Lives: Identity and the Politics of (Re)Presentation in the United States.* Minneapolis: University of Minnesota Press, 1995.

Olivares, Cecilia. "Seeking Divine Intervention: Votive Iconography and Processes of U.S.-Mexican Migration." In *Mediating Chicana/o Culture: Multicultural American Vernacular,* edited by Scott L. Baugh, 100–112. Newcastle, UK: Cambridge Scholars Press, 2006.

Palumbo-Liu, David. *Asian/American: Historical Crossings of a Racial Frontier.* Stanford: Stanford University Press, 1999.

Parker, Kevin. "The 'True' Nanny Experience." Introduction to Nandi, *The True Nanny Diaries,* unnumbered pages. Brooklyn: Bread for Brick, 2009.

Passel, Jeffrey S., and D'Vera Cohn. *A Portrait of Unauthorized Immigrants in the United States.* Pew Research Center Report, 14 April 2009, pewhispanic.org /files/reports/107.pdf (accessed 19 July 2013).

———. *Unauthorized Immigrant Population: National and State Trends, 2010.* Pew Research Center Report, 1 February 2011, pewhispanic.org/2011/02/01 /unauthorized-immigrant-population-brnational-and-state-trends-2010/ (accessed 19 July 2013).

———. *U.S. Unauthorized Immigration Flows Are Down Sharply since Mid-Decade.* Pew Research Center Report, 1 September 2010, pewhispanic.org /files/reports/126.pdf (accessed 3 September 2010).

Passel, Jeffrey S., D'Vera Cohn, and Ana Gonzalez-Barrera. *Population Decline of Unauthorized Immigrants Stalls, May Have Reversed.* Pew Research Center Report, 23 September 2013, pewhispanic.org/2013/09/23/population -decline-of-unauthorized-immigrants-stalls-may-have-reversed/ (accessed 23 September 2013).

Passel, Jeffrey S., and Paul Taylor. *Unauthorized Immigrants and Their U.S.-Born Children.* Pew Research Center Report, 11 August 2010, pewhispanic.org /files/reports/125.pdf (accessed 13 September 2010).

Pérez, Ramón "Tianguis." *Diary of an Undocumented Immigrant*. Translated by Dick J. Reavis. Houston: Arte Público Press, 1991.

Prado, Anayansi, director. *Maid in America*, DVD. Los Angeles: Impacto Films, 2004.

Puchner, Martin. *Poetry of the Revolution: Marx, Manifestos, and the Avant-Gardes*. Princeton: Princeton University Press, 2006.

Ramírez, Elizabeth C. *Chicanas/Latinas in American Theatre: A History of Performance*. Bloomington: Indiana University Press, 2000.

Roach, Joseph. *Cities of the Dead: Circum-Atlantic Performance*. New York: Columbia University Press, 1996.

Rollins, Judith. *Between Women: Domestics and Their Employers*. Philadelphia: Temple University Press, 1985.

Román, Ediberto. *Those Damned Immigrants: America's Hysteria over Undocumented Immigration*. New York: New York University Press, 2013.

Romero, Elaine. "Memories on the Border." *American Theatre* 25, no. 10 (December 2008): 64–65.

Romero, Mary. *Maid in the U.S.A.* 10th anniversary ed. New York: Routledge, 2002.

Rossini, Jon D. *Contemporary Latina/o Theater: Wrighting Ethnicity*. Carbondale: Southern Illinois University Press, 2008.

———. "Teatro Visión and the Limits of Chicano Politics in Neoliberal Space." In Nielsen and Ybarra, *Neoliberalism and Global Theatres*, 209–20.

Saborío, Linda. *Embodying Difference: Scripting Social Images of the Female Body in Latina Theatre*. Madison: Fairleigh Dickinson University Press, 2012.

Said, Edward. *Orientalism*. New York: Vintage Books, 1978.

Salazar-Parreñas, Rhacel. *The Force of Domesticity: Filipina Migrants and Globalization* New York: New York University Press, 2008.

Salinas, Ricardo. Introduction to *The Mission*. In Culture Clash, *Culture Clash: Life, Death and Revolutionary Comedy*, 3–7.

Salyer, Lucy. *Laws Harsh as Tigers: Chinese Immigrants and the Shaping of Modern Immigration Law*. Chapel Hill: University of North Carolina Press, 1995.

Samora, Julian, with the assistance of Jorge A. Bustamante F. and Gilbert Cardenas. *Los Mojados: The Wetback Story*. Notre Dame: University of Notre Dame Press, 1971.

Sánchez-Scott, Milcha. Introduction to *Roosters*. In *On New Ground: Contemporary Hispanic-American Plays*, edited by M. Elizabeth Osborn, 244–47. New York: Theatre Communications Group, 1987.

Sandoval, Trino, ed. *Borders on Stage: Plays Produced by Teatro Bravo*. Phoenix: The Lion & The Seagoat, 2008.

Schriro, Dora. *Immigration Detention Overview and Recommendations*. Report to DHS, 6 October 2009, available at www.iaumc.org/console/files/oFiles_Library_XZXLCZ/2010HomelandSecurityImmigrationDetentionOverview_MJERXUXV.pdf (accessed 21 September 2013).

Schuck, Peter H. *Citizens, Strangers, and In-Betweens: Essays on Immigration and Citizenship*. Boulder: Westview Press, 1998.

Shimakawa, Karen. *National Abjection: The Asian American Body Onstage.* Durham: Duke University Press, 2002.

———. "Staging a Moving Map in Byron Au Yong's and Aaron Jafferis's *Stuck Elevator.*" In Nielsen and Ybarra, *Neoliberalism and Global Theatres*, 97–112.

Smith, Peggy R. "Organizing the Unorganizable: Private Paid Household Workers and Approaches to Employee Representation." *North Carolina Law Review* 79, no. 1 (2000): 45–110.

Soltero, Carlos R. *Latinos and American Law: Landmark Supreme Court Cases.* Austin: University of Texas Press, 2006.

Somers, Margaret R. *Genealogies of Citizenship: Markets, Statelessness, and the Right to Have Rights.* Cambridge: Cambridge University Press, 2008.

Stanislavski, Konstantin. *An Actor's Work: A Student's Diary.* Translated by Jean Benedetti. New York: Routledge, 2008.

Storm, Margaret, and Elsie Ginnett. *Home Maid Spanish.* Los Angeles: Brooke House, 1976.

Sumida, Stephen H. "The More Things Change: Paradigm Shifts in Asian American Studies." *American Studies International* 38, no. 2 (June 2000): 97–114.

Sung, Betty Lee. *The Story of the Chinese in America.* New York: Collier Books, 1967.

Suro, Roberto. Featured in "Democracy in the Age of New Media: A Report on the Media and the Immigration Debate." Panel presentation at Brookings Institution in Washington, DC, 25 September 2008. Transcript available through the Brookings Institution website, www.brookings.edu/events /2008/0925_media_immigration.aspx (accessed 15 September 2013).

Taylor, Diana. "Afterword: War Play." *PMLA* 124, no. 5 (October 2009): 1886–95.

———. *The Archive and the Repertoire: Performing Cultural Memory in the Americas.* Durham: Duke University Press, 2003.

———. *Disappearing Acts: Spectacles of Gender and Nationalism in Argentina's "Dirty War."* Durham: Duke University Press, 1997.

———. "Double-Blind: The Torture Case." *Critical Inquiry* 33, no. 4 (Summer 2007): 710–33.

Thompson, John B. "Editor's Introduction." In Bourdieu, *Language & Symbolic Power*, 1–31.

Thorpe, Helen. *Just Like Us: The True Story of Four Mexican Girls Coming of Age in America.* New York: Scribner, 2009.

Trinch, Shonna L. *Latinas' Narratives of Domestic Abuse: Discrepant Versions of Violence.* Amsterdam: John Benjamins, 2003.

Tucker, Joe A. "Assimilation to the United States: A Study of the Adjustment of Status and the Immigration Marriage Fraud Statutes." *Yale Law & Policy Review* 7, no. 1 (1989): 20–100.

Uno, Roberta, ed. *Unbroken Thread: An Anthology of Plays by Asian American Women.* Amherst: University of Massachusetts Press, 1993.

Wada, Karen. Afterword. In Rodgers, Hammerstein, and Hwang, *Flower Drum Song*, 99–115.

Wall, Eamonn. *From the Sin-é Café to the Black Hills: Notes on the New Irish.* Madison: University of Wisconsin Press, 1999.

Williams, Dave. Introduction to *The Chinese Other, 1850–1925: An Anthology of Plays*, edited by Williams, xii–xiii. Lanham, MD: University Press of America, 1997.

Wolf, Linda. *Politely Tell a Maid.* Canoga Park, CA: Tell-a-Maid, 1981.

Wong, Sau-ling C. "Diverted Mothering: Representations of Caregivers of Color in the Age of Multiculturalism.'" In *Mothering: Ideology, Experience, and Agency*, edited by Evelyn Nakano Glenn, Grace Chang, and Linda Rennie Forcey, 67–91. New York: Routledge, 1994.

Woo, Miseong. "Diaspora and Geographies of Identity: Genny Lim's *Paper Angels* and *Bitter Cane.*" *Journal of Modern British and American Drama* 17, no. 1 (April 2004): 177–200.

Woodyard, George. "Rompiendo las fronteras: El teatro de Guillermo Reyes." In *Théâtre et territoires Espagne et Amérique Hispanique, 1950–1996/Teatro y territorios España e Hispanoamérica*, edited by Sara Bonnardel and Geneviève Champeau, 333–43. Bordeaux: Maison des Pays Ibériques, 1998.

Yarbro-Bejarano, Yvonne. "The Female Subject in Chicano Theatre: Sexuality, 'Race,' and Class." *Theatre Journal* 38, no. 4 (December 1986): 389–407.

Yoxall, Peter. "The Minuteman Project, Gone in a Minute or Here to Stay? The Origin, History and Future of Citizen Activism on the United States-Mexico Border," *University of Miami Inter-American Law Review* 37, no. 3 (Spring–Summer 2006): 517–66.

Yukich, Grace. *One Family under God: Immigration Politics and Progressive Religion in America.* Oxford: Oxford University Press, 2013.

Index

Printed in Great Britain
by Amazon